Critical Choices

Applying Sociological Insight in Your Life, Family, and Community

Scott Sernau
Indiana University

Roxbury Publishing Company
Los Angeles, California

Library of Congress Cataloging-in-Publication Data

Sernau, Scott.
Critical choices : applying sociological insight in your life,
    family, and community/Scott Sernau.
    p.   cm.
    Includes bibliographical references and index.
    ISBN 0-935732-82-9
    1. Sociology.   I. Title.
    HM51.S44   1997
    301—dc20   96-46533
                                                     CIP

**Critical Choices: Applying Sociological Insight
in Your Life, Family, and Community**

Publisher and Editor: Claude Teweles
Line Editing: Anton Diether
Production Supervisor: Dawn VanDercreek
Production Assistants: Joyce Rappaport, Colleen O'Brien, C. Max-Ryan
Cover Design: Marnie Deacon Kenney
Typography: Synergistic Data Systems

Printed on acid-free paper in the United States of America. This paper
meets the standards for recycling of the Environmental Protection
Agency.

ISBN: 0-935732-82-9

Figure 4.1 on page 103 reprinted from page 72 of Gilbert and Kahl,
The American Class Structure, 4th Edition, © 1993 Wadsworth Publishing Co. Reprinted by permission.

Roxbury Publishing Company
P.O. Box 491044
Los Angeles, California 90049-9044
(213) 653-1068
Fax: (213) 653-4140
Email: roxbury@crl.com

Dedication

For my most promising students, those who went beyond note-taking to inquire, to explore, to critique, and to act. They have inspired me as well as this book.

Contents

Acknowledgments

The road between the first flash of an idea for a book and the reality of its development and completion is a long one. This is especially true at the stage when the idea for a book is merely a concept. Many, it would seem, are the muses scattering ideas; much rarer are the guides and coaches willing to travel the road to put those ideas into print. I am very grateful for having more than my share of the latter.

I have benefitted from a wife who is both a patient partner and a gifted teacher, as well as three children who are always enthusiastic boosters—even though I didn't agree to let them decorate the margins. Many thanks need to go to Dean Dorn for the initial contact with Roxbury Publishing Company and for his encouragement, and also to Anton Diether for his careful—and at times eloquent—copy editing. Special thanks go to Claude Teweles for being exactly what an editor and publisher of academic books should be: at the same time both an enthusiastic coach and a careful, methodical guide willing to walk that long road to completion. The book is much improved due to his efforts in bringing together an impressive list of committed and gifted instructors willing to commit their time to careful reviews of various drafts of both the book proposal and the final manuscript. Particular thanks go to:

Arnold Arluke, *Northeastern University*
Spencer Cahill, *University of South Florida*
Irene Fiala, *Baldwin-Wallace College*
Rebecca Glass, *SUNY Geneseo*
David F. Gordon, *SUNY Geneseo*
John W. Heeren, *California State University-San Bernardino*
Jeremy Hein, *University of Wisconsin-Eau Claire*
Valerie Jenness, *Washington State University*
Rachel Kahn-Hut, *San Francisco State University*

Betty Frankle Kirschner, *Kent State University*
Peter Kivisto, *Augustana College*
Michael Lovaglia, *University of Iowa*
Kim MacInnis, *Bridgewater State College*
Harold L. Orbach, *Kansas State University*
Edward Ponczek, *Harper College*
Frank R. Scarpitti, *University of Delaware*
William L. Tolone, *Illinois State University*

Preface

Getting the Most From This Book

Features

Instructors often long to see their students integrate sociological insight into their own world in ways that challenge complacency and easy answers. *Critical Choices* is an invitation for students to explore the connections between their social world and their day-to-day lives. They are called on to apply social understanding to personal experience and to reflect on the implications of social forces and social change for their plans, aspirations, and choices. As students apply sociological insight to their lives and communities, they begin to cultivate a lifelong habit of critical thinking and using the sociological imagination.

Several emphases distinguish this approach:

An emphasis on personal experience. One of the most difficult tasks facing a sociology instructor is to help students grasp the many links between the private world of their own experience and the social world they inhabit. Students may fall into the trap of finding sociological insight implausible because it challenges their individualized view of the world, or irrelevant and distant because it does not appear to touch them. *Critical Choices* helps instructors communicate that sociology is vital because it is the study of our common life and as such can make us more savvy, more successful, more empathetic, and maybe even more compassionate social actors.

Critical thinking. The book's interactive approach calls on students to: apply data on trends and patterns; confront myth-challenging facts; examine tables, charts and thought-provoking scenarios; explore the social underpinnings of current controversies; and to dig deeper into their own communities and culture. Challenging questions for individual, small-group, or whole-class use offer a careful probing of implications, applications, and personal choices and values.

Active learning. "Reaching Out" sections include a wide variety of hands-on learning experiences, short field projects, content analyses, ethnographic writing, brief service projects, and other community-based activities to build habits of thoughtful social involvement.

Cooperative learning. *Critical Choices* provides a valuable tool for launching active class discussions. Upon completing a chapter, students will have grappled with and thought through vital issues and are more likely to come to class prepared to discuss, debate, and defend their ideas. The book provides a key resource to instructors seeking to create a vital, interactive learning environment, to convey both the intrigue and the practicality of sociology, and to spark fresh sociological imaginations.

Organization

Critical Choices is organized to reinforce the major sections and themes of an introductory sociology course. The book may be used as a supplement to either a full-length or a brief text; or it can stand alone as a brief core text to link together a variety of readings or books. In courses consisting of a large lecture section and smaller discussion sections, *Critical Choices* may serve as a guide for the discussion sections, helping the discussion leader as well as students to prepare to interact more personally with lecture topics. For those who are using *Critical Choices* as a supplement, the chapters are organized to parallel the order used in many major introductory textbooks. However, each chapter stands independently and may be used in any order.

Chapter	Related textbook and semester topics
Introduction	Introduction and Methods
1. Global Village	Culture and Society, Social Structure
2. A Long Way	Socialization and Interaction; Gender and Mass Media

Chapter	Related textbook and semester topics
3. Corporate Life	Groups and Organizations; Deviance and Social Control
4. Planning Ahead	Stratification; Education, Economy, and Work
5. Many Colors	Race and Ethnic Relations; Multiculturalism
6. Family Values	Family and other Social Institutions; Religion and Politics, Aging and Life Course
7. Humanity	Urbanization, Population, and Environment; Social Change, the World System and Modernity; Social Movements

Making the Most of the Book's Special Features

Students are often unsure of what to do with special inserts, boxes, maps, and figures—and may ignore them entirely while reading quickly. The questions and activities in *Critical Choices*, and the tables and figures that accompany them, are intended to be used as part of a dialogue of learning. They may be employed in several ways.

'For Reflection'

Each major section ends with a "For Reflection" section. These may be used in a variety of ways, and several approaches may be combined. Here are a few suggestions:

1. Journaling. The value of having students respond to course material and compile their thoughts in an ongoing journal or log is recognized across many academic disciplines. Journals stress interaction and develop writing skills. The probing, open-ended nature of these "For Reflection" sections guide students in the journaling process. These questions may be supplemented by the student's own reactions, questions, and comments.

2. Short writing assignments. One way to insure that students come to class prepared to engage in discussion is to assign short writing assignments due at the beginning of class. "For Reflection" sections are ideally suited to this type of assignment. The completed assignments can be reviewed by the instructor, by a teaching assistant, or by other students in a peer review process.

3. Class discussion. Each of the sections can launch a class discussion. Some sections specifically encourage students to share their ideas with classmates. Because students have the questions in hand in advance of class, they can think about, or write out, answers in preparation for class discussion. In courses that have designated discussion sections, these can be structured around the "For Reflection" questions. In each case, students should be encouraged to prepare in advance to allow deeper, richer discussions.

4. Discussion groups. Smaller groups of four to seven can be used to facilitate discussion in larger classes. The groups can discuss the questions and then report their conclusions back to the whole group, or they can write out their answers. One way to encourage broad participation is to insist that the task of "secretary" or "reporter" be rotated within the group for each question. Students can also write out individual answers before the group meets to encourage advance preparation. If preferred, discussion pairs, usually changing partners each time, can be used in place of groups.

Instructors may assign some sections for individual work, some for small groups, and some for whole-class discussion. On topics of particular interest, a layered structure may be created in which students respond individually, then in groups or discussion sections, and then compare conclusions in the whole-class setting.

'Reaching Out, Digging Deeper'

Each chapter concludes with a section that suggests readings and activities to extend the learning and probing process. These may be used in a variety of ways.

1. The suggested readings may be left for the students' own reference or may become the basis of a writing assignment. Such a paper can comment on and critique the authors' points, and draw connections to other class themes. This type of assignment may also be used as an option or extra credit. The "Digging Deeper" section at the end of Chapter 7, for example, is a good exercise in becoming familiar with basic data sources and library reference materials. It can be assigned independently or used in conjunction with a class session in the library, perhaps with a reference librarian.

2. Numerous options are offered in each "Reaching Out, Digging Deeper" section to give students maximum flexibility to mesh with their particular interests and life situation. How many are assigned will vary with the instructor's preference, the length of the course period, and other demands. All of the options may be left for optional or extra credit assignment. The student may be asked to select one or two activities for the entire semester, quarter, or block. The instructor may select one or more activities that are particularly pertinent to a course theme or to an issue in the local community. A heavily applied focus will be created by asking students to select one option from each chapter. An intermediate possibility is to ask students to select one "In Your Family" assignment from any chapter, one "In Your Community" assignment, and one "In the Media" assignment. This gives the students a wide range of topics from which to choose, while ensuring that they will have three different types of experiences.

3. "Reaching Out, Digging Deeper" sections may also be used for group or collaborative work. A group of students may work together on a common "In Your Community" assignment. Students may also work semi-collaboratively, in which case they discuss their research plans, each student does an independent project, and then all come back to discuss and compile results. This arrangement can help balance group interaction with personal accountability. In smaller classes or discussion sections, students can report back to the whole class or section on their projects and field experiences.

4. Activities that are beyond the scope of the semester or the possibilities of the local community can also be offered as "thought experiments" or opportunities for students to reflect on past experiences. While current, well-chosen experiences are the most valuable, students nonetheless have a variety of experience with family, community, and media to offer useful insights. An increasingly diverse student body provides the opportunity for wide-ranging exchange of ideas and experiences.

Having examined the wide range of options offered in *Critical Choices*, students may also ask to revise an idea or create of their own. This can be a good way of helping students to begin to think about how they can investigate and critically reflect on a changing social world. This is a habit and a disposition that will serve them well beyond the confines of the course.

Introduction

At the Juncture of History and Biography

To be human is to be social. How long would any of us last alone and empty-handed in almost any environment? How long would an infant last in this state, and what would it be if it could survive? Humans form groups, and groups form humans. We can examine individuals in isolation, which may be useful for laboratory purposes; but real people, no matter how solitary, always exist in a social context. To understand our lives we must understand that context. In a now-classic essay, C. Wright Mills (1959) termed this the *sociological imagination*. This imagination, he contended, is the ability to see the interconnectedness of biography (individual human experience) and history (the broad sweep and play of human endeavor).

Americans live in a society that stresses the individual and exalts individual effort. It is not surprising, then, that Americans often place little emphasis on history, except as the tale of heroic individuals. Revolutionary socialist societies and highly centralized states, on the other hand, exalt the group, the heroic masses. They place great stress on a particular version of history, but individual biographies—except those of certain key leaders—matter little. Both perspectives are misleading. Humans form groups, and groups form humans; losing sight of either side loses the essential nature of humanity. Whatever specific information you may learn through the study of sociology, if you gain an understanding of the links between

1

social context and personal experience and develop the skill to perceive these connections, you will have learned a great deal.

Critical Choices: Applying Sociological Insight in Your Life, Family, and Community is a guide to help you personalize your studies, so that you can refer to your own experiences and situations and the choices that confront you. Its focus, however, is to encourage you to do this in context: to develop the sociological imagination and critical thinking ability to make informed, sophisticated choices.

The good life is life under consideration. Across time and place, humanity has shown a great need and desire to not only live and live well but also to make sense of our common life. That life is one of cultural experience and social relationships. We live our days in what Kenneth Boulding has called the *sociosphere.* To "know thyself," as Socrates has admonished us, we must know our world.

Understanding the Sociological Perspective

Before proceeding any further, it would be best to address some common objections head on. The first goes something like this: "People are all different, so you can't generalize. Theories about groups or categories of people are always wrong, because everyone is an individual. Everyone is unique."

Think about this analogy for a moment: It has been said that no two snowflakes are alike, so each one is unique. This is not necessarily true: The crystalline shape of a snowflake can take about six million forms, but in any given snowstorm, some of them must indeed be identical. Nevertheless, let's assume that any two snowflakes are unlikely to be the same. If we examined these different snowflakes, we would find that they are not in random patterns but variations on common themes. They are full of hexagonal patterns, for example, based on the common molecular forces in water. They are different yet similar because they were created by similar forces.

Further, although examining individual characteristics of snowflakes may be of some interest, we usually want to know more about their *group* characteristics; e.g., how much snow, how fast, how heavy, how much blowing and drifting. The uniqueness of each snowflake in no way prohibits us from examining—and trying to predict—the collective aspects of snow that matter to our lives, such as whether we'll be able to drive through it or ski on it. We can also be misled by group stereotypes. If we believe that all snow is light and fluffy and falls softly, then a wet, harsh blizzard may come as a rude surprise. Hence, regardless of the beauty and wonder of the intricate composition of an individual snowflake, when we want information on snow, we seek out accurate assessments of group characteristics.

The more snow matters to us, the more nuances we will notice. It is commonly believed that the Inuit peoples of the far north, the "Eskimos," have hundreds of words for snow. In actual fact, they have about 16 words. Some of these words refer to snow characteristics (wet or dry, heavy or light, etc.) and snow configurations or structures (snow banks, snowdrifts, etc.). The cultural difference between us and the Inuit is not as great as you might imagine: Just as we have unique words for various forms of liquid water (pond, stream, creek, etc.) but use compound words for frozen water (iceberg, snowball, etc.), the Inuit have unique and separate words for the forms of water that are most important to them (frozen, freezing, thawing, etc.). Likewise, skiers have developed a specialized vocabulary of snow conditions. When snow matters a great deal, we take the time to analyze and describe subtleties that others might not notice.

Now let us return to people. It is true that we are all different but in many ways, we are more alike than different. All of us are shaped by common forces—particularly social forces. Further, what we often need to know are group characteristics; e.g., how many, how old, how smart, how poor, and so forth. The uniqueness of the individual in no way negates these generalizations any more than the uniqueness of snowflakes negates a blizzard warning.

Most of us would agree that people matter a great deal to all of us. This being so, like the Inuit and the skier, we will want to tune in to the subtleties of group characteristics and configurations of group structures. The more people matter to us, the more nuanced we will want our generalizations to be. This will likely require a broader and more sophisticated terminology, as we shun stereotypes and seek instead to carefully note commonalities and distinctions. Finally, we may try to make some predictions, which is risky but not so much as being oblivious to trends and patterns that will shape our future. Such is the task of sociology.

Even as their understanding of groups emerges, people are often reluctant to apply sociological insight to themselves: "See me as an individual, not just as a representative of a group." This is a valid assertion, but individual uniqueness does not exist in isolation. One problem with being perceived solely as a representative of a single group—women, freshmen, African Americans, honor students, and so forth—comes not so much from overemphasizing the group affiliation as from failing to recognize the multiplicity of group affiliations. Groups are made up of individuals, certainly, but it can also be argued that individuals are made up of a multiplicity of group characteristics.

Any given person stands at the locus of many group affiliations. Hence, that person's uniqueness can derive partially from his or her position at a unique intersection of groups. Unless you are enrolled with a twin sibling, you are the only member of your family and your age group who is also a member of your sociology class. To this could be added ethnic group, hometown, high school class, church, civic group, sports team, and many others. To focus on the impact of group forces in no way diminishes individual uniqueness, because we each stand at that unique intersection of groups and have been shaped—*socialized*—by a unique combination of multiple group forces.

Choice and Constraint

This discussion of group forces often spawns another objection in regard to the sociological perspective: "What about free will and personal choice?" This is an ancient question that has echoed for eons through the halls of philosophy, ethics, and theology, but a few guidelines can help you to better grasp it from the sociological perspective.

Sociology is often best known for emphasizing the constraints placed on our choices in society. There is good reason to emphasize this, particularly in the midst of popular culture that exalts personal choice and decries any talk of the inevitability of social constraint. American sociology has frequently drawn disapproving frowns for its willingness to challenge the American Dream of personal freedom, endless choice, and boundless opportunity. The task of sociology is not to defeat this dream but to bring it back to its moorings in reality: The exercise of personal freedom always involves social cooperation and conflict; choices are made within the context of socially constructed values and socially structured constraints; and opportunity is structured by position and power.

None of this denies freedom of choice. In fact, one sociological message is that our choices and our actions are *more* powerful than we might have thought. They not only shape our lives but they contribute to the reordering of society, thereby shaping many other lives. Yet social choice is always choice in context. A constant and permanent interaction is played out between constraint and choice, between social structure and social action. Too much emphasis on the first, and we fall into the trap of unfounded conspiracy theories. We start playing the victim: "It is no use, everything is controlled anyway by the media, big corporations, international bankers, the CIA, crooked politicians. . ." or whichever group we most distrust. Too much emphasis on the latter, and we lapse into naive individualism. We start blaming the victim: "Whatever anyone says, it just comes down to punks, hooligans, irresponsible moms, deadbeat dads, decadent youth, lazy freeloaders, common trash. . ." or whichever group, real or imagined, we happen to dislike the most.

To avoid these pitfalls and the pointless debates they too often engender, we need a foot in each camp and both hands firmly on the evidence. We are not powerless, because we are social actors reshaping our world. Nor are we omnipotent, for the social world and our place in it is constantly shaping our choices. Sociological imagination is the ability to see both sides, structure and constraint on the one hand and personal choice and action on the other. And— most importantly—it is the ability to see the connections between them.

A proverb states, "The pessimist curses the wind, the optimist hopes it will change, the realist adjusts the sail." Social forces, like the wind, are powerful, sweeping, and global in origin and extent. But just as crucial is the on-board response, the decisions and adjustments that determine where that wind will carry us. A contemporary analogy is the typical helicopter traffic report that radio stations in large cities provide. Just hearing the report won't get you anywhere; you still need a car and still need to drive. But getting the big picture may be more important to where you go and how long it takes you to get there than how fast your car is or how skillful a driver you are. Social theory provides a map of the community, while social research provides the data on current conditions: Both can be very helpful as we plan ahead, estimate our arrival, and choose our course.

Social Thought

The social sciences in their present form are quite new, going back about a century and a half. Social thinking, however, is an ancient occupation. The earliest piece of literature we have could be the Sumerian saga of Gilgamesh, which consists of stories drawn from the very dawn of writing itself. Yet it is filled with sociological themes: the nature of humanity, the contrast between civilized urban life and life in the wild, power relations between rulers and subjects, the trials and possibilities of cross-cultural friendship, and the power of social relations to dramatically alter our personhood. From Gilgamesh to Plato, Aristotle, Confucius, Lao Tzu, Isaiah, and on through the centuries, philosophers and theologians have pondered the nature of a just and meaningful social order. At times, these thinkers sought data and a more analytical framework, but more often the stress was on moral authority, eloquence, and literary or rhetorical style. Gradually, a few European states gained world dominance, and their global voyages brought new and challenging information and ideas. These powerful and newly centralized states began collecting vital statistics on their populations that provided a new data source. At the same time, the impressive early investigations into the natural world created new admiration for scientific methods.

Out of this intellectual ferment, the various social sciences began to crystallize. Economics emerged, as states entered into vigorous competition with each other, sometimes trying to monopolize and dominate, other times trying to standardize currencies and cooperate in their search for a science of commerce and finance. Political science emerged, as monarchs, nobles, republicans, and revolutionaries struggled for control of these states and wealthy empires, and writers attempted to justify or condemn the ideals of the various factions. Geography, an ancient pursuit, gained new importance, as regional empires became global pursuits, and maps and knowledge of alternate trade routes and resources took on new importance. Anthropology came into its own, as these far-flung travelers encountered people and cultures dramatically different from their own. Psychology separated from philosophy, as emerging medical models created interest in a science of the mind akin to the science of the body.

Finally, sociology began as thinkers moved from the more immediate issues of laws and taxes to the broader questions of what is happening to societies as a whole in urbanizing, industrializing, capitalist environments. The turmoil of the times provided the questions, and newly urban industrial societies with their growing collections of maps, vital statistics, and social information provided the data sources.

Clearly, there is nothing absolute about any of these disciplinary boundaries, and they remained quite fluid for decades before settling down into their present form. Now in recent decades, the domains and boundaries of these disciplines are again being rearranged by new interest in interdisciplinary work, cross-pollenization of theory and methods between disciplines, and the establishment of new frameworks for study; e.g., regional and ethnic studies, women's studies, urban studies, and so forth.

Concepts and Theories

In any introductory overview course, particularly in sociology, it is easy to be overwhelmed by new terminology and a host of names and theories. The danger is that some of the interest inherent in investigating human social lives can be lost in the process. At worst, students can feel they are only getting "common sense with terms." But don't be fooled. There is more to both common sense and terminology than you may realize.

Entering any new field is like visiting a new country, so it is very helpful to have some familiarity with the language. In itself, language building can be very helpful. Learning new terms and phrases makes us more aware, makes new connections possible, and allows us to think about vague ideas more concretely. Language and thought are closely related. Many linguists believe that we can think with sophistication, only because we have a complex linguistic system with which to gather, sort, and organize thoughts. So, for instance, a relatively new term such as "sexual harassment" can be overused, misused, and debated as to content and context. Yet having the term also allows us to perceive and discuss behavior and maybe even be more aware of the nature of that behavior. Many terms are not just offhanded definitions but concepts with a great deal of depth and a history of research and thought.

A good first step, the one used in this book, is to explore and apply some of these concepts. In so doing, you may further appreciate the depth and complexity embraced by certain social concepts and even have a desire to probe more deeply into social theory and research.

And what about the "common sense" nature of some sociological assertions? Again, this is partly the problem of a broad and general overview that may not have time to probe into the deeper dimensions of social issues. Social theory has a particular problem in this regard, though. Its subject matter is close to home, so it tends to go through three stages:

Stage One: "You're Wrong." A new theory can seem radical when it debunks popular notions. In this position, social theories can seem absurd, cynical, biased, or just plain wrong to the observer. When sociologists challenge the cherished notions of our society—the nature of family, freedom, faith, success, and so forth—they can seem to us to be out of touch with the mainstream. Students sometimes have this reaction when they read provocative monographs by "radical" thinkers.

Stage Two: "Who knows?" At this point, the theory has been around long enough to have spawned more sophisticated counterarguments, and the debate is on. This can make for interesting reading and discussion, but it can also give the impression that social scientists have no agreed-upon principles or accepted findings; they merely like to argue with one another. Students sometimes get this impression when they read collections that present conflicting approaches to a problem or issue.

Stage Three: "Who cares?" At this stage, the theory has matured and survived the debates. It has been around long enough to have entered the mainstream. Its terminology has shown up in the popular press so much that it is now perceived as "common sense." Cries of "you're wrong!" now give way to "well, we knew it all along." Students sometimes have this reaction when they read comprehensive textbooks. You should be aware of just how much our accepted tenets, our "common sense," has been shaped by the social sciences over the last century and a half. If you read something to the effect that "a positive self-image and good self-esteem are central to social well-being," you may think, "So what, isn't that obvious?" It certainly was not obvious to people a century ago. The terms "self-image" and "self-esteem" would have been largely unintelligible and sounded dangerously like the sin of spiritual pride. The connections between them, and between living well, would have seemed obscure and somewhat strange.

As you encounter theories, try not to get bogged down in terms but push through to get a glimpse of the key concepts—the new ways of seeing—that these theories are trying to package and organize. Then try to place them in their historical context: Is this a new challenge to accepted thought, is this a current debate among scholars, or has this become an accepted way of seeing the social world that is now generating new ideas and concepts?

Getting a handle on social theory can also be difficult, because the textbooks often present broad perspectives that are only infrequently referred to in actual current research and writing. This is partly because these orienting perspectives are in the background as "things understood," while the debate rages over specifics. The key theoretical debates are also constantly shifting. For this reason, it can be helpful to sketch out a simple map of the terrain before plunging further into sociological topics.

Sociology, for all its diversity and divisions, has essentially two main topics: *social interaction* and *social organization.* The first is the primary concern of micro-sociology, the second the primary concern of macro-sociology. Because interaction and organization are in a constant interrelationship or "conversation" with each other, certain lines of theory also seek to bridge between the two.

Micro-sociology currently has two main approaches. Exchange theory sees social interaction as an exchange of good and bad, both tangible and intangible, between actors who are rational and therefore concerned about getting the "best deal." This is a very simple idea, but its very simplicity allows it to be applied to a wide range of complex situations to predict and interpret behavior. If you have had any economics, you should know that this is essentially the fundamental idea of micro-economics. This line of thinking has long roots, especially in what in Britain is commonly known as utilitarianism. The stated goal of utilitarianism is the greatest good for the greatest number; or to put it in more contemporary terms, everyone gets the best deal possible. The term "exchange theory" was brought into the discipline by sociologist George Homans, who noted its strong affinity to a key tenet of behaviorist psychology: People are more likely to do more often that for which they get the most reward. The resurgence of this line of thought has come not so much from psychology, however, as from economics. For example, economist cum sociologist Gary Becker won the Nobel Prize for economics for using this line of thinking to study the family. Sociologists working from this perspective often draw on and extend economic theory and concepts, as in the work of James S. Coleman (1990). Often termed *rational choice theory* (or *rational action theory*), it has stirred a great debate in sociology and renewed interest in social action and micro-sociology from otherwise more quantitatively oriented thinkers. Some are not so sure that this is a truly "sociological" perspective, and it is only mentioned as an aside in some introductory texts.

The other micro-approach to social interaction has the long but descriptive title of *symbolic interactionism*. For this group, "society is in the mind," its meanings and definitions turned into symbols for social communication. In contrast to the more nuts-and-bolts approach of rational actor exchange theorists, this approach is more concerned about intangibles, such as perception of self and the situation, and how these translate into the social interactions that build a society. Its origins are largely American, going back to the early sociologist Charles Horton Cooley and the philosopher George Herbert Mead, whose ideas were systemized by Herbert Blumer earlier in this century. Although often covering much of the same terrain as the exchange theorists, this approach is closer in roots to philosophy than to economics and to cognitive rather than to behaviorist psychology. Its focus on culturally defined knowledge and meanings also brings it very close to current ideas in cultural anthropology (Spradley, 1994).

The macro-study of social organization has also tended to fall into two camps. Ideas on social conflict were systematized by Karl Marx and Max Weber as they studied European societies from the vantage point of Germany, which had stood at the center of centuries of conflict, both international and internal. Their ideas gave rise to much European sociology and gained strength in the United States in the conflict-ridden 1960s. Conflict theorists focus on the component groups of a society and their struggle for dominance. In practice, conflict theorists are most likely to identify themselves by the particular locus of power and conflict that interests them. Those interested in the struggle between social classes and their political allies may claim such labels as "Marxist" or "Neo-Marxist"—stressing that they have revised or updated Marx's thinking—or they may borrow the older term of "political economy," which Marx himself preferred to "sociology." Those interested in similar struggles, but who see politics and economics as more separate realms, may adopt the label of "Weberian." Feminist theorists are also often interested in social conflict but stress power, dominance, and subordination between genders.

Another line of thought emerging in the last century stressed the foundations of social order. Emile Durkheim studied the changing social order of industrialized France and its neighbors, as village life gave way to urban life. The social order approach was greatly influenced by advances in biology and borrowed evolutionary ideas, as well as the image of society as a body whose different organs worked in systems to allow the functioning of the whole. This approach came to be known as *structural functionalism,* or *functionalism* for short, and was established in the United States through the prominence of such social theorists as Talcott Parsons and Robert Merton. Functionalist thinking also fit in with anthropologists' attempt to make sense of the structure and functioning of well-integrated simpler societies, so it became an important perspective in anthropology.

The dominance that this approach once had in American sociology means that it is still often given first billing in textbook discussions of social theory. The problem confronting the interested student, however, is that one can read long and hard in current sociology journals before finding anyone who claims to be a functionalist. This approach came to be associated with a conservative view of the social order that well fit the 1950s but seemed out of step with the changing world of the 1960s. Parsons' complicated schemes, long descriptions, and difficult prose probably also did little for sociology's image or the appeal of this approach. Yet Durkheim, in his original questions about how societies can maintain order and essential functions, was probing some of the most basic and fundamental questions of sociology. Thus, Randall Collins (1994), himself a Weberian conflict theorist, finds in this approach some of sociology's deepest and most profound insights. The heirs to the Durkheimian tradition have often shunned the functionalist label to go back to terms that are more in accord with the original: systems theory, ecological-evolutionary theory (Lenski, 1966), human ecology (Park and Burgess, 1921; Hawley, 1986) or just ecological theory.

Social theorists in this stream now have a better analogy in biology, the ecosystem. An ecosystem has order, structure, and balance but also competition and conflict between elements. As such, some in this line of thinking hope to bridge the gap between conflict theory and functionalism (Lenski, 1966). For the present, however, those drawn to ecological approaches tend to stress the effects of numbers, natural selection processes, and equilibrium; those drawn to conflict theory are more inclined to shift the discussion to topics of power, dominance, subordination, and exploitation.

Although it is helpful to lay out the terrain in terms of ideas and historical traditions, sociologists are also very human and tend to be attracted to lines of inquiry that agree with their dispositions and experiences. You will probably do the same. As long as we all remain open to new ideas and evidence, this gives the discipline some of its fervor and human interest. In fact, a line of thinking known as *post-modernism* is creating a stir in both the humanities and the social sciences, stressing subjective meanings and the importance of understanding the role and personal characteristics (especially race, class, and gender) of the observer or researcher. Post-modernism has been influenced in part by feminist theory and the larger numbers of women entering academic disciplines, at times challenging the existing perspectives and body of theory.

Differing approaches may often have complementary viewpoints. Although they may debate over the importance of micro and macro forces, rational choice theories and functional or ecological theories have a certain affinity. They both tend to stress the natural and empirical order of the social world and often use quantitative methods to describe this order. New institutional theory, for instance, accepts micro-economic models of behavior but also looks at how these are bounded by the norms, values, and understandings of social institutions—themes reminiscent of functional analysis. On the other side, conflict theorists and symbolic interactionists may also focus on different levels, but both tend to stress the humanly constructed and interpretive nature of the social order. Feminist theory, for example, is rooted in the conflict perspective of dominance and subordination but also draws freely from symbolic interactionism in its interest in language, meaning, and social roles. One can then envision a four-cell picture of prevailing social theory.

Four Traditions of Social Theory

	Micro Focus	Macro Focus
Stress on empirical/ natural order	Rational Action/ Exchange Theory	Functionalism, Human Ecology
Stress on interpretive/ constructed order	Symbolic Interactionism	Conflict Theory

There is value in working with a theoretical tradition that one finds persuasive and compelling, as insights generate new insights. Scholars working from similar but slightly different perspectives can extend and refine one another's thinking. There is also considerable value, especially at the beginning, in using the differing perspectives together as different lenses, each giving new insight into the social world. Social organization is in constant tension between order and conflict, while social interaction encompasses both social symbols and social goods.

The best way to understand a concept or perspective is to apply it. Educator Paulo Freire speaks about the dialectic between action and reflection. That is the goal in this book: not to provide extended discussion of theory and research results in hopes that enlightened action will follow, but to stress learning by doing—a use it or lose it approach—trying out ideas and approaches then coming back to reflect on their successes and failures, insights, and misunderstandings.

Digging Deeper

This introduction is intended to give you enough background in sociological thinking to understand and appreciate the approaches in the following chapters. You may wish to probe deeper into one or more of these perspectives. A good condensation of the rise of the social sciences and the development of the four theoretical perspectives discussed here can be found in Randall Collins' *Four Sociological Traditions* (1994). The differing approaches of sociology's founding thinkers can be sampled in reasonably accessible form in Marx and Engel's *Communist Manifesto*, Weber's *The Protestant Ethic and the Spirit of Capitalism* (1996), and Durkheim's *Suicide* (1951).

One useful exercise is to look through recent issues of major, comprehensive sociology journals, such as *American Sociological Review* and *American Journal of Sociology*. After stating problems of interest, articles often provide a literature review in which they trace their theoretical and intellectual lineage. What theories and theoretical perspectives are frequently cited? How do these fit into the broad spectrum of sociological theory outlined in this introduction?

The importance and relevance of social theory as a guide will become more apparent as we examine aspects of society and social relationships in the chapters that follow. We will begin with the interwoven strands of culture and social structure and how these shape and color our lives.

1

Building Bridges in the Global Village

The world is growing smaller. Our global neighbors are getting much closer to us every day. The expansion of popular media and multinational corporations spans a globe bound together by busy air routes and congested migration routes, by superhighways of concrete and supernetworks of fiber-optic cable. Closeness, however, does not guarantee understanding. Consider the complaints from families alone: "My spouse doesn't understand me," "My parents don't understand me," "I don't understand my children," and so forth. We can hardly expect the global family of humanity to fare much better. Closeness also does not guarantee harmony. Ethnography and anecdote point to villages, small towns, and urban enclaves as filled with rivalry, competition, backbiting, and gossip. Again, it should be no surprise that the emerging global village is plagued with similar problems. Closeness brings new opportunities for contact but also new problems of conflict, misunderstanding, exploitation, and violence.

Yet, if we can seize the opportunities for contact with a willingness for understanding and flexibility, we can become bridge-builders between cultures and find new worlds of possibility. As our world becomes ever more woven together economically, politically, and electronically—and as our own society becomes ever more culturally diverse—we need to grow in our understanding of the nature of culture and society, as well as our exposure to world cultures and societies.

The Social Tapestry

Each culture is as unique as each person within that culture. Our awareness of this should make us cautious about stereotypes and help us to value the contributions of each culture and each person without excluding, trivializing, or crushing the uniqueness of any of them. Diversity is a hallmark of strength in human social systems, just as it is in natural ecosystems; yet diversity is derived from many common elements. One of the tasks of social scientists is to find the building blocks of diversity in several key concepts.

Social Structure

Social structure is the enduring pattern of relationships between people. It may well be the central concept of sociology. The element of interest, or what researchers refer to as "the unit of analysis," is neither the individual person nor any particular aggregate of persons, large or small, but the relationship between them. Here is where many, from introductory sociology students to government officials, often encounter problems. How can the basic building block of understanding be something so intangible? We can see (and hear, meet, examine, etc.) individuals, but what is the pattern of relationships?

Two analogies may help. Linguists eager to understand a language want to know its sounds, its syllables, and its words. But if they are to make sense of the language, they will soon need to learn its grammar. But what is grammar? Words can be spoken, written, and collected, but grammar is more elusive. Even native speakers of a language may not be able to help. Unless they are teachers or linguists themselves, they may be largely unaware of the rules of their own grammar. Grammar is the way words and phrases are organized, the relationship between parts of speech. Whether conscious or not, grammatical structure shapes how people speak and interact. It is the enduring pattern of relationships between spoken and written symbols, its rules comprised of many differences yet many similarities. Children grasp it long before they learn these rules in school. Even their mistakes have a certain logic (e.g., my four-year-old's favorite expression, "No, I amn't!"). They take to it so readily that some suggest that a universal grammar may be hardwired into our brains from birth. Social structure is the grammar of human relationships.

Another analogy to social structure can be found in a coral reef. Coral are tiny organisms that have a brief, independent existence. What is most striking, however, is not the minute individual coral but the imposing structures they create. Long after the individual is gone, its tough skeleton is linked with millions of other fantastically diverse and colorful forms that, in turn, provide for an entire community of organisms. The reef is created by the welding together of many individuals, but in time it takes on a shape and importance of its own. Likewise, social structure is created by individual action, but over time it takes on a presence and an importance far beyond the individual actor.

Social organization is the broad outline of this structure, social interaction the daily workings of the structure. These are the two primary components of sociology. Organization is the concern of macro-sociology, while interaction is the concern of micro-sociology.

Society

Here we have another elusive term. Most textbook definitions generally describe a society as a group of people sharing territory and culture. This is certainly the essence of the idea when we speak of American society, Japanese society, or ancient Egyptian society. Yet many groups who identify themselves as one people do not share a common, independent, or even well-defined territory (e.g., Palestinians, Kurds, etc.). At the same time, most large societies in the world are multicultural; although they may share a common dominant culture, they have many diverse subcultures.

It may be better to define a society as a group of people who share common relationships with each other and a particular environment. A society is created as members of a population relate to one another in common ways (organization and interaction) in a common context (environment as well as technology). Ancient Egypt emerged, in this case over centuries, from a growing population that structured itself to make a living by growing plants on the fertile Nile flood plain. Of course, as Egyptians interacted over time, they must have developed common understandings and a common heritage to pass on; thus began Egyptian culture.

One simple yet revealing way to group the vast number of human societies is by their basic way of making a living—their subsistence. Hunting and gathering societies existed for millennia by harvesting the natural abundance of their environments. Horticultural societies are based on gardens, which supply basic needs through the small-scale cultivation of plants. Pastoral or herding societies survive through the control and use of herd animals. Agrarian or agricultural societies depend on the intensive cultivation of large fields to feed denser populations. Industrial societies harness machine power to provide food, shelter, and basic needs. Which societal type is preferable may depend on the particular example and the criteria used (e.g., social, environmental, etc.). But each step, from hunting and gathering to industrial society, reflects a more powerful form as other types have gradually been incorporated, often by force, into larger agrarian and industrial states.

The wealthy nations of the world base their wealth on industrial power. Poor nations are often largely agrarian with many poor peasant farmers in states eager to industrialize. Tribal peoples are often threatened by larger entities and face a precarious future. Today, many observers suggest that advanced industrial societies are becoming post-industrial, by which the dominant activity that shapes all others is the control and movement of information. These are societies dependent on electronic processing and the communication of information, with most people working in services.

Similar societies tend to create similar cultures. Agrarian societies, for instance, often stress respect for elders, life-long marriages, and similar cultural values. Industrial societies tend to place greater emphasis on personal achievement and broader opportunities for both men and women. Some changes we may see as beneficial and others as detrimental, but the changes do not reflect so much moral advancement or decline as they do the new demands of industrial society. An important question is how the demands of post-industrial society will shape future changes. Some popular accounts are optimistic, in that the future holds greater opportunities for interaction, creativity, and productivity (see, for example, Nesbitt in *Megatrends*, 1982; Toffler in *The Third Wave*, 1980). Others see only new forms of domination and control and still greater inequalities. Both sides agree, however, that both structure and culture will change in response to new demands.

Culture

Definitions of culture also abound. They reflect a common understanding of culture as a shared way of life but stress somewhat different aspects. One problem with the broadest definitions of culture is that they seem to include everything, thus raising the question, what is *not* culture? In general, sociologists and anthropologists agree on four points of what exactly is culture:

1. *Learned.* Culture is distinguished from instinctive and biological traits.

2. *Shared.* All societies have deviance or "rule breakers" but also shared values that allow them, for example, to determine who the "deviants" are.

3. *Symbolic.* Symbols make culture possible, as they convey shared meaning.

4. *Integrated.* Elements are closely related to one another, interwoven like a rich and varied tapestry; changing one aspect will likely alter many others.

One definition that stresses this shared understanding is that culture is acquired knowledge used to generate behavior and interpret experience (Spradley, 1994). We all need to know how to act and make sense of the world. Culture is the knowledge that is passed along and allows us to do this. Culture may be likened to a map that tells us where we are, so we can know how we should proceed. This includes norms (proper behavior), values (what is good), and interpretations (what is real). People who share a culture may not always agree, but they can at least understand the basis of their disagreement because they are likely to agree on some common foundations.

Variations of culture give the world its richness and variety. Culture and social structure are intricately bound together. If social structure is more basic and fundamental, culture is often the most striking and appealing. If we think of social structure as the grammar of society, then culture is its vocabulary: describing, defining, organizing, and giving shape to our experience so that it may be interpreted and shared. To borrow the imagery of the tapestry, structure is the horizontal and vertical threads that bind the social fabric together, the "warp and woof" of society. Culture is the design woven into that fabric and the colors and patterns chosen to give meaning and order, as well as beauty, to the tapestry.

Cultural Politics

Sociological explanations, as well as popular explanations of social situations, are sometimes grouped together as cultural and structural explanations. The first stress values and norms; the second, situations and blocked opportunities. A cultural emphasis looks to *attributes*, especially how values and perceptions shape behavior. A structural emphasis looks to *position* in a larger system whose opportunities and constraints shape behavior. This distinction underscores countless political and social debates. For instance, are poor people or poor nations impoverished because of their cultural values or because of the structure of power, wealth, and opportunity?

The distinction can blur, however, especially when the terms are loosely applied. To argue, for instance, that poor African Americans suffer from a broken family structure is to advance a "cultural" argument (note the implication of values); whereas, to counter that the problem lies in our racist culture is to advance a "structural" argument (note the implication of discrimination and blocked opportunity). For this reason, it is sometimes better to distinguish *social-psychological arguments*—those that stress learned values (socialization), self-confidence, habits, and tendencies—from *social-structural arguments*—those that stress the organization of position and power in society. As you might guess, micro-sociologists are more likely to advance social-psychological explanations, macro-sociologists to advance social-structural explanations.

The approaches noted in the introduction may also affect these emphases. For example, functionalism has traditionally focused a great deal on norms and values, thus its underlying cultural/social-psychological approach. The conflict approach almost always leads researchers into structural arguments. Exchange theory usually begins with individual choices, but because these are assumed to be rational, much of the interest quickly shifts toward the structure of rewards and penalties. Both approaches are valid and potentially useful. Frequently, however, these positions are cited in opposition to one another, which is like asking which matters most, the coral or the reef, the vocabulary or the grammar?

Initially, people often gravitate to the micro social-psychological explanation. This is closest to our immediate experience, in the same way that casual contact with a language may give us a few words and phrases but probably not much insight into the grammar. It is easier to observe values and tendencies than a more abstract or hidden social structure. Political tradition often divides these perspectives as well. Political conservatives share a heritage that has often stressed the norms and values of groups and individuals; political liberals come from a tradition of seeking more progressive social structures, so they think more often in structural terms.

For Reflection

1. Look at Figure 1.1a below. What do you see? Now look at Figure 1.1b. Does this change or confirm your initial response to 1.1a? Now look at Figure 1.1c and compare that with 1.1a. Does this change or confirm your first response? Think about culture as a way of perceiving. In what ways has your cultural background prepared you to see more than just a random ink blot? How did looking at Figures 1.1b. and 1.1c. affect your preconceptions of what to look for in 1.1a? Cultural experience affects our perception in simple ways like this, as well as in more subtle ways. Is the woman in Figure 1.1b fashionable or outlandish? Is the woman in Figure 1.1c. dignified or dowdy? How do your responses to these questions reflect your cultural background?

Figure 1.1

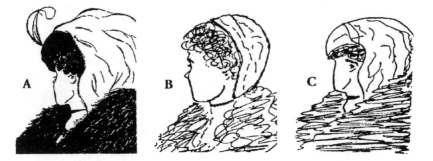

2. In upcoming chapters, we will continue to examine the dynamic interplay of culture and structure and explore the implications of social-psychological and social-structural arguments in various contexts. For the moment, however, consider different explanations that each argument might provide to the following questions. Even if you know very little about the following situations, you may be surprised by how much you can anticipate competing perspectives by thinking in cul-

tural/social-psychological and social-structural terms. Try to provide an answer from each perspective to the following:

    a. Why do men in the workforce continue to earn, on average, more than their female counterparts?

    b. Why have some immigrant groups to the United States achieved relatively rapid economic success, whereas others have struggled with low wages and frequent unemployment?

    c. Why are the outbreaks of violence so common and so difficult to resolve between Israelis and Palestinians (or between Catholics and Protestants in Northern Ireland)?

    d. Why are the economies of some nations growing rapidly and the economies of others stagnating or declining?

3. Can you see ways that cultural forces (norms, values, perspectives) and structural forces (patterns of opportunity and constraints) might work together in explaining the four questions above?

4. Similar basic types of societies often show broad similarities in their structure and culture. How might the shift from an industrial society to a post-industrial or information society change our social structure and our culture? Do you envision new or more restricted opportunities? Do you envision changes in norms, values, and lifestyle?

Seeing Ourselves: Cultural Icons

Culture is learned, shared, symbolic, and integrated. Woven together, these symbols that we learn and share allow us to make sense out of what would otherwise be a confusing deluge of daily experience. Like viewing a complex mosaic or tapestry with an expert eye and from a good vantage point, a pattern emerges out of a profusion of colors. They help us to sort through our past, understand our present, and anticipate future actions and outcomes. They make us feel at home. Sometimes, a particular structure or enterprise so encapsulates the essence of this tapestry of symbols that it comes to epitomize a society and its culture. Think of the pyramids of ancient Egypt, the Acropolis of ancient Athens with its pillar-lined Parthenon, or the Roman Coliseum. These become ready identifiers of a culture, or cultural icons.

Does the United States have cultural icons? Generations ago, we might have pointed to structures such as the Statue of Liberty and the Golden Gate Bridge as identifiable symbols of American power and opportunity. The American cowboy in his Stetson may be in danger of being relegated to cigarette billboards but nonetheless continues to evoke something of American character values: independence, self-reliance, quiet strength, and rugged determination. Around the world, however, two other cultural icons stand out as representing the American way of life. Appropriately, both are large corporations: Disney and McDonald's.

Before Premier Khrushchev visited the United States, he was asked what place would he most like to see. His choice—Disneyland. Subsequent decades have seen the development of Disney World in Florida, a Disney park near Tokyo, and Euro-Disney near Paris. Countless people around the world are familiar with Disney films and products, and Mickey Mouse is recognized virtually everywhere.

As a filmmaker, Walt Disney cultivated an image that was wholesome and "all-American." Despite changes over the years, this image continues to be well-preserved, with various results. For example, Japanese female employees seem to have few problems with Disney dress requirements. However, young French women have objected to Disney's requirements that employees not wear mini-skirts and "inappropriate clothing" (as well as "excessive" jewelry or make-up), always maintain a demeanor of extreme politeness and cheerfulness, and always answer questions about their personal life. To many French, this was considered corporate intrusiveness. What they resented was the "all-American girl" image they were required to project.

What is "all-American?" For Disney, this includes family orientation, traditional gender roles, an emphasis on technology, fun, and leisure, and clear-cut struggles of good versus evil, during which good always prevails. Anthropologist Conrad Kottack notes that a visit to Disney World is filled with myth and ritual that is distinctly American, combined with a sense of both awe and amusement.

Likewise, the Golden Arches of McDonald's offer much more than the assurance of a meal. To enter under the arches is to enter a world that stresses speed (i.e., "fast food" and fast service), efficiency, uniformity, family-oriented fun (e.g., playgrounds in a restaurant), cheerful service, shiny machines, clean rest rooms, disposable packaging, and more. In *The McDonaldization of Society,* George Ritzer (1996) argues that many of these values of uniform organization and efficiency are permeating our society. They did not originate with McDonald's restaurants, of course. Rather, the franchise chain has seen explosive growth because it has encapsulized these values into a package that can be replicated around the world. A successful McDonald's restaurant requires more than access to enormous quantities of ground beef; it also needs to transport cultural practices. When McDonald's opened in Moscow, the most difficult aspect was not getting a steady supply of food products but training Russian employees to smile cheerfully, respond promptly, and wish customers the Russian equivalent of "have a nice day."

For Reflection

1. An advertisement in family-oriented magazines promoted a collector's doll named "You Deserve a Break Today," offered by McMemories, "the official McDonald's Collectors Club." Its illustration showed the porcelain doll of a toddler with big blue eyes hugging a smaller Ronald McDonald doll, with the title underneath asking, "Isn't it wonderful to have a friend like Ronald?" The copy read as follows:

   What a hectic day it's been! Mom hasn't even had time for a game of peek-a-boo. But her chubby-cheeked baby boy is happy to play quietly as she goes about her chores. After all, he has Ronald McDonald—his very best friend—to keep him company.

What cultural themes and values permeate this advertisement? What cultural details might be confusing or unintelligible to someone from a different society or worldview, even if this person knows about McDonald's restaurants?

2. What symbols, slogans, and images come to mind when you think of Disney and McDonald's? What values, attitudes, and ideals do these convey? How do they reflect broader American values and themes?

3. Think of Disney films and their products and promotions. What views of life and the world are presented? What values are stressed? Have these changed over time?

4. What has contributed to the popularity of McDonald's restaurants and Disney products? What image of Americans would be conveyed to others entering a McDonald's or a Disney theme park for the first time?

5. One aspect of culture is that it is integrated. While this is often easier to see in smaller, simpler societies, consider the cultural integration that comes from corporate interconnections. It is no accident that products based on new Disney movies are often heavily promoted at McDonald's. Disney and McDonald's recently signed a ten-year contract giving McDonald's restaurants the exclusive promotional rights on Disney-related products. How might this arrangement benefit both the film company and the restaurant? How does this arrangement serve to reinforce common cultural messages? Do you believe such corporate "cooperation" results in cultural uniformity? Does it foster or limit cultural creativity?

Culture and Communication

Culture as shared learning affects our perception and our worldview. Culture is a way of seeing the world. We often don't realize how powerful this is until we see alternative ways of perceiving the world. The naive view is that "reality is reality," and everyone everywhere sees things in about the same way (presumably *our way*). Yet our view of the world is socially and culturally constructed far more than we are aware. Peter Berger and Thomas Luckmann (1967) dubbed this "the social construction of reality." Culture and society provide the means of making sense of our social experience. People who were born blind and later in life have their sight suddenly given to them through surgery take a while to become effective in their use of this new sight. Their eyes work fine, but they need to learn to make sense of all the new visual stimuli and how to use it to judge size, distance, depth, angle, and so forth. Painters need to study the same things as they learn to convey these impressions on a two-dimensional canvas.

A classic example of culturally constructed perception is described by Colin Turnbull (1961). He took a Mbuti "pygmy" from a dense rain forest to the overlook of an open plain for the first time in the man's life. The pygmy saw faraway cape buffalo and asked what sort of insect they were. As they moved nearer and the buffalo "grew" in size, it seemed to be magic to him. The problem was not that the pygmy was not clever or sophisticated enough—he was extraordinarily adept at judging sound and scent—it was that the dense rain forest did not provide any perception of distance. This example raises the question of how much our own perceptions have been shaped and perhaps limited by our personal experience.

The first response to encountering other ways of seeing the world and living in it is often ethnocentrism: *Our* way is the best way. We place our experience and cultural viewpoint at the center of the world. Look at various maps of the world. A longstanding map still in common use is the Mercator projection, which flattens our round planet into a rectangle. The center of this rectangle is Germany (no surprise, since Mercator was German). Of course, this distorts most of the world. Higher latitudes are stretched, and tropical latitudes are compressed. Since this map centers on Europe, the shifted equator leaves the entire southern hemisphere shrunken in size. Similarly, some suggest that our "Western" view of the world places greater emphasis on the North (including Europe and North America) and ignores the South. Mercator's world is split open along the Pacific, emphasizing the closeness of Europe and North America which seems literally worlds apart from Asia, even though the two continents almost touch at the Bering Strait.

The point is that the ethnocentrism inherent in the map distorts the world. The modified Mercator map in my elementary school classroom, as I recall, placed the United States in the center and split

China and Asia down the middle, two halves on each side (see Figure 1.2). We are not alone in this practice. Japanese maps consistently place Japan in the center. We all tend toward ethnocentrism. Maps, like observers, face an inherent problem. The only accurate representation of the world is a globe, whose surface cannot be seen all at once. A viewer needs at least two vantage points to see it all.

Ethnocentrism, therefore, is the practice of positioning our viewpoint in the middle and judging all others against that standard. Of course, most of them do not measure up very well. To be more encompassing, we need a viewpoint that is geocentric or global. As in the case of maps, our viewpoint must be multicentric with several vantage points. The term that has come to express this is *multiculturalism.*

Multicultural individuals, like multicultural schools and societies, have the advantage of several viewpoints. Have you ever used a stereoscope or 3-D viewer? It requires at least two pictures of the same subject taken from different vantage points to create the 3-D image. One picture by itself looks flat. Learning new vantage points adds dimension to our perspectives. Sharing the perspective of another culture helps us to perceive our own culture, just as learning another language helps us to better understand our own.

One ideal way to gain many vantage points is extensive travel. Even this, however, would only help if we have enough time in each location to learn to see it as the locals do. Travel is wonderful, extended cross-cultural experiences even better. But with so much of the world and its many cultures crossing our doorstep daily, we simply need to be open to new ways of perceiving and understanding.

The goal of ethnography, a technique used in both sociology and anthropology, is to gain an insider's view of a cultural setting. At times, social scientists study people to learn, for example, more about structures that may be obscured even from the people involved. Ethnography, however, seeks to learn how people see their world and their place in it. What is needed are not experimental subjects or survey respondents but informants—teachers—who can show us their world from an insider's perspective and teach us a new way to perceive them. Studying underlying structures can provide important insights and make us more astute social actors. To be more empathetic actors drawing from a broader, richer, multidimensional world of experience, however, we also need the humbler techniques of ethnography.

An attitude of empathy, an interest in novelty, and a willingness to learn are crucial in successful cross-cultural encounters. The tremendous diversity of cultures and the subtleties of differences make it as difficult to be knowledgeable about cultures as it is to be fluent in languages. Often, the best we can do is adopt attitudes and perspectives that promote mutual learning and understanding. Although there is no simple way to organize all cultural patterns, scholars from a variety of perspectives (along with travelers from a variety of regions) have noticed a common distinction between the cultural patterns of many small-scale societies with long, stable traditions and those of many large-scale, ever changing, urban-industrial societies. In a classic statement of this dichotomy, Ferdinand Toennies (1988 [1887]) distinguished between the face-to-face norms and habits of *gemeinschaft* (personal-community) societies, and the more impersonal, fluid norms and habits of *gesellschaft* (impersonal-society) communities. Durkheim and Parsons both speak of similar basic shifts that marked the movement from "traditional" to "modern" society. Many scholars today are troubled by the glib use of the terms *modern* and *traditional* and the value judgments they imply. One alternate way of noting these cultural distinctions comes from the linguist Edward Hall (1966, 1976), who terms them *high-context* and *low-context* societies. High-context cultures tend to be more indirect, stressing the emotional content of communication and engaging in what is termed *dependence training*; that is, socializing people to be mutually interdependent group members. Low-context cultures stress direct, logical communication and focus more on *independence training*.

Distinctions between gemeinschaft and gesellschaft, high- and low-context, are at best *ideal types* that highlight certain distinctions. Any particular culture may blend elements of both, yet these distinctions will hold with considerable consistency. American society is typically placed in the low-context category, though its many subcultures and minorities tend to be more high-context. Certainly Native Americans, possibly African Americans and Latinos, and perhaps even Italian Americans possess more high-context characteristics. Western Europe is primarily low-context, though many would note variations between Irish and English or between Germans and Dutch on the one hand and Spanish and Italians on the other. Insofar as families have preserved these distinctions, the variations also explain some of the stereotypes that we have of the tendencies of American ethnic groups.

The distinctions also explain many of the frustrations that American tourists (as well as Canadians, British, Germans, and other low-context cultural groups) have in Latin America or the Caribbean. Much of Asia and Africa are also decidedly high-context. One might ask, for example, why don't Japanese business people ever seem to get to the point? Why do Mexican tellers and clerks always seem to be taking care of things other than your business? Why does it seem that you have to "know someone" to get anything done in many foreign bureaucracies? Why do Latins and Caribbeans always seem to be late? Why do so many consider Anglo Americans to be rigid and uptight? In each case, the answer seems to lie in the differing positions of Hall's cultural distinctions.

Cultural differences, even the most subtle ones, can greatly complicate communication. As Hall reminds us, this is partly because communication is easiest when we share a common context or common experience. Also, much of what we have learned about how to express ourselves is "tacit culture" rather than "explicit culture." When our elementary teachers reminded us that "there ain't no such word as ain't," they were explicitly reminding us of a rule. But many rules of communication are tacit: how loud, how close, in what context, etc. Children frequently embarrass their parents by breaking tacit rules, such as asking brazenly, "Why doesn't that fat man have any hair on top of his head?" After a childhood full of hushes and shrugs, we come to learn these tacit rules. Many of them apply not just to our words but also to the communication that envelops our words. Communication specialists are fond of noting that "you cannot *not* communicate." That is, whether we are speaking or not, we are sending messages.

Sometimes, stony silences express a great deal. Communication that wraps around language includes how we use our body, voice, space, and social position.

Some cross-cultural differences in body language can be dramatic: The American "OK" sign is an obscene gesture in some cultures. Standing by the road with one's thumb out may be asking for a ride in our culture, but it may be telling motorists "where to go" in another. Other gestures are more subtle. Smiles may suggest pleasure and agreement, or they may indicate polite disagreement. Casting down one's eyes is perceived in American society as a sign of guilt and avoidance. In other cultures (even some American sub-cultures), this is merely a sign of respect. A teacher who demands that a wayward student from another culture "look me in the eye" may be sending a very confusing cross-cultural message to that student.

How we say things also communicates a great deal. In some languages, a change in tone or pitch can completely change the message, a frequent source of confusion and embarrassment for non-native speakers. English is not a true "tone" language, yet speed, pitch, and other qualities can also dramatically alter our communication. Imagine asking a friend how the previous night's date went. Downcast eyes and a response of "O.K." with a falling pitch means one thing. A shrug, a nod, and an even response of "O.K." means another. Raising one's eyebrows and pitch with an enthusiastic "O.K.!" means quite another. Even as that unusual American expression "O.K." becomes understood around the world, the hearer must also correctly interpret the inflection.

Cultures also differ markedly in their use of space and distance. Too far apart seems impersonal; too close seems intrusive. In much of the world, people are used to "claiming" much less personal space. Men in particular often stand much closer to one another in other cultures than in the United States. At the same time, men and women might stand farther apart when possible to maintain a "respectable" distance. Here again, differences can lead to discomfort and misinterpretation.

In one setting, for example, Arab diplomats were left wondering why Americans at receptions always seemed to talk with their backs to a wall. What happened, in fact, was that the Arabs and Americans were inching oddly across the room together as they conversed. Because Arab men tend to stand much closer in accordance with their idea of conversational distance, the Arab diplomats were unconsciously stepping closer. This was too close for the Americans— who were unconsciously backing up. As conversations progressed, the Americans kept retreating until they reached a wall and could go no further.

Sociolinguistics examines language use and structure based on social position: class, ethnicity, and region. The accent or dialect used in speaking can have a major effect on how the communication is perceived. Studies have shown that the same speech is likely to be considered more intelligent and thoughtful when delivered with a British accent than with an American southern drawl. Foreign accents tend to be assigned a hierarchy, with British and French near the top, Eastern European lower, and Spanish often the lowest. A similar pattern holds for regional and ethnic dialects, such as Appalachian English and African American English. The distinctive sound of Appalachian dialects are believed to have their roots in Elizabethan English but are usually more perceived as "hillbilly" than as Shakespearean. Likewise, linguists note that some of the distinctions of African American English are similar to West African and Caribbean Creole grammar, suggesting that as such it should be considered a dialect not unlike New England or Southern speech. Yet it has often been interpreted by white educators and employers as simply "uneducated" or "improper" speech. In each case, the actual dialect or accent and its origins are not nearly as important as the social context and interpretation given them. No one seemed to think that Henry Kissinger's or Albert Einstein's accents made them seem "uneducated" or that Alastair Cook's accent made him seem "improper."

Realizing that not all styles of speech are equally well-received in all contexts, many with a distinctive style engage in *code switching:* changing style to fit the situation. Distinctive styles and idioms become more pronounced when on home turf, then are modified or suppressed when in a more public or mixed setting. The challenge for effective communication is to code switch just enough to be understood and at the same time, to withhold judgments about other styles and accents.

No one can be fluent in all possible cultural rules. Much can be gained, however, by becoming familiar with a wider range and by withholding judgment on cross-cultural intentions, until one learns the context and familiarizes oneself more with the practices and their meaning.

For Reflection

1. Look at the two maps in Figure 1.2. Both have their limitations. The Mercator map preserves the shape of continents and the direction of travel between them but

Figure 1.2

Mercator Projection of the World

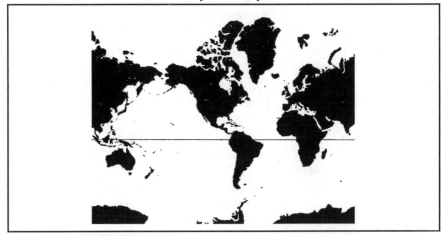

Peters Projection of the World

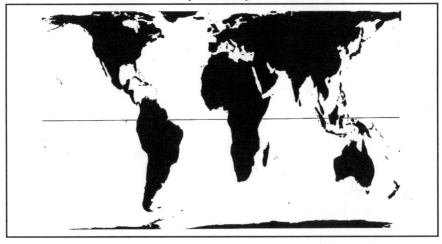

badly distorts their size. This was long the preferred map of mariners who cared mostly about which direction to sail. The Peters projection accurately preserves size but distorts shape. It is now the preferred map of many United Nations agencies. Bradshaw and Wallace (1996) note the differences in age: The Mercator map is over 400 years old, while the Peters map is a "new and improved" projection. Both maps distort reality in their own way, and which is better depends on our purposes. What impressions of the world do you get from the Mercator projection? What strikes you about the Peters projection? Why might U.N. agencies concerned about the developing nations of Africa, South America, and southern Asia prefer to promote the Peters projection? How might displaying the Peters rather than the Mercator projection in a classroom affect students' perceptions of the world?

2. Think of a misunderstanding you have experienced in communication. What caused the misunderstanding: differing assumptions, missing information, differing contexts, opposing definitions, or something else? How might cultural difference increase the likelihood of these misunderstandings? What could be done to avoid such a misunderstanding?

3. Are your own habits toward the high- or low-context side? How did you arrive at this conclusion? Can you think of situations where you were interacting with people from an opposite cultural tendency? What were the results?

4. Come up with as many non-verbal messages you can think of. Would everyone in the United States interpret these actions the same way?

5. Facing a partner, try conversing while standing at varying distances: two arms length, arms length, 12 inches, and six inches. Where is your comfort zone? Would this change in a different situation: an elevator, a business conversation, an intimate conversation, a new acquaintance? Have men and women try this exercise in different combinations: male-female, male-male, female-female. Note the distances as well as body alignment (direct or at an angle). How does this change? Do cultural patterns start to emerge?

6. What interpretations or misinterpretations do we sometimes make about someone's dialect and style of

speech? Brainstorm a few examples. Can you think of
instances of code switching that you have used or
heard?

Cultures in Collision

Our understanding of culture can be limited by a museum view
that suggests that culture is fixed and unchanging. We are especially
prone to this assumption about those simpler or earlier cultures
whose creations we are most likely to encounter on display in mu-
seums. In fact, although the core aspects of culture can be very enduring, many facets constantly change, converge, diverge, mingle,
and innovate. During times of severe environmental or social up-
heaval, these changes can be quite dramatic.

What comes to mind when you picture classical Native American culture? For many, it may be a feathered warrior with a lance
on an Indian pony in pursuit of bison herds. Yet horses and the
mounted pursuit of buffalo came quite late to plains cultures, only
after they had tamed and traded enough escaped Spanish horses to
adopt this lifestyle. Long before they took to the high plains, the
Cheyenne were settled farmers, growing the American staples of
corn, squash, and beans in relatively peaceful villages. Warrior images aside, many of the Native American contributions to the world
are in the wealth of horticultural skills and domesticated plants they
had accumulated, providing both food and medicine (Weatherford,
1988). Many groups gave up the life of settled farmers for the greater
abundance and adventure of the open plains that the horse made
possible. This, in turn, led to other changes in dress and custom.

Similarly, the classic image of the Navaho and Apache is bound
up with the desert Southwest, depicting wild horses and mesas,
great herds of sheep, and beautifully woven wool rugs. But like
horses, sheep were a European import. The Navaho and Apache are
linguistically related to tribes in Canada, where they may have once
been skilled northwoods hunters and gatherers. When they arrived
in the Southwest, the Navaho became bean farmers, which they
learned from Pueblo neighbors. Only with the arrival of large stock
animals could a herding society and culture emerge.

The rapid diffusion of European peoples, ideas, and diseases
around the world in the 1500s set off many cultural changes and for
some at least, social and cultural calamities. We are once again wit-

nessing a period of the incredibly rapid movement of people and ideas (as well as pollutants and diseases) around the world. In our electronic age, "remote" now refers to electronic controls rather than to locations. We live in an age of remarkable diffusion (spreading ideas), innovation (new ideas), syncretism (blending ideas), and attempts at cultural preservation (resisting threatening or destructive ideas).

Amidst the high-speed flying shuttles of the contemporary world, new tapestry patterns are woven and others are remade; still others seem to be fraying at the edges, on the verge of unraveling.

In the midst of these changes, one's cultural identity has become a complex—and at times contentious and political—matter. In resort locales, such as Mexico's Pacific "Riviera," the wholesale transplant of North Americans and American culture is particularly obvious. But between the aging glitter of Acapulco and the new glitter of American, Japanese, and European hotels sprouting up farther south is a fascinating blend of cultures. Dubbed Mexico's African Coast, this region just south of Acapulco contains the remnants of a West African group brought over to work the sugar plantations. They have retained their cultural distinctiveness over the last 400 years, so much so that neighboring Zapotecs shake their head and claim, "'Los Negros' have no culture and no religion." On the contrary, they have maintained both but with distinctly African forms. Houses are built in the rural southern Mexican style with only vertical sticks providing a screen from the outdoors. The shape, however, is not the classic Mexican rectangle of their Indian and mestizo neighbors but a round form that gives the black villages a distinctively African look. In small towns, the black Mexican population tends to adhere to specific neighborhoods with distinct traditions. A funeral procession through one of these neighborhoods at first looks much like others in rural south Mexico: A truck carries the casket and grieving widow, while mourners follow behind, led by a small band. But this line of musicians is not the usual mournful trumpet players but four black men with sunglasses playing the blues on saxophones. This instrument's association with "black" music fits better with these black Mexicans' sense of self and identity than a "Mexican" trumpet.

Diffusion, innovation, and syncretism take on a world of fascinating forms as people attempt to retain, define, and express their cultural identity. However, none is so pervasive worldwide as the influence of contemporary, especially American, commercial pop culture. Walking through a "remote" black Mexican village of stick huts, one must be careful not to trip on the long chains of extension cords that snake their way into each small home. Their purpose is evidenced by the flashes of light filtering through the gaps in the stick walls—the ubiquitous television set. The programming may be Mexican soap operas, or it may be American MTV featuring black sax players. Cosmopolitan consumer culture reaches every corner of the world.

In a small town nearby is the countryside's only billboard, advertising Bancomer VISA credit cards. In the local cantina next to the river where people are washing their clothes, you can pay with plastic. The cantina owners complain that many locals are already badly in debt.

This dominant form of diffusion and change based on Western urban industrial patterns has been labeled, for better or worse, *modernization*. Its impact has varied greatly around the world. The Japanese are famous cultural borrowers, for centuries from the Chinese, then from Western Europe in the last century. Today, the favorite cultural source for Japan is the United States, and the choices are wide-ranging. Spurs jingle in Japanese country-western bars, and the songs are pure Nashville, albeit with a slightly different accent. If that music doesn't suit one, across the street, a band with blond wigs harmonizes old Beach Boy songs. English words and phrases are everywhere. Yet few who have spent time in Japan seem to feel that Japan is losing its distinctiveness or becoming any less Japanese. Everything that is borrowed is eventually conformed to specific Japanese patterns. Having sufficient wealth, autonomy, and power seems to allow one to pick and choose without having one's cultural core threatened.

American culture itself is the product of two hundred years of this picking and choosing, borrowing and reinventing. The American hamburger looks slightly different from anything created in Hamburg, Germany, American wieners and frankfurters are distinct from the sausages of Vienna or Frankfurt, and pizza has become "all-American." But the names all remind us of their foreign origins.

In some places, the spread of modern technology and Western, especially American, culture has proved to be a mixed experience.

In an Amazonian village, the elders bemoan how few people are left at the story-telling circles around the evening fires. One by one, villagers have fallen victim to the "White Ghost." Each night, the White Ghost flickers through the village, and people disappear. Young people are especially vulnerable. We could have warned them about the mysterious powers of the White Ghost, for flickering television sets claim large portions of the evenings of most Americans.

Yet this same "ghost" can have another face. In the city bustle of Lagos, Nigeria, urbanites now tune in to a favorite program, *The Village Elder,* to hear rural wisdom and feel a part of a culture they can now only occasionally visit. By means of their television sets, they can still connect with their cultural roots and heritage and the village life that remains part of their identity.

In other places, the forces of rapid and uncontrolled cultural change have been far more devastating. Urban streets and slums around the world are filling with what Jack Weatherford (1994) calls "cultural castaways," displaced people with lost roots, little future, and few choices. Latin American street children may spend the day selling Chiclets gum, wearing T-shirts advertising some rock band's world tour, stealing car parts, and sleeping under a movie marquee advertising the latest Chuck Norris karate movie. They are immersed in modern, cosmopolitan cultural trappings, yet they are a part of no enduring culture and claimed by no society. It is fitting that American policymakers looking at the needs of our own communities and children have struck upon an African proverb: "It takes a village to raise a child." We have yet to see if the new global village is up to the task.

For Reflection

1. What is the appeal of Western, especially American, culture and images for people in many non-Western societies? Why do you think there is so much more social acceptance of Western culture in Japan than in Iran, Saudi Arabia, or China? Why have the Japanese been able to adopt many Western cultural forms while retaining their own distinct culture?

2. How has technology, especially communications tech-
    nology, contributed to cultural diffusion and cultural
    retention? Can you think of some examples?

3. Must modernization be painful and destructive? Is
    there an answer for cultural castaways and displaced
    peoples?

4. Do you believe that the world is headed toward one
    cosmopolitan culture? Would this be good or bad?
    What might that culture look like? Can it cope with
    global problems?

5. Do you have a sense of cultural identity or heritage?
    Are there ways in which you pick and choose from a
    variety of cultures in foods, dress, music, and leisure
    activities? What impact might your choices have on the
    rest of the world?

Reaching Out, Digging Deeper

Designs for Living

American culture has come under scrutiny and criticism in a
variety of books over the years. A good recent example is Robert
Bellah and co-authors' *Habits of the Heart* (1985) and *The Good Society*
(1991). A broader view can be found in Jack Weatherford's *Savages
and Civilization* (1994), which looks at tribal culture, national cultural, and world culture and their interrelationships in a sweeping
and interesting account. A controversial but fascinating account of
the origins of cultural practices can be found in Marvin Harris' *Cows,
Pigs, Wars, and Witches: The Riddles of Culture* (1974). To further explore the dimensions of culture, consider the following project ideas:

In Your Family

1. Examine a cultural tradition in your family: a distinc-
    tive holiday celebration, language use, religious obser-
    vance, or other practice that goes back for several
    generations. Talk about this with older family mem-
    bers. What are the roots of this tradition: ethnic, re-
    gional, local, or other? How does this particular
    practice relate to your family's broader cultural heri-

tage? Has the tradition changed over time? Do you wish to continue, modify, or abandon this practice?

In the Community

2. The ethnographic interview: A complex society such as ours contains many *microcultures,* settings that each have their own terminology and routines. The task of ethnography in this context is to gain an insider's view of the microculture. Locations can range from the very ordinary (counter work at McDonald's or a neighborhood bar) to the somewhat more unusual (a local nudist colony or the local "punk" scene and its clubs). The more well-defined the setting and the microculture, the easier your task will be. The informant should be someone well enough versed in the setting to give you a true insider's view. The informant can be a friend (although this is not always the easiest) or acquaintance, and the setting may be one with which you are already somewhat familiar (e.g., a nursing home or police station where you have worked). Because listening skills are an important part of the assignment, however, you should not be your own informant.

    a. Establish friendly rapport and respect and let your informant be your teacher about his or her world.

    b. Begin the interview with a "grand tour question," asking the informant to verbally (if not literally) show you around, focusing on typical activities.

    c. Listen for specialized terms and categories of people and things (e.g., "the burn-outs," "the big shots upstairs," "the basket cases," etc.). Try to group these into a taxonomy that describes people and events in the insider's own words. Is there a status system of hierarchy of positions? Are there clear categories of activities?

    d. Listen for cultural themes and values—honesty, hard work, dedications, and so forth—as well as ways of interacting, such as getting ahead, getting even, getting along, and so forth.

    e. Probe for more categories by asking structural questions, "Are there different kinds of . . ."

    f. Probe for more detailed description by asking attribute questions, such as "What is this like?"

How does the respondent use this information to shape and construct behavior? How does their insider's view differ from yours as an outsider?

3. Oral history: Anthropologists working in non-literate, oral societies must depend on oral histories. Others have discovered this as an important way to record experiences that do not make the history books: stories of "ordinary" people and neglected groups. The informant need not be elderly but should be old enough to have had enough substantial life experience that he or she can relate to you. This could be the history of an ethnic or social group, of a particular social institution or cultural practice, or of an extended family through the recollections of a senior member of that group. If you are related to the informant, you will still need to sit down with this person and get an organized account rather than trying to recreate an account from bits and pieces you may have heard in the past. Focus on structures, cultural domains, and cultural themes, as well as the sequence of events. Try to keep the focus on culture and cultural change.

4. Cross-cultural communication: Discuss the challenges of cross-cultural communication with an international student or someone else from another cultural background. Focus on cultural attitudes that may affect communication and could lead to conflict or misunderstanding: formality/informality, signs of respect or deference, views of time, appropriate behavior between men and women, appropriate distance, voice, etc. How

do these differ, and what effects do these differences have?

5. Culture and religion: Visit a church or place of worship whose traditions are rooted in a culture distinctively different from your own. Talk as much as possible with congregation members or leaders. How are cultural traditions and themes retained in the worship and life of the congregation?

6. Visit a group dedicated to the preservation and performance of a traditional style of dance or music. What are the origins and history of this art form? How has it changed? How is it being maintained?

7. Visit a museum or cultural center dedicated to the experiences of a distinctive ethnic or cultural group. You may be surprised at the diversity of possibilities in your community. What cultural practices and values are emphasized, and what is their basis? How has this group been treated or received? How have they maintained their cultural identity?

8. Visit a campus or community art museum with a diverse collection. Examine art from one region in detail or compare regions. In particular, you may wish to focus on a non-Western culture. What aspects of cultural beliefs and practices are conveyed in the art of different times and places? Look for views of religion, gender, authority, aesthetics, nature, daily life, and so forth. How are cultural ideas conveyed in this art form?

9. See if your community has outlets for "alternative traders," stores dedicated to selling crafts and indigenous art from various places in the world with no middleman profits. These include United Nations Stores and UNESCO outlets, Ten Thousand Villages, SERVE, and Pueblo to People. If you are unaware of local possibilities, the Yellow Pages under "Crafts" or "Gifts" may provide leads. What crafts are represented from what regions, and how do they reflect the art and culture of the region? How does this store attempt to cope with

the problems and inequity of the global economy? Clerks and volunteers are often eager to talk about the products and the programs. Conversely, find an outlet for local traditional handicrafts: regional pottery, woodworking, basketmaking, or other ethnic or indigenous crafts. What are the origins, history, and tradition of this art form? How has it been maintained? Is it in danger of disappearing or of succumbing to excessive commercial influences?

In the Media

10. Look through old editions of *National Geographic Magazine* (many libraries have issues going back to the early part of the century). How have perceptions of others changed? What differences of others have been emphasized? You may wish to focus on a particular group: Native Americans, African peoples, etc.

11. Look through old issues of *Life* or *Look* magazines (many libraries have issues going back to the 1940s). What cultural themes are presented? You may wish to focus on one aspect: home and family, material goods, popular culture, etc.

12. Look through popular magazines from another country: *Stern* (Germany), *Paris Match* (France), *Epoca* (Italy), etc. Magazines are also available on life in Russia, China, and the Middle East (ARAMCO), though you should realize they are official magazines intended to portray a positive impression. Look for cultural themes, cultural differences, differences in views of work, gender, home life, popular culture, etc.

13. Examine children's books and textbooks for attempts at multicultural representation. How effective are they in representing cultural diversity? Do you find examples of stereotyping? Do you see evidence of change over time?

14. Follow the history and development of a style of music with an extended cultural tradition (rhythm and blues,

gospel, salsa, calypso and reggae, cajun and zydeco, etc.). Listen carefully or read the lyrics to a number of songs. How has this music been intertwined with its culture of origin? Are there examples of cultural borrowing, diffusion, and syncretism? What cultural themes are reflected in the music?

15. Examine older and recent Disney productions, either on film or through the many books and promotional spin-offs. Are there common themes you note in Disney films? In female roles (from Minnie Mouse and Snow White to *Beauty and the Beast*, the *Little Mermaid*, and *Aladdin*)? In male roles? How are other cultures represented? Think of Middle Easterners in *Aladdin* or Native Americans in *Pocahontas*, for example; or in older films, look at the "Asian" Siamese cats in *Lady and the Tramp*, or the southern "black" crows in *Dumbo*. Do you note any change or consistency in these themes and images?

2

You've Come a Long Way, Maybe

Socialization: Traits and Roles

Socialization is the term that sociologists use to describe the way people learn their society's norms, values, and expectations. Socialization shapes our personality traits—what we are like—and our roles—what we claim as our legitimate expectations and obligations, and how we live out our place in society. Nowhere have we seen as many changes and controversies as in the area of gender: what men and women are like (gender traits) and what should be expected in the behavior of each (gender roles). Because our views of gender have undergone significant change and continue to stir controversy, they make a good arena in which to explore the power—and the limits—of socialization.

The understanding that led Emile Durkheim to pioneer the newborn discipline of sociology is that people are thoroughly social beings; they are social products and cannot be understood apart from social processes. We should not try to imagine a linear process that starts with individual persons who get together to form a society, because apart from some form of society, we cannot develop into fully human beings. Humans form societies, certainly, but societies also form humans. People and society create one another in a constant cycle of interrelationship. "To love society," Durkheim wrote, "is to love something beyond us and something in ourselves."

The importance of socialization in creating people and their personalities relative to the importance of genetics and biology has generated the long and largely fruitless "nature versus nurture" debate. The debate has subsided with both sides recognizing that they have overstated their case. Human development and behavior is a complex and continuing interaction of nature and nurture. Not only do both matter but they cannot be separated. Inherited temperament affects how a child is perceived and treated, aspects of nurture and experience actually alter brain chemistry, and in the midst of all this is the experiencing, interpreting child trying to make sense of it all.

Despite these difficulties, the debate continually resurfaces in discussions of sex and gender. Do biological differences between the sexes lead to different gender traits (the characteristics of men and women) and cause society to assign men and women different roles? Or do different social role expectations cause men and women to take on different traits? Is our development guided by our heroes or by our hormones? Easy answers have been discounted, but the questions seem to continually tantalize and plague us.

An old anthropological theory proposed quite simply that men had been dominant throughout history simply because they had bigger brains than women. When a female anthropologist decided to actually do some measurements and found out that the smallest brain in the university belonged to a distinguished male colleague, the theory found much less favor. In fact, women may have more neurons than men—but only in certain regions of the brain. This is the new line of inquiry: Are there male/female differences in brain chemistry and activity? Perhaps dominance of one hemisphere over the other, or greater activity in one region or another, gives men an edge in math and spatial reasoning and women an edge in language and interaction. To some, this would explain why men read maps and figure gas mileage, while women ask directions and how far it is to the next gas station. To others, this is just culture-bound sexism with a thin gloss of dubious science.

At the same time, researchers have demonstrated that gender socialization is at work right from birth, if not before. The birth announcement exclaims "It's a boy!" or "It's a girl!" so that well-wishers know whether to send the pink sleepers with kittens and flowers or the blue sleepers with toy trucks and trains. In one example, mothers (who all claimed to be non-sexist) who were given baby Elizabeth held, cuddled, and talked with her much more than later when they were given baby Adam. But Elizabeth and Adam were the same baby, only the color of their diapers had changed. This may explain in part why the real Elizabeths will grow up to be more nurturing and talkative, while the real Adams will learn the expectation of self-reliance.

"I tried to give my boy Barbies, but he turned them into 'shooters,' " complains a mother. Is this biology or society? Primatologists have observed young male chimps shaking big sticks to show off their strength. Power play may have deep roots, but of course, guns are cultural creations. The best we can say at this point is that there seems to be some difference between male and female behavior that has biological roots, but that societies greatly magnify (or diminish) this difference.

Social expectations can minimize differences: Girls on average become better readers early on, but most schools make sure the boys catch up. Social expectations can also magnify differences: Later on, boys seem to take the lead in math, but this time the difference is often seen as inevitable and "natural." The math-gap widens rather than narrows.

Differences in ability and behavior are at best probability distributions that tell about likelihoods. For clarity, however, cultures tend to turn tendencies into categories. Small differences with a large overlap become large differences, in some cases with no overlap (see Figure 2.1).

Figure 2.1

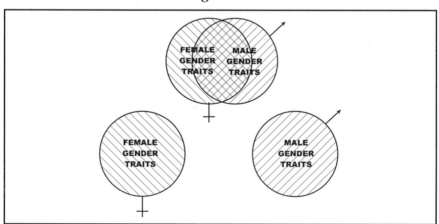

This has proven especially tempting with gender: Girls are neat, boys are messy; girls are quiet, boys are noisy, and so on. Probabilities can be helpful when considering large numbers: What is the likelihood that taking 100 Boy Scouts to see the *Nutcracker* ballet will result in uncontrolled chaos versus the likelihood of chaos when taking 100 Girl Scouts? Small probability differences on a single dimension do not tell us much about individual differences. Generalizations are useful when exploring group effects (for instance, the persistent case that men, on average, are paid considerably more than women). Generalizations degenerate into stereotypes when applied uncritically to individual cases. Because male and female differences are small relative to individual differences, it is far safer to avoid gender expectations about individuals whom we encounter: our children, our students, our classmates, or ourselves.

For Reflection

1. Make a list of traditional gender traits for men and for women. Which are still valid, and which are changing? Can you think of evidence that might indicate whether any of these are primarily biological or social in origin? How well do these lists describe you? Have you had to struggle against gender expectations that don't fit who you are?

2. What male and female role models did you encounter in childhood? Did they influence your ideas about sex roles? Have you taken on the same roles as your same-sex parent?

3. Gender roles provide a good example of how differing perspectives might generate different questions. Think of the four theoretical perspectives presented earlier:

    a. Functionalist/ecological: Were clearly divided gender roles functional in earlier times? What are the benefits and problems with clear gender role expectations? Have changing gender roles kept pace with social change?

    b. Conflict: What gender role conflicts have emerged with recent social change? How strongly do men resist changes in traditional gender roles? Do men have more to gain or lose from changing gender expectations?

c. Exchange: One traditional gender role exchange had men providing the income for the family and women providing the nurture. Was this a fair and equitable exchange? Have gender role changes balanced the exchange, or have women become overburdened with responsibilities? Why would women put up with an unequal exchange?

d. Symbolic interaction and gender role meanings: Has our society equally valued male and female traits and roles? Why or why not? Women have moved more rapidly into traditional male domains and occupations than men have moved into traditionally female areas. What would explain this? Do men or women now have broader roles? Are roles changing faster for men or for women?

Gender Socialization: Media and Messages

While we may speak of gender roles as "traditional" or "modern," what was expected of men and women has varied over our history. American society has also offered different messages about gender traits and what it means to be masculine and feminine. The following offers examples of how much these messages have shifted back and forth during past American historical periods and decades, given different social situations:

Colonial Period. Through sermons and essays, couples were commanded to be affectionate. Yet partly arranged marriages and very different worlds of work and leisure meant that many married couples probably did not share much emotional intimacy or romantic fervor. For many, the relationship with same-sex peers was more important. Remember the tale of Rip Van Winkle who sleeps for twenty years in Sleepy Hollow and then wakes to a happier life? In the original tale, the reason his life is happier is that his nagging wife is now dead and he can spend more time at the local tavern with his buddies! Such tales may not say much for the family values of our forefathers, but the reality is that marriage in most agrarian societies carried important economic and social functions and was rarely based on emotional fervor. The amount of male intimacy seen in letters from the colonial period surprises many. Those upper-class men writing letters to one another in which they pledge their deepest love and undying affection were not all homosexual, but rather using the language of a time in which emotional intimacy was more likely with the same sex than with the opposite sex. Women held largely subordinate roles and were accordingly seen as morally inferior. As a result, men were called upon to provide moral authority in the home. Because both men and women were seen as unable to control their powerful sexual urges, there was considerable suspicion of sexuality. Unlike in later times, sex was widely talked about but most often in cautionary sermons, and chaperons were expected. Still by some estimates, one-third of women were pregnant at the time of marriage. Maybe the suspicions in those sermons were correct.

Jacksonian Period. In the early 1800s, men and women were more likely to be seen as equals, but their domains became even more separate. The growing commercial marketplace was the man's world, and he was expected to prove himself a good provider. Women were expected to tend to the social and domestic worlds. Judging from the fairly large numbers of men who deserted their fiancees, wives, and families, many men must have found the role of sole economic supporter to be a difficult one to maintain.

Victorian Period. In the middle to late 1800s, the growing focus on home life idealized the domestic woman who was devoted to home and family. Glorification of motherhood as the highest female calling promoted the ideal of the nurturing woman. Men in competition with one another in the workplace were expected to be reserved. Now it was women who were viewed as morally higher and purer, as well as more passionless. Child-rearing was now the task of the devoted mother, who disciplined with guilt rather than physical punishment. To counter all this female-centered socialization, groups emerged to preserve the manliness of the growing boys: boys' clubs, Boy Scouts, and so forth. Not all women seemed delighted with their social roles at this time, for now more women than men deserted the home. This period also saw the first rise of feminism. The 1848 Seneca Falls Declaration denounced the "domestic slavery" of women.

Roaring Twenties. The *Progressive period* of the first two decades of this century brought new roles and demands and new uncertainty about the "proper" behavior for men and women. These changes culminated in the "mini-sexual revolution" of the 1920s. Dating became more common as couples went to activities, socials, and even jazz clubs together—usually unchaperoned. Sexuality and companionship were now expected to be part of male-female relationships. Couples could freely show affection, and romance was highly desired, but sex was still to wait until after marriage. Nonetheless, there was considerable worry about the new morality. Traditionalists thought female "liberation" was leading to "degenerate and immoral behavior." Some feminists thought that earlier feminist goals were being trivialized.

Depression Era. The Great Depression saw delayed marriage and child-bearing as a result of the economic hard times. High unemployment rates took their toll on the ideals of male providers.

Forties. World War II saw relationships disrupted by war, and many women were suddenly needed in the paid work force to replace men in military service. This decade produced the highest divorce rates seen up to that time.

Fifties. The "all-American" decade was in many ways an atypical period that saw a reverse in many trends: Women left the paid work force, people married younger and had more children, and they were less likely to divorce. The Fifties also saw the return of the domestic woman, but now she was both a loving companion to her husband (as in the 1920s ideal) and devoted to her children (as in the Victorian ideal). She kept a "hope chest" ready for her dream of marriage then became a devoted "housewife."

Sixties and Seventies. These two decades seemed to bring forth radical changes, although this was in many ways resuming earlier trends at a more rapid pace. The domestic ideal gave way to rapidly changing roles and with them a new round of uncertainty and worry about values and expectations.

Norms and expectations have clearly changed, but males and females both seem to get conflicting messages. Often, subtle messages are more powerful than the best-intentioned efforts. For example, even children sometimes hold on to stereotypes with a vengeance. One teacher reports how after visiting a hospital, her second-graders still insisted that only boys could be doctors and only girls could be nurses. "But then how do you explain the man we met who was a nurse and the woman who told us about her work as doctor?" the teacher asked. The children's answer was simple: "They lied."

These persistent stereotypes would be amusing were it not for the alarming evidence that girls still face a difficult challenge to their self-esteem and self-confidence as they mature. Emily Hancock, in *The Girl Within* (1989), asks the question: What happened to all the self-confident eight- and nine-year-old girls who were going to be astronauts when they grew up? By the time they reached high school, their self-evaluation had dropped markedly. They no longer seemed so sure of who they were or what they could do. Certainly, adolescence is hard on everyone's self-confidence. Boys also experience this drop in self-esteem, but they often find various ways of proving themselves through academics, sports, social skills, mechanical skills, and other activities. Girls, judged largely by their appearance, find fewer ways to prove themselves and often never regain their self-confidence. Somehow, the limiting messages, however subtle they may be, too often become internalized.

Gender messages come to us from family, school and peers, media and advertising, and the broader community. Often, they are mixed messages.

Families are changing, but they often still send strong gender messages to children. Choice of toys and activities, assignments of chores, and different styles of interaction can all relay powerful messages about differing expectations. Families can also challenge and refute other gender messages, but few seem to see this as a problem. Minority parents often speak frankly to their children about the challenges of overcoming racism and prejudice, but few parents talk with sons and daughters about overcoming gender-based bias.

School messages have also changed but still contain many mixed signals. Boys are consistently given more attention in class: They are called on more and given more encouragement, often by female teachers, even those who insist that they treat everyone equally. Some have suggested that boys simply demand more attention. Regardless of the reasons, boys and girls are frequently channeled into different courses and tracks based on gender expectations.

Television and advertising messages are often the most blatant. Walk through almost any toy department, and you are likely to find a "pink aisle" and a "khaki aisle"; girls and boys quickly learn which is theirs. In the one aisle, a dozen different Barbies all say, "Be attractive and fashionable," while the baby dolls all communicate the same message, "Be nurturing." In the other aisle, rugged and sometimes grotesque "action figures" all command the message, "Be strong, be tough, be active, be a hero."

In his study, *Gender Advertisements*, Erving Goffman (1979) demonstrated that similar messages are communicated to adults. Males are continually portrayed as powerful and dominant, looming physically over their women. In contrast, females are portrayed as dependent and subordinate, sometimes quite literally at the feet of their men.

In lectures across the country, Jean Kilbourne maintains that biased advertisements have a powerfully cumulative and unconscious effect on us that is "still killing us softly." She points to ads that portray an impossible ideal as the only acceptable look for women, thus communicating, "You're ugly, you're disgusting; buy something." She maintains that these ads' tendencies to treat women's bodies as objects for sale further leads to dehumanization, sometimes resulting in violence against women.

In a film about men in advertising, titled *Stale Roles and Tight Buns*, the men's group ACORN contends that men are portrayed as rugged, isolated individualists like the Marlboro Man and his hard-hatted Winston alter ego. None of these, they suggest, provide very helpful images for building healthy relationships.

For Reflection

1. Think about the ways that the following groups and institutions socialize children, both explicitly and intentionally, as well as tacitly and unconsciously. What gender messages have you observed or experienced from each? Consider the following:

    a. Family messages: What can families do to counter negative messages?

    b. School messages: Are school-based gender messages changing or persisting? In what ways?

    c. Peer messages: Do peers undermine or reinforce gender messages from home and school?

2. Media messages change with the times but also contain persistent themes. Cigarette ads are especially interesting in that they often focus less on the actual product than on the smoker's personal image and lifestyle. Virginia Slims has long promoted its cigarettes with an ad line that says more about women's self-image than product quality: "You've come a long way, baby." Their new advertisements use a similar slogan, "It's a woman thing." In one example from the new ad campaign, an attractive woman in a swimsuit is glancing back over her shoulder. The copy reads, "When we're wearing a swimsuit, there is no such thing as constructive criticism. Virginia Slims: It's a woman thing." An ad for Merit cigarettes, a product from the same manufacturer targeted at men, shows an attractive man in an open denim workshirt sitting on what appears to be a completed project with his arms outstretched in triumph. The copy reads, "You can too! You've got Merit." What messages about masculinity and femininity do you find here? What gives these ads their intended appeal? Think of the way that product and smoker are intertwined in these ads. Does "Virginia Slims" refer to the slender cigarettes or the slender models? Does "Merit" refer to the cigarette or the men who smoke them? Mentally switch the gender in the two ads and imagine a man in the first ad and a woman in the second. Do the ads' messages still work?

3. Erving Goffman found that in the ads he studied, women are often shown subordinate to men: behind them, leaning on them, or underneath them. In many ads, they are cast in childlike poses, in the midst of exuberant "body clowning," or looking dreamily away. Men grasp objects; women tenderly or dreamily caress them. He suggests that the extent to which these ads are "gendered" can be demonstrated by trying to imagine the ad with men in the women's roles and women

in the men's. Study the ads for each gender in a magazine with which you are familiar. Have these patterns persisted? What messages do they convey about masculinity and femininity and about how men and women relate to each other and to the world?

Gender Interaction: Changing Roles and Rules

The rules that guide our interactions may be reflections of broad social norms, or they may be specific to one's role in a relationship. Formal, explicit social rules are written into law or policy. Informal, implicit social rules become part of social mores, norms, and folkways. Groups, organizations, families, and even one-on-one relationships also develop rules that are both explicit and implicit. These are embedded in a broader social understanding, but in a complex, diverse society such as our own, people give their own twist and emphasis to their group role. For example, one couple is "traditional," while another is "liberated;" this group is "stodgy," while that one is "laid-back."

Gender relations have become especially complex, as both the accepted roles and rules have shifted. In a romantic relationship, who should play the role of the pursuer or the initiator? How is this communicated without appearing "aggressive," "over-eager," or "suffocating?" Rules have also changed: who brings up which topics, who pays for meals and when do they "go Dutch," and what is appropriate or inappropriate behavior? Rapid role transition, both personal and social, often leads to role confusion. People may also experience role conflict: "How can I be a competitive, competent classmate or colleague and still be the playful romantic?" Or they may experience role strain: "How can I be everything to everyone? How can I do it all?"

Traditional roles and rules have given men more power, more options, and more space, although at times also more demands for provision and performance. Some of these persist in interaction patterns. Social psychologists continue to find that in mixed-gender group interactions, men talk more, interrupt more, occupy more space, and are more likely to initiate a touch. Women, on the other hand, ask more questions, smile more, and nod and agree more. In more intimate interactions, particularly in same-gender or one-on-one settings, women are more likely to talk about feelings and to use more expressiveness and eye contact. For women, problems are often confronted "face to face." Men are more likely to stress activity-oriented interaction, in which a problem is tackled "shoulder to shoulder." In fact, when American men talk with one another, they are more likely than women to face partially outward toward something else: a television set, a fishing pole, or just passersby.

Anthropologist Helen Fisher (1992) argues that this is rooted in our past as male hunters and female gatherers. Women's talk, she claims, is the glue of society. To build lasting relationships, men need to sit down with the important women in their lives and talk face to face. Fisher further states that men are born to wander, and the women in their lives need to find a common activity that they both enjoy and can do together, side by side. Whether these differences are rooted in our common evolutionary past or more currently socialized by the pink and khaki aisles, they need to be overcome in many intimate female-male relationships. In *You Just Don't Understand*, Deborah Tannen (1990) writes:

> From the earliest ages through adulthood, boy and girls create different worlds, which men and women go on living in. It is no surprise that women and men who are trying to do things right in relationships with each other so often find themselves criticized. We try to talk to each other honestly, but it seems at times that we are speaking different languages—or at least different genderlects. (p. 279)

A frequent source of tension in male-female relationships and conversation is the tendency for women to be more feeling-focused and men to be more solution-focused. This can leave women frustrated with men who will neither "open up to them" nor "hear them out" without interrupting and offering a quick-fix or a noncommittal "who knows?" Men, on the other hand, can become impatient with talk that "goes nowhere," wishing the women would just "cut to the core" and lay out the problem; or they may be left wondering, "What does she want from me anyway?" Lillian Glass (1992) suggests that men can help this situation with better eye contact and non-verbal affirmation, fewer interruptions, and a greater willingness to hear and reflect on emotions and give and receive praise and condolence. Women can help by offering greater directness and fewer assumptions and by accepting offers of solutions as expressions of a desire to help rather than as put-downs.

Two areas in which changing rules have confronted gender and power are in the growing interest in sexual harassment and in sexual coercion and assault, sometimes called "date rape." Three broad approaches in sociology can help to sketch out the bigger arena in which these issues are debated.

First, the functional/ecological approach points to problems with rapid social and economic change and the resistance to quick change in social norms, so that we face a cultural lag. Many of our social rules became the norm at a time when fewer women were in the paid work force, especially in professional careers, and when relations between men and women were more likely chaperoned. We have yet to work out an accepted set of rules and roles for settings in which men and women interact in both economic and social settings as equals without sanctioned "supervision."

Second, the conflict approach emphasizes the element of power. Harassment is not just about sex but about sex *and* power. If a male subordinate is given to crude jokes and inappropriate comments in the presence of a female employer, it is usually easy for her to send him the message to "put a lid on it." If, however, he is the employer, supervisor, instructor, or other power holder, the situation can become much more difficult. If both are equal-status associates, the level of difficulty may depend on the attitudes and distribution of power within the organization as a whole.

Third, the interactionist approach finds problems in different styles of interaction and in changing role expectations and meanings. New roles are often ill-defined, and new settings can have different meanings for different people. Men and women now find themselves in situations of role confusion, in which expectations are not clear. In a dating situation, men may still carry the old baggage of the double standard, in which women were expected to protest any increase of physical intimacy as a sign of their basic "decency." This attitude can be extremely frustrating—and in some cases dangerous—to a woman who does not see her role or actions in those terms and simply wants to know, "What part of the word 'no' don't you understand?" Similarly, men who bring a competitive business ethic that emphasizes power, intimidation, aggressively seizing the moment, not taking no for an answer, and seeking conquest into

their relationships with female colleagues are well-situated to become harassers. Without justifying the actions of such men, we should
take into account the complex changes of cross-gender interaction, as
well as the changing ground rules and meanings attached to it.

For Reflection

1. Look closely at the interactions between men and
    women whom you pass in hallways, lounges, cafete-
    rias, the outdoors, or other settings. What do their body
    positions suggest about the differences in interaction
    styles between men and women? Do these reflect
    broader social attitudes?

2. Think of your cross-gender relationships. Have the
    rules changed? In what ways? Are there new traditions
    and patterns? Are there rules you would like to change
    or eliminate?

3. Observe cross-gender interactions in various settings.
    Do you notice such differences as who talks more in
    what settings, who interrupts more, who occupies more
    space (e.g., the spreading of one's arms and legs, as well
    as personal belongings), who is more likely to initiate
    a touch, ask more questions, smile more, or nod and
    agree more? How do these patterns change in different
    settings? Think of small gatherings around a cafeteria
    or lounge table, a business-oriented meeting, or the
    mingling at a party or social gathering. How do these
    interpersonal patterns reflect broader social roles and
    rules?

4. What has led to the growing interest in sexual harass-
    ment? Is this a key change in norms? In what ways
    might sexual harassment stem from role confusion,
    from changing social rules or norms, and from power
    differences between men and women?

Reaching Out, Digging Deeper

New Views on Gender

This chapter has focused on gender socialization and gender messages as an example of a "society within us." Gender is a status that cuts across all social interaction and organization, so we will return to gender issues in subsequent chapters. The following chapter will consider the changing role of women in the workplace. Then we will look at gender inequality in income and changing gender expectations in families.

Gender issues have received new attention throughout the social sciences, in part due to the large number of female scholars entering these once male-dominated domains. Psychology and education have begun to rethink the gender bias in our models of human development. See, for example, Carol Gilligan's widely cited book, *In A Different Voice* (1982). Anthropology has given a new and more central place to the understanding of the roles and contributions of women in cultures; the "study of man" has become much more of an inclusive study of humanity. Political science and economics have shifted their perspectives more slowly, perhaps because women's entry into these disciplines has come at a slightly slower pace. Nonetheless, new attention is being paid to women's contributions and roles in economic development and political change. Sociology has been fortunate to have had prominent female scholars, such as Jesse Bernard, for a long time but has also benefitted from the infusion of new and different voices. You may want to examine the ways in which your own areas of interest have become more gender-inclusive and gender-aware over time.

A fascinating tour of the media with a master guide to social drama and social meaning is Goffman's *Gender Advertisements* (1976). The hair and clothing styles illustrated in this book will seem dated, but see what you think about Goffman's assessment of gender portrayal. Jeanne Kilbourne's widely acclaimed lectures are captured in *Still Killing Us Softly*, a 30-minute video that is a good starter for class or group discussion. If you are intrigued by media messages, you might also find Kilbourne's new video on cigarette industry advertising, *Pack of Lies*, equally provocative. There are now many accounts of differing styles of communication between men and women. One that is quite readable yet also based on sound research is Deborah Tannen's *You Just Don't Understand: Men and Women in Conversation* (1990).

To further explore the dimensions of socialization, gender roles, and media messages, consider the following project ideas:

In Your Family

1. Examine gender socialization in your family of origin. Talk with a parent or parents about their own background, as well as their hopes and intentions for you and possibly your siblings. Look at old photos, old toys, birthday cards, or whatever other memorabilia may be around. What types of role models were offered by them? What types of gender messages were conveyed, both consciously and unconsciously? If siblings or grandparents are available, get their perspectives as well. How do such perspectives differ? How does the picture that emerges confirm or alter your own perceptions and memories of childhood messages?

2. If you have a spouse, partner, or significant other, compare the gender socialization that you each received while growing up. Do you note similarities or differences? Can you see the effects of these in the ways that you relate now? Have you attempted to make conscious changes in patterns? What traditional messages would you like to pass on to children, whether your own or others? What scripts would you like to revise?

In Your Community

3. Find out what your community offers for women's shelters, rape and crisis hotlines, violence prevention programs, etc. A good place to begin may be the local YWCA, which may offer programs or provide referrals. Visit or participate in such a program or facility. What are the most common needs and situations? Do common causal factors seem to emerge? Reflect on the societal and cultural messages in attitudes toward gender and gender relations that seem to underlie the individual situations.

4. Visit a local department store or equivalent. Browse through the toy department. Is there a "pink aisle" and a "khaki aisle?" At what age do toys diverge into "boys' toys" and "girls' toys?" What themes and expectations are stressed in these toys, and how do they differ? Play, among other things, is socialization and a rehearsal for adult roles. What types of adult roles are being rehearsed by children playing with these toys? Think beyond a specific status, such as "astronaut," to the expectations and norms of inclusive behavior.

5. Visit a local department store and browse through the infant and toddler clothing departments. Note differences in clothing for boys and girls: colors, patterns, styles, fabrics, prevailing themes, and common accessories. What gender messages are conveyed about the meaning of masculinity and femininity? How might wearing certain clothing affect a child's self-image, imagination, and behavior? How might it affect the way the child is treated or the types of activities the child is likely to pursue? Think about styles and trends in adult clothing: Do they reinforce or challenge this early socialization?

In the Media

6. Examine children's books or magazines and look specifically for gender roles. In what ways are these agents of enculturation? What do they teach about our society's gender expectations? Are role models and expectations changing?

7. Look at old issues of popular magazines with a long history, such as *Life, Look,* and *The Ladies' Home Journal.* Focus on the views of gender roles and traits in a particular decade, changes in gender roles and the views of family and gender between decades (e.g., the 1950s and 1970s), and how the views and interests of women have changed.

8. Gender relations in film: From romantic ideals to cigarettes and slaps in the face, films have portrayed and

created enduring gender images. What have been the main messages of these images and how have they changed? What are the newest themes? Do you see shortcomings with these? Review and critique one of the following, or substitute a film of your choice:

Alice Doesn't Live Here Any More. Think about women's roles, abusive relationships, and self-esteem.

Disclosure. Consider the growing awareness of sexual harassment in the workplace.

The Joy Luck Club, the novel or the movie. Consider this forceful account of mother-daughter relationships in Chinese and Chinese American families.

Kramer vs. Kramer. What problems in the divorce and custody process are illustrated?

When a Man Loves a Woman. Study the problems of family and alcoholism in this film.

9. Look through current magazines of your choice. Do you find evidence for the assessments given by Erving Goffman and Jean Kilbourne of media gender portrayals? Do you see changes or new trends? If possible, include clippings or photocopies.

10. Contrast the views of gender traits and roles in a variety of popular magazines (for instance, *Self, Cosmopolitan, Woman's Day* or *Woman's World, Christian Woman,* and *Working Woman* for women; *Esquire, Gentleman's Quarterly, Sports Illustrated,* and *Playboy* for men). What are the values, lifestyles, and subcultures emphasized? How do their views differ? Which perspectives resonate with your own values?

11. Look at the activities and articles featured in parenting magazines (*Parents, Parenting, Mothering, Family Circle,* etc.). What aspects of gender and gender socialization are emphasized?

3

The Corporate Life

Webs, Wheels, and Scripts:
Group Structure and Microculture

Not all of us will spend our careers in large corporations. Most of us will, however, spend our days intertwined in corporate living within groups, committees, associations, and communities. Some will be formal in structure, such as a licensed and chartered corporation; others will be very informal, such as a group of friends who get together regularly to talk over coffee. The smaller, informal collectives are studied as *groups and group processes;* the larger, more formal as *formal organizations* and *organizational behavior;* and the connections and links between people in each as *social networks.* An important insight that we have learned from decades of sociological research into groups, organizations, and networks is that the different levels of organization have more in common than might at first be apparent.

Groups that meet regularly over time develop a structure, even if an informal one, that includes leadership roles (who gets people together and gets things started), rules of engagement (what are good topics for discussion, which are off-limits, how long should meetings run, etc.), and enduring patterns of relationships (who talks the most, who uses humor, who tells long stories, etc.). Over time, the group may develop a microculture with inside jokes, specialized vocabulary, and common ways of seeing the world.

Likewise, at the other end of the spectrum, large formal organizations often have important inner circles of power and informal networks of information ("the grapevine," the "old boys network," "the gossip line," etc.). Learning the ropes for a newcomer often means learning not only about what is in the procedures manual but about the informal groups (or cliques) and the informal networks that link them together. There is also likely to be a prevalent corporate culture (in reality, a microculture) that embodies information on what is appropriate and inappropriate attire, conversation, and attitudes.

The newcomer does well to have a mentor, akin to the anthropologist's informant, who can acquaint him or her with the informal structure and microculture, thereby preventing any embarrassment from trial-and-error learning. At the same time, knowing general principles that structure group dynamics in a wide variety of contexts can prove to be valuable tools in making your way through the corporate jungle without being roasted alive by hostile natives.

In a new group setting, you may find it helpful to quickly assess key elements of the group's structure and culture:

1. Leadership Style. Groups may have formal leaders or just commonly recognized informal leaders. Some may have both. Many may have an instrumental leader, who moves the group as efficiently as possible toward its task, and expressive leaders, who are sensitive to emotions, misunderstandings, and relationship building. A few skilled leaders may be able to function in both roles. The group may be highly leader-directed, or the agenda may emerge from the group as a whole.

One classic study, conducted by Ralph White and Ronald Lippitt (1953), tested three types of leadership: *authoritarian, democratic,* and *laissez-faire.* Boys' craft clubs were provided leaders who either dictated the terms of the project, held group discussions and outlined goals, or did very little at all. In democratic groups, the leaders fostered the greatest group efforts and the most group solidarity. This study seemed geared to validating democratic styles, given the preferences of the researchers and the political climate of the 1950s, during which American researchers were more likely to show the superiority of democracy over authoritarian (i.e., Soviet) regimes.

The most effective style of leadership may depend on the group (is it primarily goal-oriented or relationship-oriented, formal or informal?) and on the situation (is there a time and place for lengthy discussion and interaction?). Recognizing the problems of extreme control or lack of control, a group may have a range of effective leadership, depending on the leader, the group, and the situation. Between the two extremes of authoritarian and laissez-faire, we could place an additional type: *authoritative*, with strong, principle-based leadership and clear ideas yet open to new suggestions and ideas for implementation. In this continuum, democratic leadership would have the leader step back and function as "town-hall moderator," sorting out ideas and guiding the group toward a common ground. The new leadership continuum would be arranged in the following order:

> Authoritarian—Authoritative—Democratic—Laissez-Faire

2. Patterns of Interaction. Leadership styles, expectations, the setting, and the affinity of some people for others tend to organize a group interaction into one of several patterns. Some groups function as webs, wherein everyone interacts with almost everyone else in a dense exchange of information and ideas. Others tend to organize themselves in a wheel-like fashion, with a central figure serving as the hub in the exchange. An evening "bull session" is likely to look more like a web; whereas, a class discussion may look more like a wheel with the professor serving as the hub. Centralized leadership is likely to produce the wheel pattern, while democratic and laissez-faire leadership are more likely to create a web.

One study of similar arrangements (Leavitt, 1951), in which participants were physically constrained to certain patterns by partitions, found the wheel to be the most efficient, even though participants preferred the web (which Leavitt termed the "circle"). A follow-up study (Shaw, 1954) with more complex information found the web to be more efficient, because in the spoke-and-wheel configuration, too much subtle information was lost in the hub.

Webs and wheels each have their own frustrations and dangers. Webs are inherently more interesting and allow for fuller participation, but they can degenerate into free-for-alls or simply go round and round with no direction or goal. The class discussion that goes nowhere, the leaderless student group that brainstorms well but cannot gel into effective action, or the argumentative legislative body that cannot craft meaningful laws are all examples of this. Frustrations with webs can make wheels far more appealing as a way to get things done. But wheels also have their dangers. The commanding committee chair can create a wheel from a web but may have too much power to use or abuse. Authoritarian governments have often come to power following a fragmented, futile attempt at web-like democracy. Creating order from chaos is often used as a rationale for creating greater executive power, such as justifying a military take-over. Of course, the hub of the new wheel, whether a dictatorial leader or junta, may cling to their position so tightly that they bring all forward progress to a halt.

A subtler danger of wheels is the process of "groupthink" (Janis, 1972). If all members merely feed their input into a central source, they may try to bolster their position by supporting and concurring with the leader-approved position. No one wants to be ostracized by holding to a dissenting opinion, hence important qualifications and alternatives are never heard. Disastrous decisions have been tied to this process of groupthink: the Japanese military command's decision to go to war with the United States in 1942, the Kennedy administration's decision to support the Bay of Pigs invasion in Cuba, the Johnson administration's escalation of the Vietnam War, and NASA's decision to launch the ill-fated Challenger space shuttle.

The most effective groups may be those whose structure is fluid enough to change form to fit the task at hand. A group may function as a web to brainstorm possibilities, crystallize into a wheel for action, then reform as a web to assess outcomes. This fluidity does not come easily, because group structures tend to become fossilized into particular patterns. Such flexibility has, however, become a cornerstone for proposed changes in corporate structure (Piore and Sabel, 1984; Kanter, 1983, 1989).

Other patterns are possible as well, such as a chain of command. A chain may be appropriate for decisions that must be assessed and approved at multiple levels. Multiple chains resulting in a pyramid may be useful for gradually refining diverse grassroots ideas into common goals and policies.

However, the oft-noted tendency of formal organizations, whether in large corporations or in government bureaucracies, is for a hierarchical sorting process to create unnecessarily long chains and tall pyramids. Ideas must go through many levels of approval and "rubber stamping" that can deplete their energy and delay their actions. "Corporate restructuring" and "reinventing government" often set their goals on shortening long, cumbersome chains and instead involving and empowering people to make decisions in more localized webs and wheels.

3. Cultural Scripts. The Constitution, Parliamentary procedures, and Robert's Rules of Order are all attempts to formally and explicitly script group behavior. Many informal scripts also underlay—and at times supersede—the formal scripts. Groups develop their own specific ways of perceiving the world and guiding members' behavior. Aspects of this microculture include specialized lan-

Figure 3.1

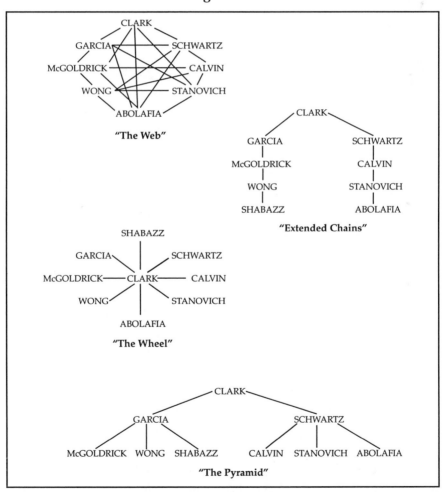

guage, the mood of the meeting (light or heavy, formal or informal), rules of engagement (how people address one another, show their desire to speak, defer to others, or indicate respect, deference, or even rebellion). These are often carefully scripted.

For Reflection

Observe a group meeting. This could be in a business, school, civic group, community organization, or any other context in which a group of people have a task at hand.

1. Note the size and shape of the room, the arrangement of tables, desks, chairs, etc., and the size of the group. How do these factors establish expectations and shape the interaction?

2. Note the leadership style. Is the interaction leader-directed or group-directed? Is the style authoritarian, authoritative, democratic, or laissez-faire? Are there informal leaders as well as formal leaders?

3. Note the patterns of interaction. Would you classify this as a web, a spoke and wheel, or some other pattern?

4. Is the mood of the meeting formal or informal? How do people address one another, show their desire to speak, or defer to others? Are there clear ways of showing respect, deference, or perhaps rebellion?

5. How are agreements achieved or attempted? Are they guided by leadership? Is there a process of groupthink, consensus, or voting, or are there struggling factions?

6. How do the interactions reflect the broader organizational attributes of structure and culture?

Dynamics of Deadlock:
When Groups Can't Get Things Done

Small groups have their own styles and structures. Many also have their own group pathologies. Some involve the dynamics of deadlock: Congress can't seem to get anything done and neither can your group project. Others involve *responsibility diffusion* ("don't blame me"), *filibusters* ("if we talk long enough, we won't have to do anything"), and *free riders* ("you do the work, I'll sign my name to it").

If groups are so problematic and committees so notorious for inefficiency, why do we have so many of them? For one thing, people enjoy socializing. Formal committees may be dreaded, in part because their formal bureaucratic structure limits what people enjoy most in groups. But group settings, in which people can brainstorm, sound off, gripe, gossip, chat, swap stories, get acquainted, and so forth, are often very popular. Humans form them every day and everywhere. People who often work in groups tend to report higher job satisfaction than those who often work alone. The worker group, focus group, and task force have become key tools in much organizational restructuring and corporate reform.

Groups do some things well: brainstorming, consolidation of ideas, networking, and building solidarity among coworkers. They are less efficient at many specific tasks. Often, this can be handled by breaking up the group into task forces and regrouping later. Imagine for a moment a committee-written version of the American Declaration of Independence:

> We hold these statements, issues, and other concerns to be essentially substantiated in regard to the general equality of the created order with respect to most persons under consideration. . . .

The Declaration of Independence does not, in fact, sound committee-written, because they let Thomas Jefferson have the quill and write from the heart. The task force then reviewed the document and returned it to the whole assembly to be signed. This smooth transition from large assembly to small group to talented individual and back again, however, assumes a willingness to relinquish control and an ability to overcome group pathologies at each level. Some groups seem to be incapable of getting past decisions on the shape of the quill or who pays for the parchment. Group pathologies need not be fatal, though, if they are diagnosed and treated early. Here are a few suggestions, many of which can be applied discreetly, even if you are merely an informal leader:

Overcoming Pathologies as a Leader

1. Intercept filibusters. Watch talk-show hosts for tips on this one. Some people talk too long because they want to stall a decision, some because they have trouble focusing their thoughts, and others because one thought leads to another, until they are inadvertently inflicting their stream of consciousness on everyone. Some may simply enjoy their moment in the limelight. Listen carefully to grasp the main point or the essence of their thought, then you can break into their ramble with a concise summary (with a tone of voice slightly louder than theirs). Most of them will pause to hear their own ideas restated, then the discussion can move on.

2. Form commitments. When you hear a lot of responsibility diffusion setting in, use your summary to turn observations into commitments: "Joan, you noted that you thought the library had good resources on that, so would you be willing to bring us the names of those resources when we get together Friday?"

3. Pull strands together. Balanced, informal summaries can be a big help in assessing what has been established and what needs to be done next: "In different ways, everyone seems to be saying that we need to move on this, but they're not sure how. Some of you want to start with the faculty, while others prefer starting with the administration. Let's try both approaches and see which group makes the most headway."

4. Balance involvement and responsibility. "I'm concerned that some of us may be taking on too much responsibility and others are getting left out. Allison, you've already got a heavy load. Mike, would you be able to pick up on this one?"

5. Intercept gripe sessions. "Sounds like everyone is fed up with the way things are. Can we turn our gripes into two concrete proposals for change?"

Strengthening Groups as a Participant

In problem-ridden groups, it is easy to either withdraw ("just leave me out of this") and become an under-responsible member or to over-commit ("just let me fix this") and become an over-responsible member. Both are understandable reactions but are likely to only increase your frustration and the group's problems. Better to take a self-responsible position and try to at least make your contribution positive. In a small group, you might create a *contagion effect* which helps others to change as well. In a larger (or more hopeless) group, your contribution might at least be remembered as a bright spot in a bad situation.

1. Provide short thoughtful responses. In many meetings (just as in many class discussions), ramblers talk too much and too long, while quiet ones say little or nothing. After a while, this pattern becomes entrenched and expected. Many concise perspectives make for better meetings and better classes. One good habit is to monitor your own participation: Try to say something—even if it's only "that's right" or "I agree"—in every discussion but always to keep input brief enough to leave ample time for others.

2. Connect ideas between members. Just as a basketball, volleyball, or soccer team that has mastered artful passing is a joy to watch, groups that manage good verbal hand-offs can also be enjoyable and productive. For example: "Right, that's a key point, Keesha, and that kind of echoes what you were saying about the source of the problem, doesn't it, Anders?"

3. Balance the leadership style. If an instrumental leader is overlooking angry, hurt, or worried group members, an open, expressive question may help: "You look worried by the direction we're taking, so do you see a problem?" A very expressive leader may need a nudge toward solutions: "Now that you've brought us to the heart of the problem, where do we go from here?"

4. Work for synergy. In his widely read book, *The Seven Habits of Highly Successful People,* Stephen Covey (1989) stresses the importance of welcoming and thriving on diverse perspectives, then bringing the diversity into *synergy* (the force of coming together). It is easy to lose this perspective, though, when we feel anxious about outcomes ("Will we ever get this group project done on time?") or about our own standing ("I don't want everyone to think I'm an idiot"). Still, the best question to ask at the onset is "what contribution can I make?" Often, seeking to contribute to synergy yields better outcomes and in the long run boosts your group standing better than any other approach.

For Reflection

1. List several groups that you have been a part of. How would you describe and diagram the patterns of interaction?

2. Have you experienced deadlock, responsibility diffu-
    sion, filibusters, or free riders? How did this occur?
    What was the outcome?

3. What group pathologies have you found to be most
    prevalent and most troublesome? Have you seen or
    used effective techniques to restore group vitality and
    efficiency?

4. Think about your contributions to class and group dis-
    cussions in this course or any other. What are your
    growing areas and your areas of difficulty? Are there
    alternate strategies that you are working on or intend
    to try?

Corporate Structure: People, Power, and Opportunity

In the 1970s, two large corporations were perplexed by a problem: They had growing numbers of women in entry and middle
management, but few of them continued into the upper levels of
management. Both companies decided to turn to social scientists for
help. One company brought in two social psychologists, Margaret
Hennig and Anne Jardim. Hennig and Jardim (1977) located the
problem in differential socialization: Women and men acted differently on the job. The only exceptions were the handful of top women
executives who approached their careers much like their male counterparts. The top men and women liked to work in groups where
they would be noticed and welcomed risk as an opportunity. They
were attuned to the internal politics of the organization and had
planned their careers carefully from the start. The female middle
managers who had not risen in the company preferred to work alone
and stay out of internal politics, hoping that their hard work and
dedication would be noticed and rewarded. They also tended to
think of their work as a job rather than a career or came too late to
the realization that this *was* their career.

What made the top executive women think differently from the
other women? Without exception, each had been an only child or
was the eldest in a family of all girls. Hennig and Jardim suggested
that they had been socialized more like boys, spending more time
with their fathers, taking more risks, and assuming greater expectations for achievement.

Note that the problem was not that the middle-level women were not good workers. You might think that employers would prefer them to be dedicated to just doing a good job rather than "playing politics." But this approach was not getting the women promoted. The social-psychological solution focused on resocializing the women through management training seminars and similar activities, in effect, teaching them to think about their work more like the men. One could also imagine resocializing the male top management to better appreciate the female managers, but this was not proposed.

The second company brought in a researcher with a more structural bent, Rosabeth Moss Kanter. Kanter (1977) conducted interviews and surveys, made observations, and ultimately located the problem not in the socialized behavior of individuals but in the structure of the corporation. Comments from interviewees suggested that women were more likely to socialize and help to mentor subordinates than to work closely with and emulate superiors. They were more reluctant to take risks. As bosses, they were more controlling and less flexible than their male counterparts. It sounded like the same problem of socialization. Kanter noted, however, three aspects of corporate structure that seemed to work against women:

Opportunity structure. People in this company knew who were in dead-end positions with few chances for promotion. They knew who were "getting old" in their present position and who were "dead in the water." People in dead-end jobs tended to lower their expectations and take satisfaction in helping others rather than promoting their own careers. This was true whether they were male or female, *but* many more women were in these types of positions than men.

Power structure. The company had high- and low-power positions, and these related more to autonomy and personal discretionary power than to the title on the office door. High-power bosses could afford to be generous and flexible with their subordinates. They knew that they could bend the rules and get away with it, and they also expected those subordinates to return the favors. Low-power bosses, on the other hand, knew that people were looking over their shoulder and had to follow the rules and be more controlling. Again, throughout the organization, women were more likely to hold low-power positions.

Demographic structure. This refers to numbers of people in a category, such as gender, age, and race. When only a handful of a group were represented, they constituted *tokens*. Tokens had to be careful: If they screwed up, people would surely remember it. Conversely, their excellence just contributed to an overall perception of high department quality, so there was little incentive for risk. Tokens were also given a host of additional duties, such as ad hoc committee assignments. They had no real power on these committees, but usually some superior wanted the token group represented. As a result, they lost time from more important work. In many departments in this company, women were often tokens.

In each case, Kanter contended, the behavior was not related so much to the *person*, whether male or female, but to the *position* and how it fit into the overall organizational structure. Her recommendations were not for seminars but for *corporate restructuring* to eliminate dead-end positions, to balance the discretionary power of positions, and to hire and promote groups of minority managers rather than isolated tokens.

These three structures can be applied to a wide variety of social organization, from small groups and formal organizations to communities and even whole societies. This poses some fundamental questions:

- How is opportunity structured? Who can get ahead, who can act on new ideas, and who is in a dead-end alley?

- How is power structured, formally and informally, explicitly and implicitly? How does power or the lack of it influence behavior? Is there a tendency by those in power to protect their position and authority by restricting the opportunity structure? (The sociological term for this is *social closure*, a prime concern of Max Weber).

- How is opportunity, power, and interaction affected by numbers and categories of people? What aspects of the demographic structure are especially salient or important: population size (e.g., too many or too few qualified applicants); age (e.g., an aging workforce with many nearing retirement); gender, race, and ethnicity; or something else?

For Reflection

1. Think back to your own socialization in light of the topics discussed in the previous chapter. How have these affected how you might act as a manager or supervisor in a position of responsibility? Have you acquired tendencies you find useful or ones you would like to change?

2. Analyze the three aspects of organizational structure—opportunity, power, and demography—for a group with which you have had experience, such as a student group, a fraternity or sorority, or a place where you have worked. How did these three elements combine to shape the climate and activities of the organization? How did they influence your own attitudes and behavior in the organization?

3. Consider the opportunity structure, power structure, and demographic structure of your college or university. How do these affect the behavior of faculty, staff, and students? How do they affect the campus climate?

Corporate Culture: Dare You Be Different?

The rapid post-World War II growth of American corporations was also accompanied by often rigid standards of corporate conformity. The ideal was the "organization man" (Whyte, 1956), his counterpart the corporate wife who supported his career. This monolithic ideal has given way to a diversity of people from various backgrounds trying to accommodate career, family, and personal life. They have brought new demands for flexibility and acceptance. At the same time, those studying corporate competitiveness in a constantly shifting world marketplace have noted that conformity and rigidity can be deadly to organizational well-being, and that the best businesses coordinate a diversity of talents and ideas into synergy, innovation, and higher productivity. The changes, however, are filled with pitfalls: workers unable to effectively communicate with management, executives fearful of losing control and doubtful about corporate commitment, employees afraid of appearing less than committed and being passed over for promotions.

In the midst of these changes, sociologists have for some time been moving into business schools and corporate consulting as experts in "organizational behavior." Recently, business anthropology has also found its place as a specialty. *Working Woman* (July, 1992) reported the movement of Marietta Baba from studying threat gestures in baboon communities to doing management consulting. Baba claims that one was good preparation for the other. McCurdy (1994) describes how applied anthropologists can get past limited surveys and "suggestion boxes" to truly understand the workings and problems of a job site. Sociology's penchant for searching for underlying structures shaping behavior and anthropology's tradition of getting the insider's view of the situation can both be invaluable to upper-level managers who may have become detached from the daily workings of the office and the shop. Network analysis can reveal patterns of communication, as well as breaks and strains in communication; participant observation can reveal why things never work "according to the book"; and corporate ethnography can reveal the subtleties of corporate culture that promote or inhibit success.

Not limited to serving management, sociologists in labor relations can work to help unions and labor to more effectively organize and press their demands. In either situation, helping people in widely different positions to understand one another's perspectives can go a long way in making the workplace more accessible, more responsive, and more human. A recent study of the most desired business skills noted, along with the usual expected skills, an ability to work with and understand people from diverse backgrounds and cultures. Few businesses can afford to frequently hire sociological and anthropological consultants. But managers, sales representatives, and many others in the business world could truly benefit from being more skilled ethnographers, by asking the right questions, listening and really hearing the answers, observing and participating in daily activities, and understanding the needs and viewpoints of others in very different situations.

One area of prime interest has been the connection between national culture and business organization, and whether international innovations can be imported. In the 1970s, considerable interest was generated by attempts in some European countries, most notably Sweden, to achieve "work humanization." Could the assembly line, the industrial shop floor, and maybe even the clerical office be made less alienating, less dehumanizing, or maybe just less boring? Suggestions included greater variety, greater autonomy, and new, more pleasant surroundings and routines. Some of these innovations started to filter into the United States. But as the American mood changed, and Swedish industry struggled while Japan's economy soared, many shifted their gaze from the Atlantic to the Pacific.

Was there a secret to Japanese success and could it be transplanted? Interestingly, some of the ideas also centered around new routines with greater variety and autonomy, but now the focus shifted from making work more humane to making it more efficient and competitive. The Japanese's team-oriented, family loyalty model included hiring and promoting teams rather than individuals, offering lifetime security in return for lifetime loyalty, total involvement with company coworkers (even in recreation and social life), broad training in many areas of the enterprise, and collective decision making (Ouchi, 1981). This approach demanded new attitudes and norms, some of which were alien to the American workplace, as well as new structures, such as "quality circles" (Florida and Kenney, 1991).

This transplant of ideas has met with mixed results. Some locations did improve their performance with the new approach. Others met considerable opposition from workers who saw the approach demanding more of them while offering little in return. New management-worker cooperative teams were sometimes seen by workers and unions not as honest cooperation but as means for management to undermine the solidarity of workers, while retaining all the important decisions. Group rewards were sometimes met with the same consternation that often greets a college instructor who announces that everyone working on a group project will get the same grade. American industry is embedded in a broader American culture with a set of attitudes about individual responsibility and reward, as well as personal privacy and independence: "This is my job, not my life." American industry is also embedded in a social structure that has tended to divide white collar and blue collar, management and labor, front office and shop floor. These attitudes and distinctions do not necessarily disappear with a new management plan.

At the same time, some principles do seem to apply across cultures. Giving workers more ability to shape the work environment and the work process, making them active and respected participants in a broader range of activities, and allowing them to use their minds as well as their hands all seem to offer advantages in morale and efficiency, whether it is implemented in Stockholm, Yokohama, or Detroit. Differing social environments do shape organizations, but changing organizations can also remake their social environments (Florida and Kenney, 1991).

One challenge will continue to be greater in the United States than in either Sweden or Japan: the challenge of diversity. Japanese teams function with an assumption of considerable homogeneity. The American workplace is ever more diverse in terms of age, gender and racial, ethnic and cultural background. If worker teams are to succeed in the United States, they will have to be composed of people who can reach across and utilize difference.

For Reflection

1. Think again about the groups and organizations that you have examined in the previous sections. How would you describe the microculture of each group? How are organizational norms and values communicated? Is deviance tolerated? By whom, and under what conditions?

2. Think about careers you have chosen or considered. What are the stereotypes and expectations of persons in that role? How well do these fit who you are as a person? What distinctions would you bring to this position (e.g., gender, age, religious background, lifestyle, etc.)?

3. What strategies might you use to gain acceptance of your particular needs and differences? (Remember that Hennig and Jardim's research indicates that just "doing a good job" may not be enough.) How might you communicate and convey your distinctions as positive contributions to the organization?

4. Think about classroom experiences you have had. Do you prefer having the opportunity to decide and develop course projects with a group, or to have an instructor give you the tasks to be completed? When has collaborative decision making and group rewards worked well, and when has it failed? What made the difference? What principles might apply to crafting successful workplace collaboration and teamwork?

The Corporate Stage and the Presentation of Self

This is where corporate culture and our own world of experience converge. How we communicate and portray our distinctions is a longstanding interest of symbolic interactionism. Erving Goffman (1959) refers to this as the *presentation of self*. His approach is termed *dramaturgy*, for it likens our behavior to actors cultivating and presenting a persona. Goffman suggests that we have both *backstage* and *frontstage* behaviors. The first, for example, is the arena of getting ready for a big date; the second is how we act and communicate on that date. Or think of a waitress who rushes back and forth through one of those swinging doors that separates the kitchen from the dining area during a busy lunch hour. Coming through the door into the dining area (the frontstage), she smiles, tries to look efficient but not rushed, and asks customers questions in a pleasant, placating tone. Back through the door into the kitchen (the backstage) she becomes more rushed and authoritative, even demanding, and the smile is gone. Back out front again, the pleasantries return. This effort to maintain the pleasant, polite cheerfulness that many frontstage positions require is what Arlie Hochschild (1979) calls *emotion work*.

The corporate "stage" often provides settings in which we hope to maintain a positive and appropriate presentation of self. Let's consider two of these.

Cocktails and Tall Tales: The Art of the Reception

The public reception has become an international modern institution, as ubiquitous as death and taxes and occurring more frequently than either. Some are gladly anticipated by the social few, others are anticipated with mild apprehension, and many others are the subject of outright fear and loathing. Receptions range from gala events following the awarding of honors and accolades to gatherings for newcomers and "informal" mingling after meetings and events. Whatever the color of the socially correct tie, in truth, these events are hardly ever informal, but they are supposed to be. Therein lies the contradiction that can make these such unwelcome events.

A host of informal knowledge and subtle social skills are a prerequisite to successful participation in receptions. Precise choreography is required to execute them well, yet all this must occur under the guise of merely talking and eating. A premium is placed on acting natural, yet nothing could be more unnatural than this exercise in social calisthenics known as "mingling." None of the other higher primates mingle—this may be why we developed opposing thumbs and not an appendage more suited to pasting thick cheese spread on fragile crackers. Tribal people do not mingle. Any tribal interaction that happens outside the immediate circle of family happens according to precise, explicit rules of conduct that have been passed down for centuries and chanted by entertaining after-dinner speakers. When these speakers are finished, the people don't mingle—they go to bed.

Even medieval notables didn't mingle. At the balls of the Italian upper classes, guests greeted their hosts and one another in the manner which befitted their rank. Dinner was served, during which troubadours sang and told ribald jokes. Group interaction occurred during the dancing, according to carefully prescribed steps. Any mingling of guests beyond this was probably either lecherous or treacherous, thus never compulsory. In any case, participants quickly learned what was expected of the encounter.

Receptions are an invention of the industrial revolution, just like the disposable utensils that usually accompany them. They were devised by the newly prosperous, who wanted to imitate the gentility of the ball but didn't know any of the rules. So they pretended there weren't any. One merely chatted with friendly faces in the most casual of manners. But the co-minglers were often not friends, merely acquaintances. In a situation where contacts were made, manners mattered and had to be refined. The great art of this new game of the reception is to learn the rules while pretending there aren't any. Machiavelli would be intrigued.

The problem with modern receptions is that none of the steps are prescribed and all are assumed. What to talk about is of course an issue, but even more tricky is knowing how to stop talking. Mingling implies moving about. But no one wants to give the impression that the current conversation partner is boring, especially if this person turns out to be a senior vice-president. The results are attempts at graceful exits. This is the main purpose served by the punchbowl and the buffet table. Of course, if the punch is alcoholic, this poses its own problems. Too many such exits, and you may become known more as a drunk than as a snob.

Another attempt to escape a talkative companion involves backing up to create more space. The shift from personal distance to social distance announces, "Someone else can break in here and join us." Of course, if the other person is known to be a long-winded bore, no one will. Further, a step backward may be followed by a step forward by the other, until you are backed against a wall like the previously mentioned American and Arab diplomats. One solution is to step to the side (preferably the side with the buffet table). If the other persists in advancing, he or she may walk right past you and start talking to someone else.

Maintaining appropriate eye contact while observing other events in the room also requires some practice. A common strategy (more often used by men than by women) is standing side by side at an open angle to one other, hence becoming co-observers of the room. This also facilitates the shift to someone else or to the vegetable dip.

Initiating conversation is an art of its own, especially breaking into a closed circle. Standing close to the circle at its widest opening will encourage the circle to open just enough to allow you in. Quietly replacing the person who is leaning toward the punch bowl or the buffet table also sometimes works.

Each of these strategies can fail and create opportunities for embarrassment: The person to whom you just introduced yourself is someone you have already met, the person you just called by name is in fact someone else, the conversation stalls without any graceful exit, or the circle draws tighter at your approach. Various face-saving actions can then come into play, usually involving jokes, gestures, or some implication that you intended something else all along. Observing masters of these tactics might make you more adept at them yourself. They might also help you enjoy the reception.

Tell Me About Yourself: The Art of the Interview

Presentation of self is hardest in new settings, such as job interviews, in which the microculture and its norms are not well-known. Learning as much as possible about the corporate culture and organization before the interview can be very helpful, not just to impress but to interpret.

At the interview, a successful self-presenter must often maintain several balancing acts. The first is between seeming too self-effacing versus too pompous. Applicants who are too timid or have been taught too well never to trumpet their own accomplishments can make a weak impression. This has long been a struggle for some female applicants. Recently, Asians and Asian Americans seeking jobs and contracts have had to face this cultural difference in expectations. On the other hand, an applicant who comes across as overbearing, self-inflated, and unrealistic may fare no better. The best strategy is often to display quiet confidence. Stress experiences rather than honors. The honors are important but are better presented on paper in your resume. Instead, talk about doing, meeting, knowing—all with enthusiasm. Positive experiences imply and demonstrate knowledge and ability, and enthusiasm implies an enjoyment of work and a willingness to learn. Of course, after a long period of job seeking and interviewing, cultivating that enthusiasm may take some emotion work.

A similar balance is best struck between appearing ignorant and knowing it all. Everyone wants to appear knowledgeable, and no one wants to be seen as a know-it-all. The challenge here is to sound informed but interested in learning more. Good ethnographic questioning techniques can be useful in this: "This is what it said in the company prospectus—is that how it really works? Have you found that to be true?" The point made is that you have done your homework but still want to learn more. You are capable but willing to allow a supervisor, mentor, or more experienced employee to be your teacher.

This presentation of self is not entirely artificial, for you are cultivating through practice the very attitudes you are hoping to project. Classic studies have shown that people internalize their socially assigned roles very quickly. It is not as though we all have a true inner self but are wearing masks or false fronts. Our true selves are social and composed, at least in part, of the sum of the roles we take on and the parts we play. Presentation of self does not mean that we are fickle and false, just sensitive to our social surroundings—to our stage.

For Reflection

1. Observe or reflect on behavior at a recent reception:

    a. How does it compare to and differ from behavior at an informal party? Does the blend of formality and informality make the event interesting or anxiety-producing?

    b. How do people move through the room? How do they initiate and close conversations? Do you notice any differing strategies?

    c. Do people with different roles adopt different demeanors? How do the topics and styles of conversation reflect different presentations of self?

2. What experiences have you had applying for jobs? How did you manage your frontstage behavior?

3. Role playing has often been shown to be an effective way to prepare for new settings. This is no surprise to dramaturgists: Since we are all called upon at some point to be "actors," we might as well rehearse. Role play a few job interview settings. Try fielding some of the classic questions: What is your greatest accomplishment? Why do you want to work for us? Why should we hire you? Try to strike a balance between pompous and self-effacing, ignorant and know-it-all. What aspects come most naturally, and which are the most difficult?

Business Ethics: Crime in the Suites

In any given year, the highest recorded income in the United States goes not to a sports or entertainment star but to a corporate star: usually the CEO of a major corporation. In 1992, the CEO of Heinz earned $75 million. Presumably, this was a very good year for ketchup. Yet the top earner for 1989 outdistanced them all: Michael Milken brought in $550 million in a single year, a feat not matched since Al Capone. The problem for Milken was that he did it by violating security and exchange laws. However, how much of a problem this was is not clear, because although convicted and banned from engaging in trading, Milken remains one of the wealthiest people in the country.

When the topic turns to crime, most people immediately think of muggers and murderers, gang members, and violence in the streets. In terms of amounts of money involved, however, these all pale in comparison to crime in the corporate suites.

The National Association of Attorneys General has estimated that white-collar fraud in the United States costs at least $100 billion a year, with anti-trust fraud adding another $160 billion. On top of this are the colossal losses, such as the $600 billion dollar bail-out of the fraud-filled savings and loan industry. Abuses appear to be both widespread and frequent. The Justice Department found that 60 percent of the 500 largest firms were guilty of criminal action, and General Electric alone managed to compile 282 counts of contract fraud (Parenti, 1995).

White-collar crimes include embezzlement, tax and credit fraud, and bribes and kick-backs (Sutherland, 1940). Some commit acts of fraud against their employers, but others do so on behalf of their employers. This kind of "corporate crime" includes anti-trust violations, price fixing, copyright and patent violations, false advertising, and failure to disclose known risks.

People in positions of power and authority have access to the flow of far more resources than anyone "on the street," so it is perhaps not surprising that criminal activity by such individuals is far more profitable. What *is* surprising is that it is also far less risky. In *Democracy for the Few*, Michael Parenti (1995) suggests that the key is to steal big. He notes the incredible disparities in sentencing: the judge who gave a stockbroker a small fine for engaging in $20 million of market manipulations and on the same day sentenced a unemployed man to one year in jail for taking a $100 television from a truck shipment; or the wealthy contractors who pocketed $1.2 million for government work never done and were fined $5,000, in contrast to a Virginia man who got ten years for stealing 87 cents or a Houston youth who received fifty years for robbing two people of one dollar.

Parenti notes that in petty cases, we as a nation are hardly soft on crime. For example, in "lenient" New York City, nine out of ten suspects for robbery are convicted and most go to prison. Mandatory sentencing laws mean that most now serve longer sentences. In contrast, only a small minority of white-collar offenders ever serve any prison time at all. Says former New York Governor Mario Cuomo, "If you're a kid from [a poor neighborhood] and you get caught stealing a loaf of bread, they'll send you to Rikers Island [prison] and you'll be sodomized the first night you're there. But if you're a businessman ripping us off for billions, they'll go out and play golf with you." (*Washington Post*, May 27, 1990).

One reason that suite criminals are treated much more leniently than street criminals is that they have far more resources for building a defense. This is especially important, because the nature of their crimes and the laws broken may be much more complex. People also tend to focus their fear and anger on street crime because they feel much more threatened by it. A street criminal with a gun is more directly frightening than a suite criminal with falsified books. Yet if we consider the lives and property lost due to faulty and unsafe products, we may all be at much greater personal and financial risk from corporate crime. Deaths attributed to tobacco products alone far exceed all the homicides ever committed in this country.

Revulsion at some of the excesses of the 1980s, capped by Milken's extraordinary earnings, did bring new attention to "corporate greed" and irresponsibility and a new emphasis on business ethics. What is the corporate culture and structure that fosters illegal and unethical business practices?

Although most sociology textbooks treat deviance and crime in the same chapter, a great deal of criminal activity is not particularly deviant from the surrounding subcultural and microcultural practices. Much family violence is perpetrated by those who experienced or observed such violence themselves. Most violent crimes are committed in violent neighborhoods by people who grew up in such neighborhoods. Likewise, fraud, bribes, and kickbacks have at times become the norm for entire cities and nations. In such contexts, it is honesty that becomes deviant and very difficult.

White-collar and corporate crime is most likely to flourish in a context in which ethically questionable practices are not especially deviant but frequent, and cut-throat competitiveness is the norm.

Businesses that foster fraud often differ from those businesses, large and small, that operate under scrupulously honest principles. They differ in their structure: Fraud-filled firms often have authoritarian leadership, with groupthink more common than open dissent and with huge rewards for those at the top. They also tend to differ in their business culture: stressing short-term gains over long-term relationships and defining a sphere of responsibility that includes owners or prominent shareholders but often does not extend to customers, employees, small investors, or the local community. Changing business structure and culture to become more supportive of ethical actions will likely require significant changes in public policy and the justice system. Such changes may accomplish little, however, unless they are supported by persistent, well-informed consumers and unswervingly ethical employees and investors.

For Reflection

1. When asked why he robbed banks, Willie Sutton gave the now-famous reply, "Because that's where the money is." The same logic would seem to suggest that law enforcement should focus on multi-million-dollar crime rather than petty crime. Do you believe that this has not been the case? Why or why not?

2. What aspects of our social structure and culture do you believe contribute to the prevalence of crime in the suites? What would it take to change these aspects: laws, citizen action, consumer watchdogs, spiritual or ethical renewal, or other factors?

3. What aspects of business structure and culture create a climate conducive to white-collar and corporate crime? What actions could you take as a small-business owner or as a corporate manager to positively affect the business climate in your firm or organization?

4. Are there core principles you can enumerate that would guide your own ethics as an employee? How would you cope if you found these to deviate from the prevailing organizational culture around you?

Reaching Out, Digging Deeper

Taking Care of Business

The shelves of major bookstores sag under the weight of books on business practices and business advice. You can learn business practices from great coaches, Eastern mystics, or in at least one popular book, Attila the Hun. Only a minority of these books take a broad sociological view that looks at how businesses fit into the bigger picture of social structure and culture. Many stress the power of the great leader without considering the overall organizational ecology, its patterns of competition and legitimacy, and the structures of opportunity constraint (Hannan and Freeman, 1989). Yet as you gain a more refined sociological perspective, try reading these books and asking about how the advice given accords with what you know about the power, opportunity, and demographic structures of our society. If you explore a bit further, you will also find more analytical treatments of organizational dynamics and change by social scientists.

To learn about personal principles, see Steven Covey's highly regarded *Seven Habits of Highly Effective People* (1989). For a comparison of American and Japanese business styles, see William Ouchi's *Theory Z* (1981) and *The M-Form Society* (1984). For a broad look at structural change from large corporate bureaucracy and mass production to flexible specialization, see Piore and Sabel's *The Second Industrial Divide* (1984). Rosabeth Moss Kanter's *Men and Women of the Corporation* (1977) is older, but its style of analysis remains very valid, and many of its conclusions are unfortunately still current. More recently, Kanter has tackled corporate change and global competitiveness in *When Giants Learn to Dance* (1989).

Sociologists and anthropologists may at times be less eager to use their skills to help management get more from its workers than to help workers get more for their efforts. For participant observation studies sympathetic to workers' struggles, see Michael Burawoy's *Manufacturing Consent* (1979) and Patricia Fernandez-Kelly's *For We Are Sold, I and My People* (1983). For a biting critique of business ideology, social class, and the criminal justice system, see Jeffrey Reiman's *The Rich Get Richer and the Poor Get Prison* (1990).

This chapter has focused on groups and organizations with an emphasis on how the business world structures its behavior. The themes of power and opportunity and how they are distributed across social class, status, and gender will be examined in more detail as we explore the broad dimensions of social stratification in the next chapter. To further explore the dynamics of groups and organizations, and how they deal with power, opportunity, gender, deviance, and social control, consider the following project ideas:

In Your Family

1. Talk with parents and/or siblings about the types of interaction you had with your mother and with your father. How did these differ between parents and between siblings? Can you see ways in which these interactions established a pattern that has been carried into interactions in school, work, or other groups? How has this affected self-confidence and risk-taking behavior? Design a "success workshop" for your family. What messages would you endorse and reaffirm? Which would you replace?

In Your Community

2. Talk with members of a formal organization, whether business-related, social, educational or community service-related. Ask about opportunities for leadership, patterns of decision making, and the composition of the group. Consolidate the answers into a brief analysis of the power, opportunity, and demographic structures of this organization.

3. Write a brief ethnography of the microculture of an organization with which you are familiar. How are organizational norms and values communicated? Is deviance tolerated? By whom and under what conditions?

In the Media

4. Consider the ideas for restructuring and improving business practices, organization, and success in magazines, such as *Business Week, Forbes, Fortune,* and others. Do the ideas focus on business culture, organizational structure, individual behaviors and attitudes, or some combination thereof? How do they relate to organization and performance? Evaluate the articles or ideas in

light of the aspects of corporate life considered in this chapter.

5. Look at the images of men and women portrayed in business-related publications, such as the ones above. Do they present an image of corporate conformity? Has this changed over time? What do the images suggest about current corporate culture? Are women and men presented in ways that suggest different expectations?

4

Planning Ahead, Getting Ahead, Keeping Your Head

W e may be created equal, as the Declaration of Independence insists, but from the moment of birth, we live in a world of stark and glaring inequalities. Central to a sociological understanding of social structure is the reality that we do not all stand on equal social ground. Access to privilege, prestige, and power vary greatly, depending on one's position within society. To describe the structure of inequality, sociologists have borrowed a term from geology: *stratification.* Just as layers of rock lie one atop the other, so too do we find a hierarchical ordering of social positions. Like a geological formation, the layers are the result of powerful underlying forces and subtle but enduring sorting processes. The harsh realities of social inequality raise several questions that will guide this chapter. Does the structure of social inequality settle out into a series of identifiable layers? Exactly how fluid is the system; how "cast in stone" are the layers? Where does each of us fit in this structure, and where are we going?

These are questions of social-class structure. Max Weber defined *social class* as one's life chances in the marketplace. For Karl Marx, social class was one's position in what he called the social relations of production, particularly whether one was an owner or worker. In the United States and Canada, we often prefer to believe that we have no rigid class divisions. India may have its castes and Europe may have its aristocracy, but the ideal here is a fluid system of social mobility up or down based on hard work and ability. Certainly, we have inequality—the United States is now one of the most unequal of the world's advanced industrial nations in both accumulated wealth and annual income.

Few would deny that inherited advantages and disadvantages also play a significant role, though we often deny this in our own experience. If we come from an advantaged background, we may prefer to believe that our own ability and hard work, rather than class advantages, have brought us to where we are. If we come from a disadvantaged background, we may readily acknowledge that it was harder for us in the past, but we may also want to believe that we will not be hindered in future success—that our ability and hard work will pull us through.

Not all of this is naive wishful thinking. The United States is more unequal than most of Europe and Japan but shows indications of somewhat more mobility; that is, people move up and down the ladder of socio-economic status (based largely on education and income) somewhat more readily. Yet when asked about the types of people likely to live in a particular location, to drive a particular car, or participate in particular activities, many people have no trouble making distinctions of social class. When people are asked to describe levels of positions in a large organization, the labels may vary, but again class divisions are often described. Since its founding, sociology has been extremely interested in stratification by class. In our society, it often plays the unwelcome role of reminding us that our successes and life chances, even our tastes and aspirations, are influenced greatly by our place in a stratified social structure. Social class is not as clear as a caste assigned at birth, and there is ambiguity and uncertainty in the classification system. Nonetheless, various ways of classifying the American strata tend to converge on some common class categories. One attempt to synthesize a century of studies of class into an outline of contemporary American class structure is offered by Gilbert and Kahl (1993). Their synthesis suggests six classes:

Capitalist Class. Comprised of investors, heirs, and executives, typically with a prestige university education and annual family incomes over $750,000, mostly from assets.

Upper Middle Class. Upper managers, professionals, mid-sized business owners with a college education, most often with an advanced degree, with family incomes (1990) of $70,000 or more.

Middle Class. Lower managers, semiprofessionals, some sales and skilled crafts, foremen and supervisors with at least a high school education, usually some college, technical training, or apprenticeship, with family incomes of about $40,000.

Working Class. High school-educated operatives, clerical workers, most retail sales clerks, routinized assembly and factory workers and related "blue collar" employees with family incomes of about $25,000.

Working Poor. Poorly paid service workers and laborers, operatives and clerical workers in low-wage sectors, usually with some high school and family incomes below $20,000.

Underclass. Persons with erratic job histories and weak attachment to the formal labor force, unemployed or only able to find seasonal or part-time work, dependent on temporary or informal employment or some form of social assistance.

This scheme emphasizes several important elements of the American class hierarchy. At the top, we are no longer talking just about high salaries but most often returns on investments and assets. That broad-band, all-American middle class divides into an upper strata of highly paid professionals and upper management, a "white-collar" core, and a largely "blue-collar" working class. Among the working poor, collar color often gives way to the smocks of poorly paid clerks and service workers; whether they actually experience poverty often depends on whether they must support dependents on their incomes. The term "underclass" is sometimes decried as demeaning, implying poor values or poor work habits, but here the category just encompasses those with poor job histories, unable for one reason or another to maintain steady, formal employment. With this scheme, imperfect as it may be, we can explore class influences on our lives and life chances: past, present, and future.

Socialization: Ways You Have Been Affected by Class

Earlier, we examined the way a variety of social institutions socialize their members to act in accord with certain social values, norms, and expectations. What messages dominate will vary by our sub-culture, our age, our gender, and also by our social class. Social class has a big effect on which institutions we are a part of and what messages we are exposed to. As a result, social class can have a powerful effect on the development of personal values, aspirations, and tastes. Much in our society denies this: Presidential candidates who wear red flannel shirts, frequent McDonald's, or listen to country music all convey a populist ideal that the "common life" is good enough for everyone, and that we all share common American ideas and ideals. In fact, however, many attitudes show a strong correlation with social class background. In more ways than we might like to admit, different classes live in different worlds and are socialized to accept and appreciate those worlds differently.

Melvin Kohn (1969) has conducted decades of interesting research that documents social class differences in socialization. Most parents agree as to the fundamentals of what children should learn, but their intentions for their children also diverge by class. Parents at the upper end of the class ladder have been more likely to stress curiosity, happiness, responsibility, and self-control. Parents at the lower end of the class ladder have been more likely to stress obedience, good manners, neatness, and honesty. Note that at issue is not "good values" versus "bad values" but an interesting difference in emphasis. In part, parents may be instilling the values most appropriate to what their children can expect in life: Highly regarded professions may reward inventive curiosity and require considerable responsibility. In contrast, a routinized occupation, such as life on the factory floor, may demand greater obedience to authority; while being seen as "respectable working people" may demand an emphasis on neatness and good manners.

Class-based socialization also has a big effect on our tastes and lifestyle. French sociologist Pierre Bourdieu (1984) has developed the concept of class *habitus:* the long-lasting dispositions of mind and body instilled in our early upbringing that affect our tastes, habits, and the places where we feel at ease and at home. To feel and act at home in elite circles, we must acquire *cultural capital:* the knowledge, tastes, and marks of distinction to show that we belong to and participate in elite culture. These marks of distinction in turn show that we are "a cut above" the rest and merit a higher place in society. Bourdieu divides tastes in art and leisure activities into categories of high brow (the most elite), middle brow (the tastes and interests of the middle class), low brow ("popular" tastes associated with lower classes), and an interesting high-low brow (folk art forms once created by the poor but now "discovered" by upper classes). He is not saying that one form of taste is better or superior; in fact, his work is intended to demonstrate that "good taste" has no meaning apart from a social context. Good taste is a means to prestige and demonstrates one's education and "good breeding." As well as prestige, lifestyle can also reflect privilege. The early sociologist Thorstein Veblen (1912) in his classic book about the wealthy, *The Theory of the Leisure Class*, described forms of *conspicuous consumption,* the ways by which people could demonstrate the extent of their wealth and privilege by the types and quantities of consumer goods they had at their disposal. At times of course, "good taste" may demand a more subdued expression of privileged consumption: the gray Mercedes rather than a yellow Cadillac. Finally, consumption and lifestyle can demonstrate social power as in the "power suit" of the young executive. People may attempt to stake a claim on a higher social position by adopting the outward trappings of that position; hence, the power suit worn by the hopeful job applicant for a managerial position.

For Reflection

1. List some of the activities, interests, and patterns of consumption that you would associate with each class below. Consider sports and other recreation: Where would you place polo, golf, bowling, professional wresting, etc.? Think also about patterns of consumption: Where would you place certain clothing styles, models of automobiles, and household items? Placements may depend in large measure, though not entirely, on the amount of discretionary income they require; for example, it is often cheaper to attend a polo match than a professional basketball game. What other criteria may affect choices: socialized taste, prestige and marks of distinction, values, social expectations, or others? Compare your list with those of your classmates. How much agreement is there? What does this indicate about our collective awareness of class differences in lifestyle?

Lifestyle by Social Class

Class	Activities	Interests	Consumption
Capitalist class:			
Upper middle class:			
Middle class:			
Working class:			
Working poor:			
Underclass:			

2. Think about cultural capital, marks of distinction, and the social distribution of taste. Where on the list below would you place the following preferences in art: nature photography, French Impressionists, Norman Rockwell paintings, Dutch Masters, posters of fashion models, Picasso, Andy Warhol, black velvet Elvis Presley prints, Navaho rugs, graffiti, or street murals? Now try the same with music. Where would you place country-western, classical, jazz, opera, rhythm and blues, rap, hip-hop, heavy metal, soft rock, or pop?

Patterns of Taste

High brow:
Middle brow:
Low brow:
High-low brow:

Compare your list with those of your classmates. Do you find general agreement or some notable exceptions? What can you conclude about the correlation between social position and personal taste?

3. Some gradations in aesthetic taste are more subtle: Why would a taste for abstract "modern art" be higher brow than a liking for Monet and Renoir? Why would a taste for more contemporary symphonic music (such as Debussy and Bartok) be higher brow than a liking for Bach and Mozart? What does this suggest

about education, socialization, and "distinction" or prestige?

4. Persons toward the upper end of the class ladder are more likely to jog, do aerobics, join health clubs, and seek a low-fat diet. Persons toward the lower end of the class ladder are more likely to smoke, be obese, have a heart attack, cancer, diabetes, and even asthma, and die at a young age. Clearly, access to quality healthcare may vary greatly by social class, but why would so many health and fitness-related behaviors also correspond to class position?

5. Consider some of your personal values. At first, you may be more likely to point to religion, family, and personal reflection as the source of these values (all of which are important), but do any correspond with your social class background? Think about what you would desire in a job (autonomy, creativity, security, etc.) and what would be your philosophy of success. Is it more important to get early work experience and work hard on the job, to emphasize getting the most formal education possible, or to emphasize having the right contacts or ideas? What you would hope to instill in your children (obedience, creativity, respectfulness, self-respect, etc.)? How might these differ if you had a different social class background?

Association: Ways You Are Being Affected by Class

Association, who you know and interact with, is an important result of class position and, in turn, reinforces one's class identity and position. We have all heard the maxim about how it's not what you know, it's who you know. Parents may seek to send their children to the right college in the hope that they will not only secure the right job but that they will adopt the right values, meet the right people, and maybe even find the right spouse.

Types of association also matter—what you know about who you know. In our more blatantly class-conscious past, association was strictly controlled by social norms and standards, often formalized, at least for the upper classes in such collections as the Social

Register. The Social Register listed prestigious families, presumably those who would make good acquaintances, good trustees and board members, and—above all—good spouses for one's children. Marriage was perhaps the most intimate association but also the one most important for reproducing class position in the next generation, thus the most guarded. Debutante balls were "coming out" parties, announcing who would soon be available for suitors and courting, so of course attendance was carefully restricted. People not on the Social Register may have had money, but they "either [were] not at ease in a ballroom or else [made] others not at ease" (quoted in Mills, 1956, p. 54).

A few such balls remain in the southern states, but one recently had to be canceled in New England when not enough young women were willing to be dubbed "debutantes" and participate in this coming out event. We must realize, however, that they flourished in a time when we were much less occupationally and residentially segregated. The elites lived and worked near the poor (who may have been their domestic help or laborers) but kept their social distance. In modern America, we may have relaxed the social rules in part, because widely separated residences, schools, and vocations assure differences in association. Residences, neighborhoods, clubs, stores, and recreational facilities still often promote themselves as "exclusive," though they rarely specify who they are excluding. Voluntary associations still tend to attract people of similar background then, in turn, reinforce those similarities (McPherson, Popielarz, and Drobnic, 1992).

For Reflection

1. List some of the associations and types of organizations that might be important to each class below. Some may be more obvious (labor union meetings or elite country clubs), wheras others may take some thought. Where would you place local civic groups? An old adage has it that "the Rotaries own the town, the Kiwanis run the town, but the Moose have the most fun." What does this suggest about the class affiliations of civic groups?

Association by Social Class

Class	Associations	Churches	Neighborhoods
Capitalist class:			
Upper middle class:			
Middle class:			
Working class:			
Working poor:			
Underclass:			

Compare your list with those of your classmates. How much consistency is there across lists? What does this indicate about our ability to recognize and categorize social class differences? Did you find exceptions or likely stereotypes? How much does your list reflect your own background?

2. Think for a moment about a form of association important to many Americans: church affiliation and participation. What churches or denominations do you associate with each social class? Why might religious affiliation be correlated with class as well as race and ethnicity?

3. The likelihood of participation and membership in formal organizations increases as one moves up the socioeconomic ladder. Even the likelihood of church membership increases moving up this hierarchy. Why would wealthier and better educated individuals be more likely to be involved in formal associations? Why would the poor be least likely to be involved? What effects might this have on opportunity and mobility?

4. One of the most important elements in association is the neighborhood of residence. This affects casual acquaintance, local organizations, and access to associations, as well as other important elements, such as the public school district. Review your list of association by social class and list local neighborhoods, areas, and subdivisions that you would associate with each class. Share your list with your classmates. Was this an easy

or difficult task? Is there common agreement? Why or why not? What effects might neighborhood of residence have on daily interactions? On future prospects and life chances?

5. Think of non-family members who have been influential in your life. Have there been neighbors, teachers, counselors, pastors, or friends of the family who have influenced your values, attitudes, and choices? Have your college and career choices been affected by this influence or information? Have you ever found a job through a personal contact? How might your choices and opportunities have been different if you had belonged to a different class listing and been part of one of the neighborhoods and the associations that you listed for that class?

Prospects: Ways You May Be Affected by Class

The profound changes occurring in our economy can leave workers and prospective workers at all levels confused and anxious. College students in particular, whether preparing for or beginning a new career or just retooling skills, often watch the various projections on trends and patterns with alternating euphoria and dismay. By some accounts you can't lose, by others you can't win. What can you expect?

Expect modest initial incomes. When working hard and paying high tuition, it is pleasant to dream that that piece of parchment at graduation will prove to be a golden fleece. Don't count on it. There is no degree, certainly no bachelor's degree, that is guaranteed gilded in our current economy. During the oil exploration boom of the 1970s, the highest paying entry-level jobs were in petroleum engineering; just a few years later, the oil glut left many hopeful graduates in this area with few job opportunities. Tight budgets (both public and private) combined with an ever increasing number of degree holders will mean that most initial job offers will be modest. It can be discouraging to realize that your first offer may be less than your parents, siblings, or friends are earning with much less education. Be patient. A new graduate is still largely "unproven" in the labor market; you will likely need to demonstrate your worth before commanding high incomes.

Expect modest upward movement, perhaps with a great deal of lateral movement. There is room at the top but not much. Moving up will take time and increasingly it may take several "lateral moves" between jobs, divisions, or locations along the way. Your education, both the skills and the habitus you are developing, will likely serve you well over the long run, but you will need patience and perseverance. Don't overestimate where you will be in a year or two after graduation, but also don't underestimate where you might be 10 or 20 years after graduation. If you are hoping to improve your class position, several factors are working in your favor. *Circulation mobility* results from space created by those experiencing downward mobility. Some older workers may lose long-time jobs or find their skills becoming obsolete, while some younger workers will find it impossible to do as well as their parents did. This is of course bad news for the people involved, but it does make room for others on their way up. Fortunately, not all gains require someone else's loss. *Structural mobility* results from growth in the upper levels of the labor market. Many people now in white-collar working-class occupations have parents who had industrial or rural working-class positions. It is not that they are all smarter than their parents, but that growth and change in the American economy created many more middle-class positions to fill (see Figure 4.1). *Structural mobility* will continue but more slowly, as the national labor market becomes more saturated with existing white-collar positions and as some firms' downsizing eliminates positions. One source of upward mobility used to be immigration. Members of an older immigrant group moved up, as a new poor group moved in "underneath" them to take the lowest-paying jobs. A much higher portion of immigration in the United States is now coming from an international middle class of professionals. Highly skilled immigrants may be deemed better for the economy as a whole than poor immigrants, but they are not going to do much to push others up the class ladder. A similar type of process, however, is continuing in *reproductive mobility*. Career-oriented, predominantly middle- and upper-middle-class individuals and couples are having fewer children or in some cases forgoing a family altogether. At the same time, many children are entering the class ladder near the bottom, as a full fifth of American children are born into and live in poverty. This is certainly not desirable for the children involved nor for the nation as a whole. Yet in an odd way, it does allow for upward mobility. As some privileged classes do not fully reproduce themselves in the next generation, room is made for some of those born poor to move up. Factors, such as limited resources, socialization, and association, may mean that most will not move up very far and some not all, but having more people entering the system near the bottom does create an "endless escalator," allowing some to move up in the system over time.

Finally, expect different experiences, depending on who and where you are. Being in the right place at the right time, both geographically and in class position, makes a big difference. Yes, ambition matters, but money doesn't hurt. For one thing, it remains a big predictor of educational outcomes. Not only does class background have a big effect on one's ability to enter college, it continues to have a big effect on the likelihood of graduating.

Cutbacks in federal and state funding mean that this is not likely to improve. One reason for this may be rooted in the class structure. With considerable *structural mobility,* schools are looked to as *human capital investments,* turning out more skilled, more capable people to fill the growing number of demanding jobs. In an economy dominated by *circulation mobility,* in which someone's gain is someone else's loss, schools can function as *gatekeepers,* passing on privileged credentials to the privileged while selectively eliminating those trying to move up. The point here is for you not to become overly cynical or discouraged but to realize and anticipate challenges that you are likely to face.

One simple way to think about class background and its effects is to think in terms of just three categories: privileged (capitalist and upper middle), threatened (middle and working), and disadvantaged (working poor and underclass). Students from privileged backgrounds of course have many advantages but may also feel the stresses of maintaining a position and reputation, attaining a position and lifestyle comparable to that of their parents, living up to family expectations, etc.

Students from threatened class backgrounds may need to deal with the insecurity of resources and family support and the lack of assurance of good future employment. They may need to explain their educational and career choices to family members whose own path may have been quite different, such as depending on hard work on the job rather than on extensive formal education for advancement. They may also feel that they are trying to reach an uncertain and moving target as the economy, the labor market, and the array of job opportunities seems to continue to shift, maybe for the worse.

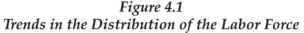

Figure 4.1
Trends in the Distribution of the Labor Force

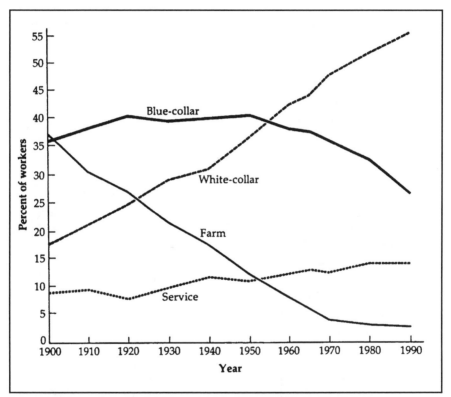

Source: Gilbert and Kahl, 1993; from U.S. Bureau of the Census and U.S. Department of Labor. Copyright © 1993 by Wadsworth Publishing Company.

Students from disadvantaged backgrounds may have the greatest stresses. They may need to "fill in the gaps" in their public school background created by overburdened and underfunded schools, family and community disruptions, and so forth. This may require extra study, personal reading, tutoring, etc. They may need to remind themselves that these gaps do not represent personal inadequacies. They may need to fill in gaps in association with supportive groups or mentoring. Finally, as they succeed in a college environment not shared by many family members or old friends, they may find themselves "living in two worlds," each with a different subculture, and have to work hard for acceptance and communication in each.

For Reflection

1. Examine Figure 4.1. What are the key changes? What social, demographic, and economic forces might account for the trends?

2. Look at Table 4.1 on the fastest-growing jobs. These are the 40 occupations that will contribute the most new jobs to the labor market by 2005. The percent growth for each category is also shown. Peruse the table. Do you find surprises? Trends? Good news or bad news? What social, demographic, and economic trends might account for some of the types of jobs that are growing? Note the substantial growth in the professions, especially health, education, and human services. The largest number of jobs will be contributed by the low-wage category, however, especially retail sales and food service, two sectors known for near-minimum wages. A major question for our future: How will we find—and how will we compensate—all the people needed to care for our children, our homes, offices and gardens, and our elderly and indigent?

3. Which of the three broad class categories—privileged, threatened, or disadvantaged—best describes your background? Do any of the challenges described for this category resonate with your own experience? If so, in what ways?

4. In thinking about your class background, what aspects helped to bring you here (financial support, socialization, association, good public or private schooling, etc.)? What class resources can you hope to draw on in the future? What might you need to compensate for or

TABLE 4.1

Occupations With the Largest Job Growth: 1992 to 2005
(Based on moderate projections; numbers in thousands)

OCCUPATION	EMPLOYMENT		PERCENT
	1992	2005	CHANGE
Professional and Managerial			
Registered nurses	1,835	2,601	42
Systems analysts	455	956	110
Teachers, secondary	1,263	1,724	37
Marketing and sales managers	2,036	2,443	20
General managers and executives	2,871	3,251	13
Teachers, elementary	1,456	1,767	21
Accountants and auditors	939	1,243	32
Teachers, special education	358	625	74
Computer engineers and scientists	211	447	112
Teachers, preschool/kindergarten	434	669	54
Food service and lodging managers	532	764	44
College and university faculty	812	1,026	26
Correction officers	282	479	70
Physicians	556	751	35
Lawyers	626	821	31
Social workers	484	676	40
Technical and Skilled			
Truck drivers, all	2,391	3,039	27
Home health aides	347	827	138
Maintenance repairers, utility	1,145	1,464	28
Licensed practical nurses	659	920	40
Clerical supervisors	1,267	1,568	24
Human services workers	189	445	136
Blue collar worker supervisors	1,757	1,974	12
Carpenters	978	1,176	20
Hairdressers and stylists	628	846	35
Low Wage			
Salespersons, retail	3,660	4,446	22
Cashiers	2,747	3,417	24
General office clerks	2,688	3,342	24
Waiters and waitresses	1,756	2,394	36
Nursing aides, orderlies	1,308	1,903	45
Janitors and cleaners	2,862	3,410	19
Food preparation workers	1,223	1,748	43
Child care workers	684	1,135	66
Guards	803	1,211	51
Teacher aides	885	1,266	43
Gardeners and groundskeepers	884	1,195	35
Food counter workers	1,564	1,872	20
Receptionists	904	1,210	34
Cooks, restaurant	602	879	46
Cooks, short order/fast food	714	971	36

Source: U.S. Census Bureau, 1995. *Statistical Abstract of the United States.* Based on U.S. Department of Labor estimates.

substitute? What lifestyle expectations will you need to support?

5. How well do you relate across social class divisions? What effects will your current educational and career choices likely have in relating to family and old friends?

Improving Your Prospects: Education and Employment

Though your prospects depend on who and where you are, having a coherent and informed strategy will certainly improve your prospects. An important part of that strategy, certainly for most college students, is education.

Education: Does it Pay?

Considering the costs in time and money coupled with uncertain prospects, it is tempting to ask, does higher education pay? Considered over a lifetime of earning, just in financial terms, the answer is a resounding yes. In fact, the wage gap between those with and those without a college education continues to grow (see Figure 4.2).

Not all years of education contribute equally, however (see Table 4.2). Key credentials matter, and higher levels pay back even more than basic levels of education. Years in school are almost irrelevant without a high school diploma. A high school diploma greatly reduces the likelihood of unemployment but doesn't provide much in wage guarantees. The greatest advantage of a high school diploma or a GED is that it allows one to go on to get more specialized education and training. The crucial edge goes to those who continue education beyond high school and get some form of technical certification, especially when coupled with apprenticeships and on-the-job learning. While a technical degree may offer better initial job prospects than some college degrees, note the big lifetime benefits that accrue to that college degree. The reason is that jobs offered to college graduates tend to have higher long-term earnings trajectories—they place the graduate in a much better position for ongoing raises and promotions.

Again, however, the credential and not the time is what is crucial. A four-year degree matters much more than just having "a few years of college." Further, years in graduate school return the highest yields of all. In terms of lifetime earnings, it is hard to find an educational degree or program that is a poor investment, no matter how high your tuition may be. One partial exception to the "more years of education equals more income" rule is that certain highly rewarded professional degrees in medicine, law, and business may return more in income than longer graduate programs leading to a Ph.D. Of course, the careers that follow such professional degrees also tend to make great demands in time and stress.

This raises the point that returns on investment go well beyond dollar returns. Many would argue that the non-tangibles of a good education—greater awareness, greater confidence, and greater sense of personal fulfillment—outweigh the financial benefits. These benefits continue beyond the years in school, in part because greater education not only prepares you for better-paying jobs but also just plain better jobs. It might be fair if people with the least desirable jobs were paid the most to compensate, but our society tends to do something of the opposite. Jobs that require greater education often have greater autonomy, greater variety and room for creativity, greater opportunities for personal growth and fulfillment, greater intrinsic interest, and higher reported levels of job satisfaction. Even if many of your criteria for a good job are non-monetary, you are more likely to achieve those criteria with stronger educational credentials.

Your choice of major will have less effect on your lifetime earnings than you might think. The reason for this is that the most technical and job-specific majors often lead to the highest starting salaries but may have less steep income trajectories. Liberal arts majors may receive slightly lower initial salary offers, but their greater flexibility (coupled with good preparation for graduate school) can lead eventually to steeper trajectories, although greater patience and perseverance may be needed. The traditional liberal arts (the Arts and Sciences majors of most universities) can offer wonderful exposure and learning that will bring both financial and personal rewards, but it still pays to begin thinking of a career plan that suits your skills and desires. A more general liberal arts degree can be followed by graduate or professional school, combined with an internship or work experience or with a more vocationally focused co-major or minor. When writing your resume, it is good to remember that employers are increasingly seeking skills rather than labels. For instance, someone promoting himself or herself in the business world with a sociology degree may want to stress technical competence: computer skills, data analysis, an understanding of statistics and complex organizations, and so forth, coupled with people skills: good communication, the ability to work with diversity and appreciate differing viewpoints, and the like.

Many of the opportunities for association and socialization are provided by one's family's class background. Yet college years can provide a number of opportunities to compensate for not having been born into a world of privilege. You can improve your prospects through association and professional socialization. Unless your family is listed in the Social Register, it will help to improve your networking ability early on. A good place to begin is with your professors. Many are more accessible to interested, enthusiastic, and curious students than most students realize. Make use of those posted office hours and inquire about future career prospects and possibilities. Find out about the possibilities for working on a research project or doing a guided independent study. These are wonderful experience that can generate some good letters of recommendation at a later time. Find out about options for professional internships, which are one way out of the Catch-22 "how to get a job without experience and how to get experience without a job" conundrum. If you can, join a student club and/or a professional association related to your major or major interests. All of these will help to socialize you to the standards and ways of thinking and acting in your prospective profession while building a network of professional associates. In the community, voluntary service and related activities can be rewarding, can provide "real world" experience, and certainly do not hurt on a resume. Try to find something that isn't hopelessly time-consuming. Maintaining a balance between curiosity and practicality is useful here. Crass single-minded resume building is not likely to be very rewarding and may be obvious to future employers. If, however, you can combine honest interests, concerns, and curiosity with practical activities to improve and enrich your college experience, you will be far ahead, personally as well as vocationally.

Fast Tracks, Off Track, Dead In Your Tracks

In a changing economy, it helps to have a plan. It also helps to be flexible. In his classic study of inequality, Christopher Jencks (1972) finds that in predicting future income, social class and family background do matter, as well as intelligence and ability, but more important than anything else is luck. Getting the right break at the right time seems to matter as much as anything we can plan or prepare for. The implication for society, Jencks suggests, is that for greater equality we simply need to reward success more modestly and penalize failure less severely. Such a "kinder, gentler" society seems to have eluded us, and so the individual implication is to have a broad view of prospects with multiple, flexible strategies.

In particular, it helps to emphasize positions with long career ladders and many possible paths. Your income and responsibilities one year after graduation are in fact a fairly weak predictor of income and occupation ten years after graduation and beyond. Most important is to avoid positions with obvious dead-ends (unless you are willing to remain at that level) or bottlenecks in upward mobility. The likely trajectories of various career choices vary considerably. Some occupations offer high initial salaries but limited growth; others offer low initial returns but steeper trajectories. It helps to have a realistic understanding of both starting salaries and likely trajectories.

It also helps to have a broad and balanced view of one's own needs, aspirations, and life situation. Those who only consider "the bottom line" in career choices can be setting themselves up for ill-fitting, unrewarding work and future "mid-life crises." At the same time, it is easy for younger college students to underestimate their future financial needs, especially if they have a family with children. Consider your particular needs and values.

Often when considering a future vocation, one has the tendency to focus almost exclusively on the aspects of the job itself and not on some of the lifestyle choices that may accompany it. Just as important as having a good, enjoyable job is having a career choice that fits with the rest of your life interests and values. A key element in job satisfaction goes beyond the job itself to how well it fits with the rest of one's life and responsibilities. For example, some people are very happy in jobs that in themselves are not that interesting, because the hours and limited demands of the work allow them to invest themselves elsewhere where they can gain more satisfaction: family, hobbies, church, or community. Some careers take a long time to become established; this is fine for some but perhaps not viable for someone with immediate financial and family demands. Some careers are very likely to require relocating. In fact, a willingness to relocate can greatly expand job options. Yet some people have strong personal and family ties to a particular area and would find relocation very disruptive.

Even in an uncertain labor market, it can help to have a realistic plan. For some plans, you may be able to sketch out a flow chart with the sequence of positions and experiences you anticipate. Given the uncertain nature of this, however, most will probably need to be contingency plans; that is, flow charts with several alternate routes down the way. If you do not have a clear vision of what you would like to be doing, try to make an incremental plan that reaches a decision point with a series of steps leading to the next decision point.

For Reflection

1. Does investment in education pay off? How well? Examine data on returns to education in the following tables.

    a. Examine Figure 4.2 on median family income. What was the overall trend in family income between the mid-1950s and 1970? What has been the trend since 1970? How has this differed by educational level? Does education make more or less difference in 1993 than it did in 1956? What levels or credentials seem to make a particularly big difference?

    b. Earning higher degrees results in higher salaries but also means time out of the workforce. How do these factors balance out? Examine Table 4.2. Does the extra earning power compensate for the time lost in the workforce? What educational credentials offer the highest lifetime returns? How do the returns to various degrees differ by gender? Does education help reduce the gender gap in income? Is education a good investment for both men and women?

    c. Table 4.3 uses average personal earnings and adds a confidence interval. As indicated, 90 percent of the earners fall within the range given after the average. How much does one's degree field affect earnings

Figure 4.2
Median Family Income by Educational Attainment

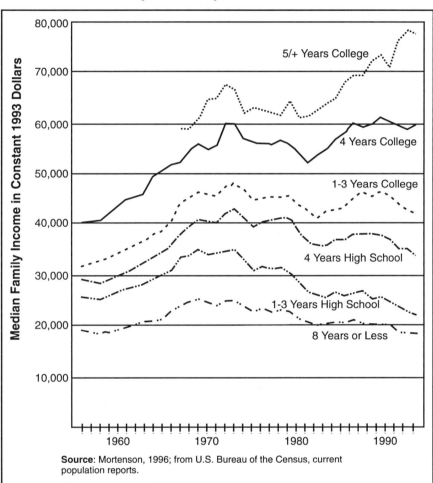

Source: Mortenson, 1996; from U.S. Bureau of the Census, current population reports.

compared to differences by degree levels and gender shown in the first table? What might be some of the factors that could explain the range in earnings by field? Which fields have the greatest range in earnings within the field? Why might this be the case?

d. It is not difficult to find income and earnings data on various groups. It is much harder to find clear evidence to explain the results. The first is readily available from the Census Bureau, the Bureau of Labor Statistics, and other agencies; the second often takes careful and detailed study. How would you go about researching the reasons for the spreading income differences in Figure 4.2, the gender differences in Table 4.2, or the differences by field in Figure 4.3? The fields in Figure 4.3 also reflect a gender difference, with top-paying fields such as engineering, agriculture/forestry, and economics being predominantly male, and lower-paying fields such as education having more women. Not shown is the lowest-paying field, home economics at $1,156, which is also overwhelmingly a female pursuit. Is it that women are more likely than men to pursue lower-paying careers, or that careers associated with women tend to become lower paying? How would you test this?

Table 4.2
Lifetime Income by Educational Attainment and Gender
(1994 estimates)

Educational Attainment	Working Years	Mean Annual Income	Lifetime Income	Gain Per Year of Post-HS
Men 25 years and older				
Doctorate	34	$76,844	$2,607,000	$98,000
Professional	37	99,323	3,681,000	336,000
Masters	37	56,016	2,045,000	71,000
Bachelors	42	46,197	1,930,000	113,000
Associate	44	32,713	1,439,000	48,000
Some College	46	30,799	1,417,000	96,000
High School	48	25,501	1,224,000	0
Not HS Grad.	52	15,622	805,000	-120,000
Women 25 years and older				
Doctorate	32	$45,389	$1,409,000	$44,000
Professional	38	47,666	1,796,000	110,000
Masters	36	34,149	1,197,000	41,000
Bachelors	42	25,579	1,069,000	65,000
Associate	44	20,486	901,000	59,000
Some College	46	17,173	790,000	62,500
High School	48	13,844	665,000	0
Not HS Grad.	52	8,775	453,000	-59,000

Source: Mortenson, 1996; from U.S. Bureau of the Census, *Current Population Reports*.

Table 4.3
**Average Monthly Earnings by Field of Degree, 1993
(Bachelor's Degree)**

Degree	Monthly Earnings	90% Confidence Interval
Average	$2,269	+/- $69
Engineering	3,189	+/- 210
Economics	2,923	+/- 595
Mathematics/statistics	2,716	+/- 338
Business/management	2,626	+/- 130
Law enforcement	2,331	+/- 338
Nursing/pharmacy/health	2,080	+/- 218
Physical/earth sciences	2,045	+/- 293
English/journalism	2,032	+/- 234
Biology	1,990	+/- 325
Psychology	1,974	+/- 280
Social Science	1,922	+/- 166
Liberal arts/humanities	1,733	+/- 146
Education	1,699	+/- 270
Home Economics	1,165	N. A.

Source: U.S. Bureau of the Census, 1995. *Current Population Reports.*

2. Reflect on your own needs and criteria in career selection. How important is income level and how much income are you likely to need? How important is initial salary versus steep income trajectories in meeting your likely needs? How willing and able are you to relocate to another city or area of the country to pursue your career? How willing and able are you to conduct a longer job search while getting more experience or education or working temporarily in another field? How willing and able are you to give long hours to a particularly demanding profession? How important to you are autonomy, variety, ability to be creative, ability to serve human needs, or other criteria? Think of several career choices that you have considered or might consider. How do they compare with the criteria you listed above? Are there some aspects about which you are unsure and could gather further information?

3. Sketch out a career plan. Even if you are undecided on your major and your future, try out a hypothetical

route. Note that you can do this at any age and place in life: for mid-career changes or even retirement. Are you able to sketch out several alternate paths to similar outcomes? Do the elements in your career plan consider likely economic and demographic trends, as well as your own likely life course changes?

4. Suppose for a moment that your career plan unravels. Do you have a contingency plan for failure? How is your sense of self and self-worth tied to professional accomplishment? Could you thrive with a less-than-ideal income? Now suppose that your plan works well. Can you live the "good life" without indifference to others who have not experienced the same successes? Will your prospective plan give you particular resources (e.g., income, time, or expertise) that will allow you to share your success? If so, in what ways?

Improving Our Prospects: Opening Doors, Opening Minds

The type of answers we seek and find are often determined by how we frame the question. By looking at prospects and life chances, we can choose to focus our attention on the individual level of personal gain: "How can I win the race?" Or we can focus on the community and societal level: "How can we improve conditions for all the runners?" Having looked at the narrower picture of what we individually hope to become, we can step back to consider what we are becoming as a society.

One massive shift in employment in North America and Europe occurred as people left farm labor for urban and industrial employment. A second great shift occurred in the United States following World War II, as significant numbers of men and women whose parents worked farming and industry shifted to white-collar employment. The third great shift began in the mid-1960s and is still making its presence felt: the loss of traditional factory employment to technological innovation, industrial downsizing, and overseas competition. Whether pessimistically termed "de-industrialization" (Bluestone and Harrison, 1982) or more optimistically called "post-industrial society" (Bell, 1973), the labor market is continuing to change rapidly. Union-protected employment in heavy industry, such as automobiles and steel, is disappearing and being replaced by service sector jobs.

Although it is tempting for those who knew more secure times to wonder what has gone wrong, it is helpful to realize that a volatile economy with many workers in low-wage, high-risk employment has often been our norm. Only in the brief period between about 1945 and 1965 did the United States so dominate the world economy that rising wages, secure employment, and unbroken economic progress became the expectation. Many young workers now face a labor market very different from that experienced by their parents. It is a situation, however, that may not be so different from that faced by their grandparents and great-grandparents, in which routine industrial and clerical workers were frequently at the mercy of business changes and closures, international struggles for economic dominance, changing technologies, and the constant strain of stagnant real wages.

Income inequality in the United States has been increasing since the 1980s, although the middle class is not in danger of vanishing overnight. The growth of the high-wage professional service sector has enlarged the ranks of the upper-middle class and spurred both the gentrification of older urban neighborhoods and much of the new housing construction of the past two decades in the "exclusive residential communities" of select suburbs. At the same time, the growth of the low-wage routine service sector has enlarged the ranks of the working poor, with workers facing downward mobility and finding the ideals of the previous generation, such as homeownership, ever more distant. Many now find that they must return to school for higher degrees to even attain the income levels that once came with only a high school diploma and a union card. The so-called shrinking middle class is largely a shrinking working class seeing the end of stable, protected blue-collar employment. This also means that those near the bottom of the occupational structure have fewer opportunities. The working-class jobs that once provided important rungs on the class ladder by demanding hard work instead of higher education are largely gone. All that is left for many is to leap from poverty into the middle class, and it is a leap many fail to make. The result is a disappearing working class, a threatened middle class, and an increasingly desperate underclass. Is there a way out of this dilemma?

Two contending perspectives provide some ideas. The *mismatch hypothesis* (Wilson, 1987) suggests that there is a growing mismatch between the needs of increasingly technical business and industry and the education and skills of the people who need those jobs. This mismatch in training is compounded by a geographic mismatch that has many unemployed in central cities or isolated rural areas and most new jobs in suburban settings. The mismatch approach suggests that what is needed is better education and job training and full employment programs. Better access to information and transportation coupled with incentive policies to bring employers back into the city might further alleviate the geographic mismatch. None of these are easy or inexpensive, but a multifaceted commitment to opening the opportunity structure would make a strong beginning. Further, in a competitive global economy, better trained and more productive workers would likely preserve and create more jobs, further expanding opportunities.

Less optimistic is the *polarization hypothesis* that suggests that service-oriented economies produce a large number of jobs at the top of the ladder, an even larger number at the bottom, and fewer in between (Harrington and Levinson, 1985; Harrison and Bluestone, 1988). It is not that people are unable to fill better jobs, but that the economy needs people to fill a host of menial jobs. The polarization approach suggests that widening gaps will not respond to better education and training but can only be reduced by a major commitment to redistribution: wage supports (e.g., a higher minimum wage), tax help (e.g., the Earned Income Tax Credit), and public investment in healthcare, childcare, housing, and other needs that bottom-ladder workers will not be able to afford nor will likely receive. The polarization approach is also more pessimistic: It points to a zero-sum situation, in which the only way to benefit the bottom is to take from the top.

There is considerable evidence to support at least part of the polarization hypotheses (Morris, Bernhardt, and Handcock, 1994). This does not necessarily negate the mismatch approach, however. One reason that wages for many service sector jobs are so low is that there are still so many people willing to work for them and skilled to do little else. Greater investment in the education and training of future employees might increase competition for jobs farther up the ladder, in effect cutting those high wages down, while leaving a smaller pool of potentially more efficient employees near the bottom, pushing their wages up somewhat. Further, fewer but better educated applicants could encourage employers to upgrade some of these positions, increasing their responsibilities and technical support, which could begin to again fill in some of the missing middle rungs on the occupational ladder.

Clearly, there are no easy solutions. One suggestion at the individual level is to make sure that you are on top of the rising income gap and not underneath. If, on the other hand, we are to have thriving communities and some measure of equity in our society, then we will also need to find community- and societal-level solutions.

A big step in this direction is reintegrating school, community, and family. Decades of research have shown the tremendous importance of home and family involvement in educational achievement (Coleman et al., 1966, 1987). When there is a congruence between home and school to make students feel "at home," effort and achievement rise. With struggling school budgets and limited resources for special needs, broader educational attainment will require strong parental involvement, both supporting and guiding the school efforts. Recent interest in "family literacy" is just one example of the new focus on helping the entire family across a range of ages to improve their education. This is neither a purely "cultural/social-psychological argument" nor a purely "structural argument," but one that stresses the importance of congruence between home subculture and what is rewarded in the broader social structure.

The links between schools and businesses can also be strengthened. It is easy for the business community to bemoan the large number of graduates who lack the most sought-after skills, but change requires employers to become more involved in the education process rather than waiting for the perfect product to emerge intact from the school system. Innovative school and business/community partnerships can include in-school projects, in-class presentations, internships and work-study programs, community-service work and service learning, and mentoring programs. Besides supporting basic skills, such programs also lower the barriers between school and work, providing a congruence between learning and earning that reinforces the significance of education for at-risk students. During a time of political and economic polarization, these can help bring a community together around common goals.

For Reflection

1. Examine Table 4.4. A variety of measures is used to chart trends and patterns in inequality. It is important to look for several distinctions. Wealth—total assets accumulated or one's "net worth"—is much more concentrated than income. For example, the wealthiest 20 percent of the American population control about 80 percent of the nation's wealth. The poorest 40 percent, on the whole, control none at all; they are as likely to be in debt as to have net assets. Income measures can be reported as personal earnings, family income, or household income. Family and household income are similar measures, but a "household" need not be made up of related members. Different measures are appropriate to different questions: Differences in personal earnings may be a useful way to examine wage differences between men and women but would be a poor way to look at the well-being of children. A common way to divide the population is into fifths, or *quintiles*, then compare across quintiles. In a perfectly equal society, each fifth of the population would receive exactly one-fifth of the income. How far the reality deviates from this ideal is one measure of a society's inequality.

Table 4.4
Trends in Inequality
Share of Household Income, by Quintile

	1968	1973	1978	1983	1988	1993
Lowest 20%	4.2	4.2	4.2	4.0	3.8	3.6
Middle 60%	53.0	52.2	51.7	50.9	49.9	48.2
Highest 20%	42.8	43.6	44.1	45.1	46.3	48.2
Top 5%	16.6	16.6	16.8	17.1	18.3	20.0

Source: U.S. Bureau of the Census, 1995. *Current Population Reports.*

a. What trends do you note in the graph for the poorest fifth, the middle three-fifths, the richest fifth, and the richest five percent? What time periods saw the greatest changes?

b. One way to measure inequality is the ratio of the income of the top quintile to the income of the bottom quintile. Note that in 1968, this was very close to 10:1 (42.8 divided by 4.2). What is the ratio for 1993? By comparison, the ratio for Japan is closer to 4:1. What factors might account for greater inequality in the United States?

2. Examine Figure 4.3. What are the interrelated factors that exclude "underclass" people and communities from full participation in economic and political life? What are the key "leading factors," that is, basic changes that might lead to a cycle of positive changes and upward mobility? Should we change focus on the poor individual or the poor community?

Figure 4.3
Cycles of Exclusion

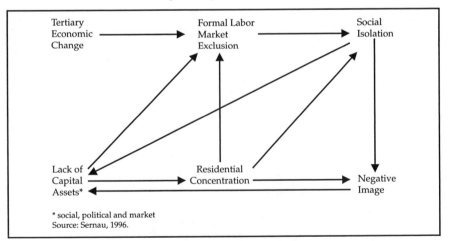

3. Examine the charts in Figures 4.4. What are the trends in poverty rates? What are the most common characteristics of people in poverty? How do these affect the

duration of poverty? What are the characteristics and
complexities that will need to be addressed to alleviate
our poverty problem?

Figures 4.4
Poverty Rates, Characteristics, and Spells

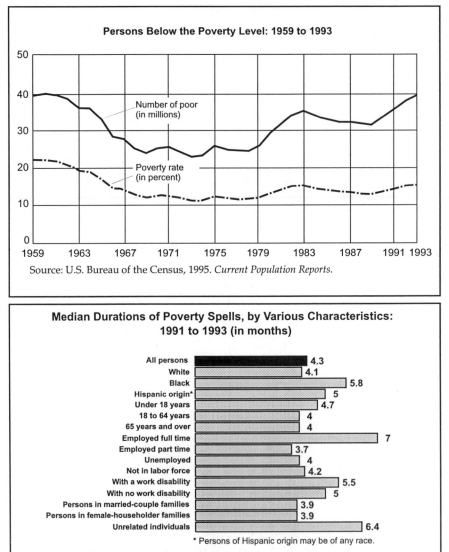

Persons Below the Poverty Level: 1959 to 1993

Source: U.S. Bureau of the Census, 1995. *Current Population Reports.*

**Median Durations of Poverty Spells, by Various Characteristics:
1991 to 1993 (in months)**

* Persons of Hispanic origin may be of any race.

Source: U.S. Bureau of the Census, 1995. *Current Population Reports.*

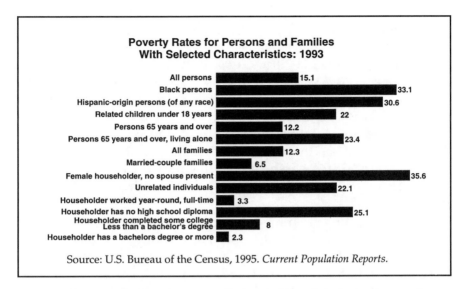

**Poverty Rates for Persons and Families
With Selected Characteristics: 1993**

Characteristic	Rate
All persons	15.1
Black persons	33.1
Hispanic-origin persons (of any race)	30.6
Related children under 18 years	22
Persons 65 years and over	12.2
Persons 65 years and over, living alone	23.4
All families	12.3
Married-couple families	6.5
Female householder, no spouse present	35.6
Unrelated individuals	22.1
Householder worked year-round, full-time	3.3
Householder has no high school diploma	25.1
Householder completed some college Less than a bachelor's degree	8
Householder has a bachelors degree or more	2.3

Source: U.S. Bureau of the Census, 1995. *Current Population Reports.*

4. How can educators work to make school a more welcoming place for all types of parents and families and encourage family involvement? How can parents enrich the home learning environment for their children and increase the congruence between home and school?

5. What are some ways that educators might begin to build community and business partnerships to increase opportunities for students? What are some ways that business persons or professionals might contribute to education (formal or informal) in your community? Which of these statuses have you occupied, or are planning to occupy? How might you contribute to meaningful solutions in that capacity?

Reaching Out, Digging Deeper

The Other America

The problems of inequality and poverty have generated a vast literature, some analyzing the problems, some offering solutions, and others documenting the experiences of people in very different circumstances. One such book, Michael Harrington's *The Other America* (1962), was instrumental in raising awareness and launching what became known as the War on Poverty. Others are continuing to raise awareness and inform the policy debate.

For analyses of the changing economy, see Bluestone and Harrison's *The Deindustrialization of America* (1982) and Harrison and Bluestone's *The Great U-Turn: Corporate Restructuring and the Polarizing of America* (1988). William J. Wilson analyzes the effects of this economic change on poor communities in *The Truly Disadvantaged* (1987) and *When Work Disappears* (1996). For policy prescriptions from an academic who has been influential in several presidential administrations, see the work of David T. Ellwood, most notably *Poor Support* (1988). A harsh and moving indictment of educational inequality in the United States is offered by Jonathan Kozol's *Savage Inequalities* (1991).

For penetrating accounts of the experiences and struggles of poor families and communities, see Alex Kotlowitz's *There Are No Children Here* (1991), Jonathan Kozol's *Amazing Grace* (1995), Mike Rose's *Lives on the Boundary* (1989), and Jay MacLeod's *Ain't No Makin' It* (1995). The particular challenges of working-class and working poor families have sometimes received much less attention. Two notable exceptions are Lillian Rubin's *Families on the Fault Line* (1994) and Schwartz and Volgy's *The Forgotten Americans* (1992).

This chapter has focused on social inequality with an emphasis on social mobility: how people move up and down through the occupational system and the class structure. The focus has been on inequality rooted in class background. American society has also seen tremendous inequality in life chances based on race and ethnic background, which we will consider in more detail in the next chapter. To further explore the class stratification of our society and its effects, consider the following project ideas:

In Your Family

1. Talk with older family members about their "class origins" and their educational and job histories. What were their aspirations and experiences? What hopes did or do they have for their children? What investments were made in promoting learning, such as private and public schooling, extra lessons (in music, sports, art, etc.), and emphasis on homework and the home learning environment? What patterns will you seek to retain, and which would you hope to change? Compare your findings and experiences with those of

siblings, friends, or a significant other. What similarities and contrasts do you notice?

In the Community

2. Major area employers: Talk with the personnel officer or any person with primary hiring authority. Look at the hiring needs and practices of a major local business or industry, such as a manufacturing firm, hospital, university, bank, large retailer, or the like. The firm should be large enough to have a diversity of positions. Focus on specifics: Who has been or is being sought, hired, promoted, etc.? Based on what criteria: experience, technical expertise, or educational credentials? What positions are hard to fill and why? How much do they promote from within? Is there continual on-the-job training? How long do people tend to stay? Seek examples. Focus on change: Have they been hiring or laying off, or remaining constant? What positions are opening, and which are disappearing? In what areas do they anticipate needing people? Focus on categories of people: What are the prospects for older workers, displaced or retrained workers, women versus men, college graduates, high school graduates, etc.? What are the essential credentials or "signals" of competence; i.e., what makes a person appear promising?

3. Family, schools, and academic aspirations: How much do preparation, achievement, and aspirations vary by socio-economic and family background? Is this due to the influence of parents, teachers, counselors, media, peers, or some combination thereof? Talk with students, teachers, counselors, or parents. If possible, survey a mixed class or classes. A good access point can be to volunteer as a classroom aide in a local elementary school, preferably one with a diverse student body. Community groups and organizations are also often eager to involve volunteers, even on a short-term basis. Head Start works with young children and their parents to encourage school readiness, and people are needed to assist teachers and relate to children one on

one. Church and community outreach centers often provide after-school tutoring and hot meals for children from low-income families.

4. High schools: Talk with counselors, long-time teachers, students, and/or concerned parents. You may also wish to focus on particular skills programs, after-school programs, or work-release and school-to-work programs. What are the reasons students choose college or vocationally oriented classes? Are students clearly "tracked" into particular paths? What are students' career ambitions or hopes? How well are these achieved? What reasons are there for dropping out or non-completion, or for variations by class and racial background?

5. Higher education and adult education: Talk with the career and placement counselors at your college. You may also find it interesting to visit other local settings: area colleges, technical colleges or adult education programs, GED programs, worker retraining programs, family literacy programs, and tutoring programs. Look at career tracks within a field of study (e.g., health, education, business, etc.). Who pursues what tracks and why? What are the job prospects for various groups? How difficult is it to return to or continue education? What is the completion rate for various programs? Focus on the placement experience of various types of graduates: Are they improving, declining, or shifting?

6. Public or private job agencies: Talk with administrators or long-time employees. Administrators of public job agencies may be busy and hard to reach but can often point you to a wide range of material on local job listings and local job training programs. Private agencies are often very accessible, but you will need to carefully sort factual information from self-promotion. What programs and services are offered? What types of job training are offered? Who tends to fill what programs? What types of people are hardest to place? Are there areas of unfilled demand? You may focus on the career

plans and prospects of a group or sector of the population: those unemployed by a plant closing, homemakers returning to the paid labor force, etc. What are the options and obstacles? How successful are people in overcoming obstacles?

7. Community programs and agencies: Study the goals, activities, effectiveness, and problems of a local agency or organization working with poverty or economic mobility. Interviews can be useful here, but perhaps the best way is to volunteer to work on a project with this organization and write about your experiences as a participant observer. Access points can include:

   • Homeless centers and shelters: Some are merely "a roof and a meal," while others provide a comprehensive range of programs to help people recover from personal and financial problems. What are the local demographic trends in homelessness: numbers, men versus women, singles versus families, etc.? What are the major local causes of homelessness: fleeing family violence and abuse, substance abuse, personal and emotional problems, lack of affordable housing, economic downturns, etc.? What is being done locally to work for the recovery and self-sufficiency of different homeless groups? How effective have they been?

   • Second-hand stores and food pantries: Salvation Army, St. Vincent De Paul, and other groups often operate thrift stores, as well as providing personal and family assistance. Church and community food pantries have expanded to meet growing demands. Talk with employees and volunteers and if possible, assist with activities. Who does this group serve? What are the biggest needs, and what causal factors lie behind those needs?

   • Community health centers and clinics serving low-income neighborhoods: administrative help, statistics, assistance with community health visits, health fairs, etc.

- Community youth programs: These are often operated from local schools and community centers. What are the biggest community needs in this area? How does this program attempt to address those needs? How effective have they been? Interacting with the youth, as well as with the employees and volunteers, can help greatly to find a fuller answer to these questions.

- Neighborhood housing services and housing groups, such as Habitat for Humanity, often need help with construction and organization and are eager to talk about local programs. What are local housing needs? Who is the most squeezed in the local housing market? How does this group hope to alleviate some of these problems? For whom are their programs targeted, and for whom are they the most effective?

In the Media

8. Consider the portrayal of social class in popular television. Which social classes are most often presented? Are some underrepresented? How do popular television programs portray the experiences and lifestyle of the wealthy, the middle class, the working class, and the poor? Do the programs offer insights or merely perpetuate stereotypes?

9. Examine the "Help Wanted" section of a local Sunday newspaper. What fields have the most listings? What are the most sought-after qualifications? What job seekers should have ample choices? Are there types of job seekers who would find this section useless or discouraging?

10. Look at a publication that targets employment issues for a population of personal interest to you: *Working Woman, Black Enterprise, Hispanic, Money Magazine,* etc.

What are the common projections concerning jobs and income in these publications? What are frequently cited as problems and obstacles? What kinds of suggestions or implications are provided for career planning?

11. Examine a political issue related to the economy and economic change, employment, income, poverty, or unequal access to social goods, such as housing or healthcare. Look at the arguments associated with the political right and those of the political left (for example, compare articles in *The Progressive* with those in *American Enterprise*). Are there points of agreement between the two sides or points of dissent within each camp? What are the root causes of the problem according to each side? How does this lead to different proposals and policies? What do you find convincing? Do you find any examples of bias or faulty reasoning?

12. Many are hopeful that the "information superhighway" will be their fast track. Certainly, this has become an important new form of media. Try exploring the World Wide Web. You can gain access through Netscape or whatever system is supported by your campus. Peruse two "homepages":

    http:\\www.occ.com

    http:\\www.careermosaic.com

    These sites are really electronic clearinghouses for a variety of career-related information. OCC and CAREER-MOSAIC allow you to look at job opportunities in various areas of specialty and various geographic locations as posted by national employers to explore college programs, to look at career and resume advice (from columnists, *The Wall Street Journal*, and various sources), and even to post resumes. These programs have relatively user-friendly menus that transfer you to the homepages of companies, universities, publishers, etc. Remember that most of these have been created to promote a particular company or organization rather than to provide objective assessments of the opportunities. Nonetheless, the amount of information available is wide-ranging and growing daily. Try these sites (or others that you may learn of) to explore educational and occupational information of interest to your own career plans. Were you able to locate interesting or useful information? Do you think that the growth of such on-line services will increase equal access to the job market, as some have contended, or create new inequalities based on the ability to access information, as others have contended? For whom would electronic career assistance likely be most useful, and who might be left out?

5

A Cohort of Many Colors

The current cohort of college students is more ethnically and racially diverse than at any point in our history. This partly reflects gains that a number of groups have made in obtaining access to higher education and higher-status careers. It also reflects the growing diversity of the United States as a whole (see Figure 5.1).

Diversity itself, however, has not paved the way for harmony and mutual accommodation among diverse groups. At Wellesley, a black professor's course emphasizing Jewish involvement in the slave trade stirs local and national controversy among African American and Jewish American students. Some even call his work a politically motivated tirade. The professor calls the criticisms "a Jewish onslaught" and subtitles his work *Notes from the Wellesley Battleground*. On other campuses, proposals for affirmative action in student admissions are denounced by some student political groups as quotas that perpetuate "campus apartheid," prompting angry rebuttals from other groups. Deans on several prominent campuses cite concern over the rising number of "racial incidents."

Race and ethnicity are the social divisions that will not go away. Karl Marx believed that these divisions would gradually give way to the dominance of the real divisions in society—those of class. Despite the efforts of property-owning capitalists, workers of all races and backgrounds would eventually come to realize their common position in capitalist society. Likewise, Max Weber believed that many primordial or ancient distinctions, including racial and ethnic distinctions, would give way to the newer, rational divisions of modern bureaucratic society. The modern bureaucracy, whether public or corporate, would not care about personal characteristics, such as skin color or personal heritage, but would rather focus on impersonal criteria, such as formal credentials. Many modern observers believe Marx was right about the importance of class divisions, and that Weber was right about the growing emphasis on formal credentials and bureaucratic organizations. In the midst of this formal, bureaucratic capitalist society, however, race and ethnicity are still very much with us (Smith, 1981). Some speak of a "return to tribalism," as Yugoslavia degenerates into warring tribes, and Miami and Los Angeles threaten to do the same. From the chaos of ethnic cleansing to the exuberance of ethnic festivals in ever more cities, race and ethnicity have become an important part of the modern world. From talk of "resurgent racism" to new ethnic studies programs, race is also very much a part of the contemporary college campus.

One way to think about race and ethnicity is to consider them an important divider or boundary between social groups (Barth, 1969). *Ethnicity* is a social boundary between groups based on each group's sense of common identity and common ancestry. It is a social boundary in the sense that it distinguishes "those like us" from "those who are different," which may affect a wide range of actions and interactions. The most important element is a group's sense of commonality, since ethnic definitions and boundaries are continually changing. At times, persons who consider themselves members of a common group may have few cultural practices or recent ancestors in common. In one setting, Cuban Americans and Chicanos (persons of Mexican American background) may be very aware of their separate and distinctive identities. In another setting, they may see themselves under the common heading of Latinos (Hispanic Americans).

Race is a social boundary between groups of presumed different ancestry that is reflected in physical differences. Again, a very subjective element has slipped into the definition. Regardless of what your elementary school teacher may have told you, *biological race* is a very weak concept when applied to human beings. People have migrated and intermarried for so long, resulting today in such a mixture and subtle variation of physical characteristics that no division of humanity into any number of races is biologically defensible. Nonetheless, because over time people have placed great emphasis on differences in color or facial features and treated people accordingly, *social race* can be a very important division. This division also varies by society: A person who is "colored" in South Africa may be considered "white" in the United States.

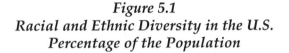

Figure 5.1
Racial and Ethnic Diversity in the U.S.
Percentage of the Population

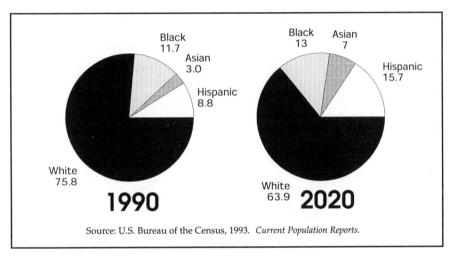

Source: U.S. Bureau of the Census, 1993. *Current Population Reports.*

Race on Campus: Are You a Racist?

Two men, one white and one black, pace about the room recounting personal experiences with *prejudice*, a biased judgment formed before all the facts are known, and with *discrimination*, biased actions that restrict a minority group. They define *racism* as the combination of prejudiced attitudes and the power to discriminate, including an *ideology* to rationalize such attitudes and actions. The black man then approaches one of the students in the room and asks with an air of innocence, "Tell me, are you a racist?" The student shifts uncomfortably. After hearing the list of common practices, this student is not so sure. "Well, at least I hope not," he replies. The question is asked of several others, each providing a somewhat evasive answer. The tension in the room is noticeable. Given the long history of racial biases and tensions in the United States and in our own communities, can anyone claim complete innocence? The tension is relieved as students break up into groups to discuss how they felt about the questions. This is the Nasca Workshop, "Put it on the Line," one of a number of attempts on campuses across the country to bring out into the open unspoken questions and problems of race.

In groups like these, contradictions often surface. Most whites claim they do not discriminate, yet most blacks can point to one or more times when they felt they were the targets of discrimination. Most students claim to believe in the benefits of interacting with a wide range of people, including those from many ethnic and racial backgrounds; yet many campus social groups show little such diversity.

One definition of ethnicity is a social boundary based on presumed ancestry. Such a boundary affects actions, those we interact with and those we do not. Boundaries are also a part of identity: They tell us who we are by means of contrast with who we are not. Boundaries separate "Us" from "Them."

Pluralism is the ability to accommodate a diverse group of people, while accepting (not eliminating) their differences. It is in essence drawing a second, more inclusive boundary.

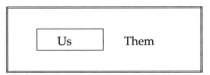

Students often ask, "Why can't we just interact as people and not worry about what group someone belongs to?" What they are really asking is a very American wish: Why can't we interact just as individuals? The school of sociology known as symbolic interactionism, however, offers an important insight here: People do not interact as isolated individuals but out of a social context that includes meaning, definitions, and power. Men and women interact differently based on their ideas of maleness and femaleness and appropriate behavior. Managers behave differently from those under their supervision because of the social definitions and expectations that accompany their role. Many of these differences are unconscious. People's responses to others are conditioned by expectations based on perceptions of group identity. This is how we categorize a world of strangers. Cues on how to approach someone may be offered by their clothes: a lab coat, a clerical collar, blue overalls, a gray vested suit, or a mini-skirt. Cues may come in the form of physical "props": a large oak desk, a podium, a stethoscope, or a wheelchair. Cues may also come in the form of personal characteristics: accent or style of speech, eye contact, vocabulary, age, gender, or color.

Attitudes are acted upon in the context of social power. Any group may hold bigoted opinions, but not all have the power to systematically discriminate. Racism in the United States is synonymous with white racism, not because only white Americans hold prejudices, but because the power structure of the United States has long been white-dominated. In this context, it is very unlikely that access to an African American-dominated institution (for instance, a black college or fraternity) will greatly limit the opportunities from an access to the power and prestige of a European American. Yet discrimination by white-dominated institutions could greatly limit the opportunities of non-whites, which is a matter of greater concern.

For Reflection

1. Sociologist Peter Rose finds American race relations deadlocked in a pattern of white denial and black anger (Rose, 1990). Most European Americans claim they don't discriminate, yet many African Americans say they experience frequent discrimination. What could account for this apparent contradiction? Do many people find it difficult to make their beliefs and actions coincide? Why or why not?

2. Think about the criteria people use to distinguish between Us and Them. List several. Do you find that you use any of these? Has there been a time when you felt walled out by a group and labeled as part of Them? What were the circumstances, and what were your feelings? Are there ways that institutions, groups and individuals can draw a more encompassing, pluralist

boundary to bring Them inside? How might they begin?

3. When is a cue likely to be informative about a person, and when is it likely to lead to prejudiced perceptions? When does a category become a stereotype?

4. Differences make interactions interesting, but they can also make people uncomfortable. Discomfort can lead to avoidance or stilted behavior, that is, actions that are unnatural: being overly evasive or overly friendly, overly guarded or overly respectful. What differences can make you uncomfortable? How do you tend to respond to this discomfort? Are any of these differences often associated with racial or ethnic differences?

5. When members of different ethnic or racial groups interact against the backdrop of a history of prejudice, discrimination, and racism, a variety of factors can interfere with natural and relaxed conversation:

Resentment	Defensiveness	Suspicion
Anger	Hurt	Awkwardness
Shyness	Hostility	Feeling put on the spot
Guilt	Stereotypes	Lack of common ground

Have you experienced any of these? In what situations?

Discuss this with someone who holds a racial or ethnic identity different from your own. What have they experienced? Do these discomforts and interfering elements decline with greater exposure? If so, under what conditions?

Wiggers Goin' Gansta: Choosing Your Ethnicity

The idea of choosing ethnicity may strike you as odd. It would seem that ethnicity, if anything, is one thing you do not choose. Yet in modern American society many aspects of life that have previously been determined by culture and class are becoming matters of choice. Ethnicity may be joining that list, as large numbers of people seek to find, and perhaps recreate, their roots. In particular, they seem eager to find the most appealing aspects of those roots.

For the first time, the 1980 census asked respondents who had checked a racial category to also list their ethnic ancestry. Mary Waters (1990) was researching ethnic differences using this new census material. She became interested by a question that underlay her data, "How did people decide what to list?" She details her findings in a book titled *Ethnic Options*. Interestingly, for many the choice of ancestry was not obvious, and involved picking among options. Many European Americans, those folks often merely lumped together as "white," have very complex ethnic ancestry. Some are not entirely aware of their entire ethnic background. How do these people establish their roots? Often they choose them.

People with last names with strong ethnic associations may emphasize that ethnicity, even when it is a small part of their background. Others may choose a heritage that is appealing: One woman who is Scottish and Irish only emphasizes the Irish—she sees the Irish as more fun-loving. Besides this, Scottish Americans don't have a holiday with as much fun and visibility as St. Patrick's day. Another who is English and Hungarian only emphasizes the Hungarian. English is too commonplace for her, and the Hungarians have better food. A young man who is Italian and four other European nationalities only emphasizes the Italian. A "very Italian" grandmother keeps this ethnic identity alive. Many Americans, upon finding some Native American ancestry in their background, are intrigued and begin learning about American Indian cultures.

Herbert Gans (1979) referred to this association process as *symbolic ethnicity*. It is not based in a closely knit socio-economic community but rather based on a desire to recapture the symbols of ethnicity: holidays, foods, music, and customs that give a sense of special belonging. Decades of assimilation of European Americans have reduced most socio-economic distinctions: Irish Americans are no longer predominantly manual laborers, Swedish Americans are no longer primarily rural farmers. Similarly, any single ancestry has become diluted by intermarriage. Even names may have been Anglicized, Rosencrantz becomes merely Rose. Yet many long for the sense of identity and belonging, of community and commonality, and of uniqueness that can accompany ethnic ties. The answer is to preserve, or in some cases revive, symbolic ethnicity. A woman who until recently was unaware of her German ancestry now has a list of meals that feature sauerkraut. A Swedish American family that only grew up with Santa Claus now begins the Christmas season with St. Lucia day.

Interestingly, some of these people may have had great-grandparents who consciously tried to hide aspects of their ethnicity. Many immigrants tried to change their names, hide their accents and eliminate identifying customs that could invoke scorn or discrimination. Few would have chosen to emphasize an Irish or Hungarian background if they also had English ancestors, for class considerations were involved. Any "non-white" ancestry might have been a point of embarrassment rather than pride.

For some groups, a similar ambivalence between pride in ancestry and concern about discrimination may remain. Some African Americans are both intrigued by rediscovering African customs, and yet worried about the price they will pay for "differentness." An African American professional has begun to celebrate Kwaanza, a new holiday based on West African harvest festivals unknown to his grandparents, yet has worked hard to achieve a polished, "white English" manner of speech. Likewise, Latinos may enjoy the sound of Spanish and the smells and sounds of their cultural heritage in private, and then find they must minimize some ethnic markers in an Anglo-dominated marketplace. Symbolic ethnicity is a luxury of a *pluralistic society* that welcomes and integrates differences, and in our society not all differences are always equally received. American society offers many individual choices, but these choices are still made in the context of constraints imposed by social structure and majority culture.

The extreme form of ethnic choice is sometimes exercised by teenagers who adopt the motif of a group to which they have no apparent ethnic affiliation. White youth may "go gansta," adopting symbols and clothes from black gangs as a way of appearing tough, cool, or just more interesting. With hats turned sideways or backwards and the latest in hip hop clothes, white teenagers are sometimes derided as *wiggers* but apparently see no incongruity in their chosen image. A blonde Anglo teenager tries out the dark lipstick and heavy make-up of the Mexican American *cholita* image, because "white is boring" (Bernstein, 1995). These may be examples of teenage foolishness to older adults, but they exemplify that in a highly cosmopolitan society, cultural identification is often a matter of taste and choice.

For Reflection

1. What is your racial and ethnic ancestry? Is this ancestry important to your self-identity?

2. Are there distinctive traditions associated with your ancestry that you maintain? How interested are you in reviving or continuing ethnic traditions with your children and grandchildren? What traditions do you enjoy and hope to continue?

3. Does an emphasis on ethnicity isolate people, cutting them off from other ethnic groups, or does it build community bonds?

4. Think about a penetrating question for a moment: Many predominantly white Americans note with pride that they are "also a little bit American Indian." Few predominantly white Americans note they are "also a little bit African American." Why are some ancestries emphasized or minimized? Why do you choose to emphasize or minimize aspects of your ancestry?

Not Our Kind: Old and New Forms of Segregation

Gunnar Myrdal (1944) titled his now-classic book on American race relations *An American Dilemma*. A close look at the American experience of race and ethnic relations reveals a number of dilemmas between seemingly contradictory ideologies and practices. One such contradiction has been the view of the United States as a melting pot of peoples and cultures and the continued attempt of some groups to isolate themselves from others. Early in this century, Chicago School Sociologist Robert Park (1914) laid out the steps in what he believed was a "natural history" of intergroup relations. Park was an urban ecologist, interested in the way humans create and divide urban space. His theory is rooted in an ecological perspective, but with its emphasis on assimilation and an eventual restoration of balance and order, it has been very influential in functionalist thinking about race and ethnic relations. Park's stages are:

1. *Invasion:* A new group arrives.

2. *Resistance:* The prior group defends its territory.

3. *Competition*: The two groups struggle for control.

4. *Accommodation and Cooperation:* Stable patterns develop.

5. *Assimilation*: The groups intermarry and merge.

During the racial turmoil of the 1960s, many began to doubt that certain groups would ever be allowed to follow the path toward assimilation that Park had laid out. Perhaps their situation was entirely different from the white immigrants groups. Robert Blauner (1972) adopted the term "Third World Peoples" for these others, because many had roots in parts of the world that comprise the so-called Third World, and because these groups seem to form a "Third World" of poverty within the First World. In fact, Blauner argued, these groups are also victims of colonial oppression, only for them the oppression has occurred within their country rather than by a foreign power. The United States has held only a few external colonies (most notably the Philippines) but has often relied upon the low-wage labor of many groups within its borders. Blauner, drawing much more on social conflict perspectives, termed this process *Internal Colonialism* and outlined four basic elements:

1. Control over a group's governance

2. Restriction of freedom of movement

3. Colonial-style labor exploitation

4. Belief in a group's inferiority

The integration and eventual assimilation that Park proposed have been the strategy of choice for many groups. Being integrated into a society as "colonial labor" is much less appealing. Some scholars have suggested that a way to avoid this is by mobilizing ethnic solidarity within a close-knit group. In this case the group works closely together, operating as small business people in otherwise poor or neglected areas (often the neighborhoods of Blauner's colonial peoples) as middleman minorities (Blalock, 1967; Bonacich, 1973). An alternate strategy is to cluster into an *ethnic enclave* (Wilson and Portes, 1980) in which ethnic entrepreneurs hire and serve the needs of co-ethnics, creating their own ethnic labor market.

The ethnic solidarity school of thought takes seriously the conflict perspective but also emphasizes issues of interaction: how hostility may create solidarity, and how this solidarity may breed new hostility if middleman minorities are perceived as clannish, greedy, or exploiters of poor neighborhoods.

The following scenarios are examples of segregation drawn from different times and places. Some represent formal or legal segregation, many are examples of informal or de facto segregation. Many are initiated or maintained by the dominant group, some by a minority group. You probably already have strong feelings about integration and segregation, but try to reserve judgment until you have thought through the scenarios.

Arkansas, 1940s: How long children go to school depends largely on who they are. Children of business and land owners begin school in September. Children of white share-croppers and farm hands continue to work in the fields and begin school in mid-October. Black children begin school, in their own building, in December. Their textbooks consist primarily of cast-offs from the white school. Professionally trained teachers cannot often afford to work only six months of the year, so most teachers in the black school have other jobs and other backgrounds. A handful of Asian American business owners win the right to attend the white school for the full school year. When the courts order desegregation, the black school is closed down and all students are moved to the over-crowded white school. Whites refuse to attend the now unused black school.

Florida, 1960s: Large numbers of Cubans flee the changes in their country occurring under Fidel Castro. They are welcomed into the U.S. as political refugees and dispersed throughout the country. Within a few years, however, many have congregated near an area of the Miami metropolitan area known as Little Havana. Over time, Miami and neighboring Hialeah become a magnet for Cuban Americans in the U.S., and for new arrivals from Cuba. More than most such ethnic enclaves, Little Havana replicates the sights, sounds and smells of Old Havana: outdoor cafes resonating with Latin Caribbean rhythms, small cigar shops with their distinctive aroma, and stores that reassure the shopper, "English spoken here." Cuban-owned businesses grow and expand, and Cuban Americans become influential in much of southern Florida. Cubans seeking employment often work for other Cubans rather than competing for jobs elsewhere. Some sociologists, such as Alejandro Portes, believe the high rate of financial success of Cuban Americans (higher than for other Latino groups) is tied in part to their spacial concentration in an ethnic enclave economy in which they can apply their skills and background without suffering discrimination and disadvantages in the broader economy.

Los Angeles, 1980s: Chinese Americans in California and New York have often been confined to "Chinatowns." Such places still thrive. Many successful Chinese Americans, however, are eager to enjoy the quality of life offered by middle-class suburbs. In Los Angeles this movement outward has accelerated in recent years. However, many Chinese Americans in Los Angeles have chosen *the same* suburb. As a result, parts of Monterey Park now have very high concentrations of Asian Americans, especially more recent immigrants from Taiwan and Hong Kong. Some say this offers the best of both worlds: the cordiality of like-minded neighbors and yet the uncrowded ambiance of a suburban life (in marked contrast to the vibrant but congested "Chinatown").

Indianapolis, 1980s: The city implements a bussing program to reduce school segregation. The implementation is such that almost all the students who are bussed are black. In one case, students ride for over an hour to their new school. "North Division" students, as they become known, are unable to participate in extra-curricular activities, because their only bus leaves immediately after school. In one instance, all North Division students are called to the cafeteria where they wait, while police investigate a telephone threat to harm them. The bussing plan is eventually abandoned.

New York City, 1990s: Entrance to one urban school is past police security and into halls lined with lockers, many of which are missing doors. Facilities are in desperate condition: Leaky pipes threaten books in several rooms, half of the bathrooms are not usable. For lack of space, many classes, especially those involving remedial or special education, meet in closets or otherwise unusable wood and metal shops. Many teachers are substitutes, both long and short term, while some classes disperse after the teacher fails to show up. The population of this school is 90 percent black and Hispanic, the graduation rate is 40 percent. Ten minutes away, a second school which is 80 percent white, is excited about the new equipment, including new microscopes and lab equipment, for its accelerated science program. Of these students, 95 percent graduate and 60 percent go on to college.

Milwaukee, 1990s: After two decades of attempts at desegregation, a proposal suggests separate schools for black males. This school would be specifically designed to meet the "special needs" of this population and attempt to reverse the climbing drop-out rates. Some in the African American community voice support for the proposal. Already the idea of "Afrocentric" education has found a place in Martin Luther King Jr. Elementary School. Swahili words accompany their English counterparts on the bulletin boards, African masks hang in the halls, and students learn about kings and queens with examples from the Zulu empire. "Children see themselves in the curriculum, this boosts self-esteem and academic performance," say the proponents. "It's ghetto-izing ideology that ignores our common participation in American culture," argue the critics.

New York, 1990s: African American students come to Cornell University from a diversity of backgrounds. Given the selective admissions, many come from high-quality and at least somewhat integrated private and public schools. A few have known mostly whites prior to college. A popular residence hall option for African American students is Ujaama House. One of several residences with a special theme or mission, Ujaama is dedicated to promoting minority cultures and perspectives. Directors say Ujaama welcomes anyone with an interest in these issues, but its population is almost entirely African American. Students often refer to it as the "black dorm." New black residents to Ujaama find friendly faces and people interested in their success and sensitive to their concerns. They also find that most of their new friends and acquaintances come from the House—and they are all black. For many of these students, coming to a major cosmopolitan campus in Upstate New York has meant their residence and circle of friends is more segregated than in the communities from which they have come.

Stanford, 1991: A group of Asian American students and professors follow the lead of African American and Latino students and call for an Asian American Study Center sponsoring a program of Asian American studies and headed by a recognized Asian American scholar. Such a scholar is invited to visit from an Ivy League University. This scholar then surprises the audience (and infuriates a few) by speaking out against the proposed program and ethnic studies in general. These programs limit the scope of inquiry, he contends; they fail to encompass the theory and methods of the traditional social sciences, and they perpetuate an apartheid-like view of American society in which ethnic difference is a permanent distinction and divider.

For Reflection

1. What racial and ethnic groups best fit Park's model of assimilation? Which groups best fit Blauner's model of internal colonialism? Which groups best exemplify ethnic solidarity? How do you explain the differences in the strategies and experiences of various groups in American society?

2. Is the separation of racial and ethnic groups always destructive? What are the costs and benefits to the majority group? What are the costs and benefits to minority groups?

3. Before the Civil Rights movement, much segregation in the southern United States was *de jure*, written into law. Most segregation in the northern United States was *de facto*, based on more subtle influences of class differences and individual discrimination. De jure segregation, since it was written into law, has proven easier to combat through legislation than de facto segregation. As a result, many northern cities are now more segregated than many southern cities. Which form do you believe is more or less harmful? For what reasons? Are there ways to combat de facto segregation?

4. During his term in office, President Carter created a brief stir by stating that desegregation did not mean eliminating the "ethnic purity" of some neighborhoods. Carter, often a civil rights advocate, later apologized and said he should have used "ethnic character." Are there legitimate ways to maintain the "ethnic character" of an area, or is this disguised racial discrimination?

5. In 1896, the Supreme Court decided in the case of Plessy vs. Ferguson that laws mandating separate facilities for

different races were constitutional as long as they were "separate but equal." In the landmark desegregation case, Brown vs. the Board of Education of Topeka, Kansas (1954), the Supreme Court declared that legal segregation of schools was unconstitutional, because "separate educational facilities are inherently unequal." Is racial balance the only way to achieve equality? Is separate always unequal? Can integrated schools be achieved without integrated neighborhoods?

6. Two divergent perspectives emerged during the Civil Rights movement, and both still have adherents. The first perspective, associated with Martin Luther King and the Southern movement, emphasized integration as the means to progress. Marches targeted segregated facilities and attempted to win equal access. The second perspective, associated with Malcolm X and the Northern movement, saw these integration efforts as naive and shortsighted. Malcolm X believed that whites would never willingly surrender real power, and that the only answer was the mixture of black self-help, black pride, and black withdrawal from white institutions, which together became known as black nationalism. Both men's views changed over time, and both were assassinated before they could come to any final conclusions on the Civil Rights movement. As you think of the events since their deaths, whose views seem to have been best borne out? Which route seems to offer the best hope for African Americans?

7. How do you feel about racial and ethnic self-segregation on campus, in sororities and fraternities, and in other clubs and organizations? Most people enjoy being among people with whom they share a great deal and among whom they can relax and feel "at home." Yet these sentiments can also lead to charges of isolation, clannishness, and exclusion. When does a "home" become a "clique?"

8. Sociologist Peter Blau (Blau and Schwartz, 1984) has pointed out that simply due to the effect of numbers, a

minority (by any criteria) will always have more out-group contacts than will a majority. For instance, many European Americans know few or no African Americans, very few African Americans know no European Americans. Some claim this makes reaching out even more important for the majority and less important for the minority. This factor, along with a history of disadvantage, is a rationale for all-black schools (in fact, many traditional black colleges do have a few white students), even in the absence of all-white schools. Is there any similar rationale for all-female or all-male schools? Are there situations in which limiting admission to a school or organization to a particular race, gender, ethnic group, or other group could be appropriate and beneficial? Are there any settings in which you would prefer a homogeneous group?

The Segregation of Knowledge

Since the 1960s, various ethnic studies programs—Africana or African American studies, Chicano or Mexican American studies, and others—have proliferated on college campuses. Some see these, along with programs such as women's studies, finally giving voice to a neglected and repressed history, literature, and culture. Others agree with Arthur Schlesinger, Jr. (1992) that these could reflect, as in the title of his book, *The Disuniting of America*. Some educators in the social sciences see these programs weakening the traditional disciplines and raise concerns about the segregation of knowledge: Can one understand the African American experience, for instance, apart from a broader understanding of race and ethnic relations? Yet many of these same people, like the Asian American scholar cited above, are invited to hold joint appointments in a traditional discipline, such as sociology, and in an ethnic studies program.

In practice, many of the directors and instructors for ethnic studies programs (as well as women's studies) have come from the humanities, particularly history and literature. Perhaps this makes sense in that these fields have generally encouraged specialization to a particular place and time rather than the search in many social sciences for generalizable models and theories (social scientists differ on how successful they believe this search has been or can be).

One could argue that the original ethnic or area studies program is one of the oldest in the curricula: classics, which is essentially the integrated study of the history, literature, art, and culture of a particular people, in this case ancient Greeks and Romans.

The debate over ethnic studies is revisited in various revisionist histories that give greater weight to neglected groups. School books have scurried to add boxes about "Famous Women in History" or "Famous African Americans." To some, this is still a form of intellectual segregation, implying that these are tangents or parenthetical comments and not a part of "real history." Latino students sometimes complain, "Why is there a Black History Month and not a Chicano History Month or a Puerto Rican History Month?" Others wonder where all this would end. These attempts at inclusiveness may be just the first faltering steps toward a truly integrated, multicultural history. Many educators believe that once students can envision themselves or their ancestors in this history, they will have a new sense of belonging—in the nation, in the community, in the school, and in academic pursuits in general. Others, such as Reginald Wilson, say while this may be valid, the real reason for multicultural history is "truth-telling." Our national history is one of many contributions and blending of heritages; to tell the story right is to present a multifaceted, multicultural account. Others wonder, without a sense of common founders and defining principles, can we be a united people?

These concerns have their counterpart in literature. Revisionists argue that the "canon" of required reading for students has been largely limited to "a few dead white men." We must open up, they contend, to include the voices of women and minorities. Others contend that this process merely confuses students, bends to ideological rather than literary standards, and robs students of the opportunity to become well-acquainted with the "great books" that have shaped our thought and language. Others worry that without a common cultural core, we will lack a common discourse and splinter into ideologically and racially defined camps.

In an attempt to balance a Eurocentric view of history, some propose an Afrocentric view that stresses the achievements of Africa. In this view, Europe receives its insights and innovations from ancient Egypt, as well as from such Africans as Hannibal of Carthage and the Moorish invaders who later ruled Spain. Often each of these is presented as "black" people. When African influences are driven out, Europe "grovels in darkness." Some propose that the first to "discover" the New World were neither Columbus nor Lief Erikson but West African sailors, bringing African culture to found American civilizations. Many anthropologists and historians view these proposals with extreme skepticism: This is not truth-telling but a new form of ethnocentrism, placing one's own culture or group at center stage, and pushing all others to the periphery. For some of us, however, it may be enlightening to be exposed to a different form of ethnocentrism than that to which we are accustomed—one in which the tables are turned—if only to gain new insight into our own biases.

For Reflection

1. What do you remember of your elementary school history? In world history, how much attention was given to non-Western experiences? In American history, how prominently did people of non-European ancestry figure in the accounts?

2. How should the American story be told: Does it begin at Plymouth Rock with the Pilgrims, or does American history include the founding of Santa Fe and the formation of the League of the Iroquois? Is it more important to stress a common American heritage and identity or to stress the diversity of our heritage and the ways different groups experienced our past differently? Can we have diversity without divisiveness?

3. Should Americans have a common literature and a common set of heroes to create unity? Should each group look to its own heritage and literature? Have you ever sought to study the heritage of your own ancestry or that of another group?

4. Is there a "canon" of essential reading that should be familiar to every educated American? If not, do we lose a common basis for dialogue and understanding? If so, what should it contain?

Race In the Workplace: The Affirmative Action Debate

Affirmative action is a government-sponsored mandate to employers and schools to develop timetables and goals for increasing the educational and employment opportunities of minorities. It began as an attempt to overcome the disadvantages imposed on minority groups by years of racial discrimination. During the Eighties, however, this idea came under increasing attack. Critics argued that it constituted *reverse discrimination*, in which white males were now placed at unfair disadvantage. Others argued it imposed harmful quotas on businesses that hindered their management. Some simply argued that the programs just weren't working. Yet many insist that some form of affirmative action is still needed to help overcome decades of discrimination. Here is a summary of some of the key arguments:

Edwin Meese, former attorney general, declared, "Counting by race is a form of racism." He argues that numerical goals perpetuate rather than alleviate discrimination by race and ethnicity, and that the only fair policy is for the government to be "color blind."

William Raspberry, a black columnist, argues that African Americans are hurt by too much emphasis on past grievances. Even though the past wrongs may have been very real, the real need now is for African Americans to improve their educational motivation, pool their savings, increase their investment in black-owned business, and emphasize self-help strategies. He cites Asian Americans as a model. In this view, affirmative action is a distraction from the real needs.

Thomas Sowell, a black economist, argues that under the banner of affirmative action, the United States has slipped into meaningless quotas. A scholar of American ethnic history, he contends that different groups have always varied in their educational and economic attainment. These differences are often due to differences in the group's age composition, cultural background, time of arrival, and subsequent history. There is just no point in trying to maintain statistical representation for all groups in all places, he contends. Unless we are going to start bussing Greeks into predominantly Irish Catholic schools and insisting on more Hispanic hockey players, these averages have no meaning. It is better to try to improve opportunities for everyone.

William J. Wilson, a black sociologist, is less critical of affirmative action but believes that it has not helped those who need it the most. The black middle class, who have the credentials to qualify for affirmative programs, have been helped; but the black *underclass*—poorly-educated, under-employed inner city residents—have been largely missed. This group, he argues, will benefit more from jobs programs and initiatives targeted at all of the urban poor and unemployed, regardless of their race, than they will from race-specific affirmative action. He also believes that such broad programs will have more voter support and create less resentment than racially-based affirmative action.

Lani Guinier, a law professor, was President Clinton's original choice for assistant attorney general for civil rights. Her nomination was withdrawn amidst charges she was the "quota queen." She denies that she supports quotas and says that instead we should think of affirmative action as the "miner's canary" that warns of an unhealthy environment for everyone. If few women and people of color are excelling on the entrance criteria for a program, this may indicate that the criteria are too narrow or are biased. For example, entrance exams may indicate who could afford to be coached and to retake the exam rather than who is most capable. Counting by race and gender is not a matter of "canary rights" but an early warning that hiring and entrance criteria may need to incorporate a broader range of criteria to reflect broader talents and backgrounds, thus creating a healthier atmosphere for all.

Benjamin Hooks, former president of the NAACP, argues that talk about quotas misses the point of affirmative action. The name refers to efforts to take positive steps to counter-balance continuing negative effects of prejudice and discrimination. Since African Americans are often not a part of powerful "old boy networks" of hiring nor in places to be noticed and promoted by primarily white superiors, they continue to experience the disadvantages built into the social structure known as *institutional racism*. When positive steps are not taken to balance these disadvantages, business and government merely acquiesce to continued institutional racism.

In *The Zero-Sum Society*, Lester Thurow (1980) argues that although we are interested in remedying an individual's experience of racism, we can never know how much any one person has been disadvantaged by race. We can only measure disadvantage in terms of groups. When there is clear evidence of disadvantage, as in the case of racial minorities, we must attempt to provide group-level remedies such as affirmative action. An individualist ethic is all right as long as the society has never violated this in the past. Since our society has violated this ethic, giving extra aid to those who were initially handicapped until they can catch up is the only way to assure a fair race in the future.

Ronald Takaki (1994), a historian of race relations, brings together the arguments of Hooks and Thurow. He contends that all prior American history is essentially the history of an affirmative action program designed to benefit white men. The advantages of this history of preferential treatment are now institutionalized, as are the disadvantages of other groups. Racial inequality is preserved by social conditions and economic structures that work to continue to exclude women and minorities, who do not have the right credentials because they have not had this history of advantage. The only way to remedy this is with affirmative action programs that generate pressure to educate, recruit, train, and employ racial minorities. The only way to monitor success is to continue to compare levels of ethnic and racial groups, "to count by race."

For Reflection

1. Should government and business be "color blind," or is there a place for monitoring hiring and promotion rates by race and ethnicity?

2. Is affirmative action unfair to whites, or does it merely compensate for continued institutional discrimination against non-whites?

3. Does affirmative action have the potential to be effective, or should it be replaced by other programs?

4. The "affirmative" in affirmative action is to be an affirmation of racial, ethnic, and cultural diversity, and a willingness to embrace that diversity in positive ways. What are ways that an organization such as a university or a business can create a climate that welcomes diversity?

Race In the Workplace: Ain't Nobody Gonna Turn Me Around

During the height of the civil rights movement in the late 1950s and the 1960s, the protest march became a favorite tool of demonstrating opposition to unjust and repressive situations. The marchers faced many obstacles, from hostile crowds to police opposition, and so it was natural that they adapted this old refrain for their rally song:

> *Ain't nobody gonna turn me around,*
> *Turn me around, turn me around.*
> *Gonna keep on walkin', keep on workin'*
> *Keep on 'til the break of dawn.*

Marches have become rare, and fewer people see marching against injustice as a particularly effective strategy. Yet in the face of slights and subtle (and not so subtle) discrimination in the workplace, many have had to repeatedly remind themselves of what they stand for, what they believe, where they want to go, and that "ain't nobody gonna turn me around." Race is not going to go away anytime soon in the workplace any more than on campus, but there are strategies for both minorities and concerned majority members to ease tensions and promote effective, and enjoyable, cooperation and collaboration.

Strategies for Majorities

Choosing your Terms. One way to help foster a respectful and congenial climate is to use terms for people's heritage that are not offensive. Some people feel uneasy about whether or not they are using the "correct" term in a time when preferred designations seem to be frequently changing. The goal, however, is not to meet an abstract standard of "political correctness" but to convey respect and regard. The simplest rule is to use the term that the person himself or herself prefers. A common aspect of being a subordinated minority is that someone else defines you; a key to self-regard and empowerment is to regain the right of self-definition. The terms most often preferred by various groups are given below. Note that the favored terms abandon designations of color in favor of region of origin. One positive result is that the terms are all parallel, without implied superiority or inferiority. Adding the designation "Ameri-

Table 5.1

Complete	Short	Poor
European American	White	WASP, Aryan
Irish American		
German American, etc.		
Jewish American		
(a religious and ethnic label that can span racial categories)		
Arab American		
("White" but not "European" or "Caucasian")		
African American	Black	Colored
Jamaican American	Black American	
Haitian American		
Asian American		Oriental
Japanese American		
Chinese American		
Filipino American		
Indian American (Asian Indian)		
Korean American, etc.		
Hispanic American	Latino	"Mexican"
Mexican American	Chicano	
Cuban American	Cubano	"Spanish"
Puerto Rican		
Portuguese American		
Native American	Indian	Redskin
American Indian		
Potawatomi		
Miami, etc.		
Inuit (Eskimo)		
Alaskan Native		

can" emphasizes that regardless of heritage and origin this person is a full member of American society. Referring to Asian Americans as "Chinese" or Hispanic Americans as "Mexicans" may not only be inaccurate, it implies they are not truly "American." Another good rule is to try to be as specific as possible. "Hispanic" is an abstraction that combines many cultural and regional backgrounds; a person is more likely to have a personal identity as Cuban American or Puerto Rican. Affirming this shows an interest in another's heritage and a step in going beyond the "they-all-look-alike-to-me" syndrome. The so-called hyphenated designations (although often used without a hyphen, *German American*) are longer and more cumbersome, and so shorthand "nicknames" remain in common use. "White" and "Black" are well-entrenched in our vocabulary, although any small child can point out that these are inaccurate labels. "Indian" remains an acceptable shorthand ("an Indian business") since it is still used by many Native Americans themselves. Again, however, specificity is better: "George is Potawatomi." Besides clearly derogatory labels, others are poor designations: "Oriental" conveys stereotypes of inscrutability and is resented by many Asian Americans, "colored" lingers in a few places in the country but carries racist overtones to many (and raises the question, What color are they?), WASP (White Anglo Saxon Protestant) is redundant (how many black Anglo Saxons do you know?) and inaccurate unless the person in question is truly English Protestant.

A few guidelines for another category of difference: persons with disabilities. "Crippled" has given way to new terms such as "physically challenged." People with disabilities often find the first demeaning, and the second unnecessarily cutesy. They ask, "who wants to be unnecessarily challenged by inaccessible facilities?" Barriers are bad. Likewise, "the specially-abled," is cumbersome and perpetuates stereotypes that all blind people have great musical talent and so forth. A good rule is to put the person first and when needed make note of the physical limitations: "persons with disabilities." Next preferred is "disabled persons." Blind is all right for some one with no sight, as is deaf for someone with no hearing. "Visually impaired" is better than "part-blind" or "half-blind," "hearing impaired" is better than "part-deaf" or "half-deaf." Terms should recognize disabilities but focus on abilities.

Breaking the Ice. Racial and ethnic questions have no place in a job interview where they can raise suspicion of bias, and many are not permitted by equal opportunity hiring laws. As you come to better know co-workers, however, informed and respectful questions can help break the ice. They show an interest in the other person as a person, and they can avoid future misunderstandings.

- Do you observe Jewish religious holidays?

- You seem so comfortable in both Spanish and English, which do you consider your first language?

- Your parents came from the Philippines? That's always struck me as a fascinating place. Have you visited there yourself?

- I have never quite understood Ramadan (Muslim period of fasting). How do you observe it?

A good caution is to avoid unwarranted assumptions—not all Chinese Americans speak Mandarin Chinese any more than all Irish Americans speak Irish Gaelic; not all Asian Americans or Mexican Americans are recent immigrants, and some may have had family members in this country longer than most European Americans. "You speak English so well," may be an insult rather than a compliment to a Japanese American Stanford graduate whose family has lived in Hawaii and California for generations.

The goal is to get to know the whole person; to learn about more than just their racial or ethnic background. Creating a welcoming climate means acknowledging differences without dwelling on them. Differences are interesting, but people are more alike than they are different. Over-awareness of difference adds unnecessary uneasiness, as when a speaker stops short and offers an awkward apology to a blind co-worker after every use of a favorite expression, "So you see," or when special note of a Jewish co-worker is made every time mention is made of Christmas. Comfort is achieved when differences become an incidental part of common interests: "You should check out that new restaurant—great sandwiches, reasonable prices, and they're nicely wheelchair accessible."

Standing Your Ground. It is possible to challenge offensive stereotypes and jokes without being unduly heavy-handed: "Come on, Steve, do I detect more than a little bias in that description?" General lightheartedness can do a lot for the workplace, but ethnic humor and teasing, if it has any place at all, should be reserved for co-ethnics and intimate friends. Barbed jokes, and all forms of sarcasm, can too readily create resentment even among otherwise cordial colleagues. A simple response: "No, spare me that joke. I don't mean to be prudish, but there are still too many put-downs going around for me to really enjoy ethnic jokes." Quiet convictions presented in a non-judgmental, non-threatening manner are more likely to win grudging respect than animosity and can go a long way in shaping the climate of the workplace.

Strategies for Minorities

The task of building strong relationships across cultural divides can be even more difficult for minorities. Various seminars are now offered to minority employees, especially professionals, on coping with less than ideal company climates. For example, see *Success Strategies for Minorities* by the Master Communications Group (Films for the Humanities and Social Sciences, 1991). Some frequently cited suggestions include:

Carry calm self-respect. Adopting a gentle non-hostile bearing is a great help, but there is no need to tolerate racial slurs and slights, even when ostensibly "good natured": "Listen Mike, to my grandma I'll always be 'young man' when she's proud and 'boy' when she's mad. But that's a grandmother's privilege. To my clients and associates I'm Mr. Johnson, and to my friends I'm Robert. I hope I can count you among the latter."

Display wit. A story has circulated about Bishop Desmond Tutu of South Africa. The bishop encountered a white South African on a narrow boardwalk across a muddy construction area. One of them would have to back up to the main sidewalk to let the other pass. "I don't step aside for monkeys," the man snarled. Tutu stepped backward and off to the side, dipped his hat elegantly and replied, "Ah, but I do."

Be aware of hidden bias. Two are common. The first is class or rank bias: High status people are often accorded more personal discretion than lower status personnel. A casually inclined vice president may stop by the office in his golf shirt, and yet secretarial help may be always expected to look "professional." A college professor may be able to wear distinctively ethnic clothing that would be frowned upon for a textbook representative. The second is racial bias. The most blatant stereotypes seem to be fading, but biased judgments about minorities often include construing personal reserve as "a chip on the shoulder" or conversely construing talkative friendliness as non-professional behavior, and interpreting most ethnic dialects as reflecting a lack of education or intelligence. These are, of course, "unfair" and can lead to anger or anxiety; it is better to just give a bit more attention to presentation of self. Like a good sociologist or anthropologist working in the field, it helps to be able to adapt behavior readily to the culture without pretending to "go native." It also doesn't hurt to develop a genuine regard and liking for the natives. "Code-switching" is changing style of speech and demeanor to fit the situation. We all speak differently among friends than among clients or employers. For minority workers, the switch may need to be greater, but need not be completely unnatural. We all adopt differing roles in differing situations.

Show true vitality. Slights and put-downs can cause us to want to withdraw. The more you are active, involved, and a vital part of the workforce team, however, the less likely your concerns are going to be perceived as personal aloofness, and the more likely any complaints and concerns you may raise will be taken seriously.

For Reflection

1. Bias can reside in rules, organizational arrangements, and institutional ways of doing business, as well as in prejudiced individuals. This is often termed institutional racism. A better term might be institutionalized bias. Just as a single stairstep without a ramp can be a major barrier to someone in a wheelchair, structural bias can be limiting to single parents as when there is no provision for childcare, to religious minorities as when there is no provision for non-Christian religious holidays, to low-income persons as when access to a private automobile is assumed, and to racial and ethnic minorities as when little or no provision is made for non-Anglo American cultural background. As you look closely at your campus or workplace, do you find evidence of institutional racism or institutionalized bias? How can these problems be best addressed and remedied?

2. Have there been times when you took a stand, or felt you should have taken a stand, against a prejudiced statement or discriminatory action? Looking back, are there things you would have done differently?

3. Many continue to face prejudice and discrimination, and yet others, most often European Americans, have

begun to complain that work relations are hurt by the hypersensitivity of persons and regulations. When does sensitivity become hypersensitivity? Does this depend on the situation or the group involved?

4. Is it possible to take a strong stand against racial and ethnic bias without being perceived as hypersensitive or hostile? What is your personal approach?

Reaching Out, Digging Deeper

Voices from the American Chorus

As the world of racial and ethnic relations intensifies rather than disappears, many Americans today seem caught between denial of differences and of the reality of discrimination on one hand, and an equally debilitating snare of accusations and anger, of guilt and blame, and of sheer hopeless frustration on the other. We can hope that the current cohort of students and new workers, the most diverse and the most educated ever, can take a lead in finding a better way.

Coming to better appreciate one's own background as well as the experiences of others is a good first step on this path. For a broad yet often poignant and personal multi-cultural history of America, see Ronald Takaki's *A Different Mirror* (1993). Studs Terkel's *Race* (1992) does a good job of letting a broad chorus of voices from different backgrounds speak of their experiences and perceptions. Autobiographical accounts can also give an inside view into a different world of experience. Powerful personal accounts include Maya Angelou's *I Know Why the Caged Bird Sings* (1969), Sarah and Elizabeth Delany's *Having Our Say* (1993), James Comer's *Maggie's American Dream* (1988), Claude Brown's now-classic *Manchild in the Promised Land* (1965), and Nathan McCall's more recent *Makes Me Wanna Holler* (1994), all on the African American experience. Other experiences include Richard Rodriquez's *Hunger of Memory* (1981; Mexican American), Piri Thomas's *Down These Mean Streets* (1967; Puerto Rican), Scott Momaday's *The Names: A Memoir* (1976; Native American), Jerre Mangione's *An Ethnic at Large* (1978; Sicilian), Jade Snow Wong's *Fifth Chinese Daughter* (1945), and J. Anthony Lukas's account of three families—black, Yankee, and Irish American—in *Common Ground* (1985). For compelling accounts of the state of race relations in the United States, see Andrew Hacker's *Two Nations*

(1992), Cornell West's *Race Matters* (1993), and Elijah Anderson's urban ethnography, *Streetwise* (1990).

To further explore the role of race and ethnicity in our society and our communities, consider the following project ideas.

In Your Family

1. Research your ancestry. Talk with family members, especially older ones, about what they know of your family background. You may be able to use official records such as birth certificates or unofficial records such as a family Bible. Are there parts of your ethnic heritage of which you were unaware?

2. Talk with older family members about their memories of holiday traditions, special customs, etc. Are there ethnic traditions that have been lost? Are there any you would like to revive?

In Your Community

3. Visit a church with a distinct racial or ethnic heritage that is different from your own: black Baptist, African Methodist Episcopal, predominantly Hispanic Catholic or Pentecostal, Polish Catholic, etc. How are racial or ethnic experiences and identity reflected in the style and content of the service? What elements of worship and congregational life do you find interesting or appealing? If possible, talk with staff and members about the church and its history.

4. Spend time in a distinctively ethnic neighborhood, preferably one with commercial or public areas. Try to choose a location with which you are not already familiar and one not centered around outsiders or tourism. Observe and interact in stores, restaurants, bars, parks, or on the street. What are your observations and reactions? Are there elements which give this area a distinctive feel? What are they? What would be appealing about this area to its residents?

5. Spend time in a neighborhood that is undergoing ethnic transition from one dominant ethnic group to a differ-

ent group. What are some of the causes of this change? What are some of the effects? How do residents and business people feel about the changes? How do remaining members of the previously dominant ethnic group feel about the changes? How do members of the incoming ethnic group feel about this area? How do the two groups perceive each other?

6. Spend time in a location—a shopping center, a public park, a bus stop, a well-traveled corner, etc.—that is on or near the boundary of two ethnically or racially distinct neighborhoods. The distinctions can be very apparent (between a predominantly African American and predominantly Asian American neighborhood), or more subtle (between a mostly working-class Italian neighborhood and a mostly upper-middle class Anglo-Saxon Protestant neighborhood). How do the physical boundaries of the area reflect the social boundaries between groups? In what ways do members of the two neighborhoods interact? Are there ways in which they never interact? How do residents convey their own sense of identity and their feelings toward the other group?

7. Visit or help out in a school that has significant ethnic or racial diversity. Be sure to obtain proper permission before your visit. Talk with teachers and students about racial attitudes, intergroup relations, and the special problems and accomplishments of various groups. Are there significant racial and ethnic differences in interests and performance? What are the trends in intergroup relations? Are there particular concerns, problems, or successes? Do perceptions of the situation vary between teachers and students, or between racial and ethnic groups?

In the Media

8. Listen to a form of music different from your own usual tastes. Seek a style that grew out of a particular ethnic or cultural group: gospel, blues, soul, reggae, zydeco, salsa, etc. How does the style reflect the culture and

experience of its originators? What are common themes in the lyrics? Do these reflect a common world view or shared life experience?

9. Select a newspaper that is indexed, such as *The New York Times* or the *Washington Post*, and find articles and editorials on affirmative action over the past five to ten years. Or use the *Reader's Guide to Periodical Literature* to find articles on affirmative action in the major news magazines. What arguments do you find on each side of the issue? How has the argument shifted over time—are there new issues gaining attention? Has the weight of opinion shifted in one direction or the other?

6

Family Values and Valuing Families

"**A**merican families are in crisis." That is clearly the consensus of many political campaigns, media reports, and public opinion. But an odd thing happens when you question people about their views on families and family change. Ask any group of Americans who have begun a family or household of their own, "Do you believe the American family is better and stronger than in generations past, or worse off and weaker?" Almost invariably, the majority will choose the latter. Then ask them, "Are *your* current close families stronger and better or worse off and weaker than those of your parents and grandparents?" Again almost invariably, a large majority will insist that theirs are better: better communication, better understanding, more balanced, more open, and more equitable. How is it that all these strong, healthy individual families add up to a collective crisis?

Bias is quite likely occurring in both directions. People often have a somewhat romanticized view of their qualities as spouses and parents, in contrast to a critical, realistic view of their family in previous generations. The reverse seems to occur when people assess general trends. They compare a critical view of present realities (often magnified by the media) with a romanticized view of past families.

From John Boy to Happy Days: The Way We Never Were

We tend to begin our assessment of current times with the latest headlines, which point to important problems but can also be misleading and out of context.

The problem is that most of us do not have the historical background to assess these problems. Because we misunderstand the past, we can easily misinterpret present trends. Alcohol consumption in 1820, for example, was three times the current rate. Addiction to cocaine and forms of opium in the late 19th century probably far exceeded current crack addictions. Family violence and abuse were rife through much of American history, though not a part of official statistics until recently, because wife and child beatings were once considered acceptable and legal. Divorce rates multiplied seven times over between 1870 and 1930; before that time, desertion, separation, and death ended most marriages after an average of ten to twelve years. Many children reached adulthood without at least one of their parents. By the 1940s, a full half of all students never finished high school, almost twice our current rate. Family poverty rates in the prosperous "happy days" of the 1950s were much higher than today's rates.

Stressing the idea that much of our view of past family life is rooted in myth, Stephanie Coontz (1992) titled her historical study of the American family *The Way We Never Were: American Families and the Nostalgia Trap.* One pattern she notes is that nostalgic adults tend to construct their golden age by picking and choosing incongruous elements from various eras. In their minds, for example, the Cleaver household of *Leave It To Beaver* was located somewhere in Walnut Grove, with Ward Cleaver playing the fiddle like Pa Ingalls and Grampa Walton whittling on the back porch. Yet the Cleavers represent the ideal of a self-contained nuclear family that is the repudiation of extended family and community interdependence. Grandparents are never seen on *Leave It To Beaver,* problems are solved within the nuclear household, and Ward Cleaver certainly never has time for anything as trivial as fiddle playing.

In discussing what she terms "the myths of the American family," social historian Tamara Hareven (1982) points out that the great extended families seen on *The Waltons* were generally uncommon. People moved too often (more often than today), and many died too young to be grandparents. Hareven's point is reinforced by a look at the real Ingalls family. In contrast to their television image of a family permanently nestled in unchanging Walnut Grove, they were driven out by grasshoppers, drought, and bad economic times—from Wisconsin to Minnesota to Kansas, back to Wisconsin, and on to South Dakota. They stayed with relatives or struck out on their own as necessity demanded, losing several children along the way to hardship and illness. Clearly, they were a family with great strengths, but theirs was no golden age.

In addition to all this incongruity from the past is the fact that the favorite decade for the "typical American family," the 1950s, may have been the most atypical, thus providing a poor baseline for comparison. Trends for divorce, women in the labor force, women's education, average marriage age, and family size all reversed themselves in the 1950s, relative to prior decades. Many "revolutions" of the late 1960s and early 1970s were continuations of trends that had been at work since the turn of the century; the only radical departure they made was from the pattern of the 1950s. This raises the issue of just what has and hasn't changed in family life. Let's examine some of the evidence.

For Analysis and Reflection

Before we examine the most commonly touted measure of family change—the divorce rate—we should look at the marriage rate. Is marriage losing popularity? As cohabitation (couples living together without formal marriage) becomes more accepted today, is marriage on the decline?

A rate always has two components: the movement of one element relative to another—miles per hour, homicides per thousand, etc. Rates help us standardize data for comparison, but it is important to understand the comparison being made. A common rate is the number of events relative to the size of the population. This is often reported in thousands.

1. Examine Figure 6.1 and consider the following questions:

   a. For every 1000 people in 1890, about how many marriages occurred?

   b. In 1920?

Figure 6.1
Marriage and Divorce

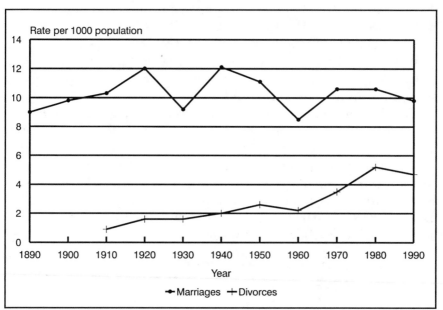

Source: *Statistical Abstract of the United States,* 1983 and 1992. U.S. Center for Health Statistics, *Vital Statistics of the United States. Historical Statistics, Colonial Times to 1970,* Series B.

    c. In 1990?

    d. Given the years in the table, what is the overall trend in marriage rates: declining, rising, or remaining stable?

The answer to the questions above would be very different if we had data on a different period of time. Tables such as this often cover only a few decades. Sometimes, data from earlier periods is not readily available, readers are assumed to be most interested in recent trends, or the author wishes to call attention only to the trends that support a particular argument.

  2. Imagine you are writing in 1960 about social change. You have data on marriage rates for the past twenty years.

    a. What is the trend?

b. Is this an accurate or misleading perception?

c. How might the answer depend on the use intended for the data?

d. If you included data going back to 1890, would this change your perception?

e. Think about what you know about some of the decades in Figure 6.1. What might account for the short-term fluctuations in the marriage rate?

Few rates are as commonly touted and as commonly misunderstood as the divorce rate. The most frequent statement about divorce is that 50 percent of all marriages today will end in divorce. This is not a rate at all but a probability: a statement about the likelihood of an event. Probabilities are based on assumptions. In this case, the assumption is that marriages occurring "today" will be subject to the same divorce rate in the future; that is, the current divorce rate. This is only a guess. If divorce rates rise, the chances of a current marriage ending in divorce in the future will increase; if divorce rates fall, these odds will be lower. We can know the likelihood of divorce for couples married in 1910, because almost all of their marriages have by now ended in either death or divorce. For more recent years, we can again only guess. Also, remember that this is a probability about marriages, not about married people. Because a few people will divorce many times and so inflate the chances, the probability of any given person experiencing divorce may be considerably less than 50 percent.

Divorce rates also reflect different comparisons. The number of divorces in a given year relative to the number of marriages in the same year is sometimes used because it implies a probability. Two hundred marriages and one hundred divorces yields a 50 percent probability of divorce. Or does it? With the exception of very short marriages, the marriages and divorces occurring in the same year are not happening to the *same people*. Because marriage rates fluctuate greatly between years, they are not likely to be a good base for calculating a divorce rate.

The number of divorces per 1000 people produces a more stable comparison. This still has the problem that some changes in the rate may be due to changes in the composition of the population. Not everyone is at risk for divorce. If those 1000 people are made up of large numbers of children, rates will be lower, just because a significant proportion of the population will not be at risk for divorce. To compensate for this, divorce rates are sometimes given per 1000 married women over age 15.

3. Look again at Figure 6.1.

    a. What is the overall trend for divorce in the United States since 1910?

    b. Which two decades deviated from this trend?

    c. What 10-year period saw the greatest change in divorce rates?

    d. How would you describe trends since 1910?

4. Rising divorce became a major concern in the late 1970s. Perhaps because it precedes an important period of social change, many tables use 1960 as a baseline year. Cover up the line prior to 1960 and after 1980 so that you can't see it. Now interpret Figure 6.1.

    a. What is your immediate perception?

    b. Is this an accurate or misleading perception?

    c. What might account for the peak in the rising divorce rate in the 1940s and for the falling rate in the 1950s?

    d. What might account for the rise beginning in the 1960s?

    e. Are divorce rates soaring? Answer this question using 1945 as a base year, then 1955, and finally 1985. What effect does this have on your answer?

Finally, remember that rates are most often based on official statistics. Official unemployment rates do not include the underemployed, discouraged workers who have given up looking, or the homeless who cannot be readily contacted. Similarly, our historical data is being compared across very different social and legal situations. Divorce was illegal or at least very difficult to obtain in many states until quite recently. We can infer from personal accounts, literature, and historical anecdotes that in earlier decades, desertion and separation—without formal divorce—were fairly frequent occurrences. How might this realization affect our understanding of recent trends in divorce?

Along with divorce, great concern has accompanied perceived changes in teenage pregnancy and single mothers. Again, isolated "statistics" (often numerical indicators of questionable statistical origin) can be cited here to make the problem sound either insignificant or enormous. The broad trends are worth examining in greater historical detail.

5. Look first at the top line of Figure 6.2, the total number of births by women between 15 and 19 per 1000 women in that age bracket.

    a. What was the birth rate in 1960?

    b. In 1980?

    c. Teen pregnancy became a major political issue in the early 1980s. What in fact had happened with teenage births between 1960 and 1980?

Figure 6.2
Teenage Birthrate

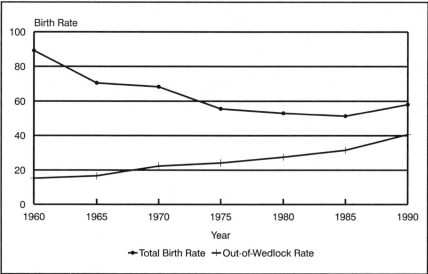

Source: See Figure 6.1.

This is part of an overall trend in the United States, as well as in almost all other societies. Birth rates are declining. Fertility, the number of children born to the average woman in her lifetime, is declining in the United States for all age groups, races, and socio-economic groups. It has been so for over a century. Something else, however, has also been occurring: Fewer teenagers are getting married, even if the girl is pregnant. Researchers have shown the popular view of the "shotgun wedding" and marrying "because we had to" as a common occurrence in the past. (See, for instance, Rubin, 1976). This changing attitude can be seen in the trends.

6. Examine again Figure 6.2.

   a. Approximately what was the out-of-wedlock birth rate for teenagers in 1960?

   b. In 1985?

   c. What proportion of teenage births in 1960 were to unmarried mothers?

   d. In 1985?

The rise in the proportion of births to unmarried women (most of whom, by the way, are in their twenties and not their teens), along with high levels of divorce, fuels concern about children growing up in single-parent households. To put this again in a historical context, however, we need to consider the effects of another major demographic trend: falling death (mortality) rates and longer life expectancy. Since our concern here is with the effects rather than just the fact of falling mortality rates, a graph of trends will not be

Table 6.1
Probability of a Marriage Broken Within the First 40 Years

Year	By Death Alone	By Death or Divorce
1900	.67	.71
1940	.50	.63
1976	.36	.60

Source: Uhlenberg, 1980. Data from U.S. Health Service, 1969; NCHS, *Vital Statistics*, 1978.

very helpful. Instead, probability tables can highlight some of these effects.

First, are marriages more or less stable than at the turn of the century? This is not an easy question since instability can have many causes. Here, we will look at two of these causes: death and divorce.

7.   According to this table, for the year 1900, the likelihood of marital disruption due to death was .67 or 67 percent. For couples marrying at the average age of marriage in 1900, 67 percent (or two-thirds) will not celebrate a for- tieth anniversary—one spouse will have already died.

   a. What is the likelihood of marital disruption due to death for an average couple in 1976?

   b. While mortality has been decreasing, we have seen that divorce has been increasing. To see which effect has been greater, examine the second column. What was the combined chance of marriage or divorce within forty years in 1900?

   c. In 1976?

   d. Given these two factors, are marriages more or less stable than in 1900?

Because of high mortality rates, many children and young adults in the past were without one parent. Since the infectious epidemics that were a major cause of death might take both parents, far more children grew up without either parent than is the case now. The notable recent increase is not in single parents but in single-parent households. Until recently, loss of a parent to death, desertion, or divorce often meant living with other relatives (with or without the remaining parent) or in some cases in an orphanage. Today, this is much more likely to mean living with only the remaining parent. What are some of the possible hardships or advantages of each situ- ation?

8.   Sociology is sometimes referred to as the "debunking science." Debunking dearly held perceptions is not al- ways popular. What are the implications for a less rosy view of American family history?

9. How does this affect how we see current family patterns and problems?

10. What do you see as the most positive and most negative changes that have taken place in the American family?

Roles, Rules, and Relationships

Defining the family is a tricky business. It is getting trickier every day, as we come to recognize the full range of diversity of family forms. Two things can be said about all families, however, under a variety of definitions. Families are *social systems. Systems theory*, often emphasized in family therapy, is based on the idea that the problems of family members cannot be understood or remedied in isolation. The family is an interconnected unit that seeks to maintain its organization and balance. Like tugging on one part of a hanging mobile, a problem, stress, or change in one family relationship affects all other family members, forcing them to rearrange their roles to restore balance to the system. This echoes a longstanding understanding of sociologists: The family is a *social institution.* As an institution, it is shaped by shared understandings about behavior and expectations—norms, values, and goals. Family norms and values are in considerable flux and vary across the diversity of family forms and backgrounds, but they give the family its character and coherence. Families as institutions are organized around *roles, rules*, and *relationships.*

Roles in the sociological sense are social positions that carry an expectation of proper behavior. Family roles define what is expected of family members and how they see themselves and each other. They can take many forms:

> *Provider roles*: breadwinner, head, supporter, dependent
>
> *Parental roles*: distant father, "liberated dad," supermom, disciplinarian, buddy, guide, enforcer, nag
>
> *Nurturing roles*: caregiver, peacemaker, ready listener
>
> *Romantic roles*: lover, "gallant knight," "lady in waiting," intimate friend, pursuer

Childhood and sibling roles: family hero, family rebel, family mascot, second mother, surrogate father, family clown, "baby" of the family

Gender roles: housewife, lady, gentleman, patriarch, "sweet thing," tomboy, "princess"

People adjust and change roles to fit the current situation. The harsh disciplinarian in one context may be the romantic lover in another. Yet if the roles associated with different status positions overlap and are contradictory, family members may experience role conflict. For example, parents may find that their ideals of being a dedicated professional and a dedicated mother or father are continually pulling them in different directions. Especially demanding roles, such as those of single parents, can result in role strain. Roles are not constant, and family members may experience gradual or sudden role transition in their relationships. For example, the strong provider has a stroke and becomes suddenly dependent on others; or the parent struggles to relate to a maturing child more as a listener and less as a disciplinarian. At times, the family environment changes so thoroughly or abruptly that family members are unsure of what is expected of them. They experience role confusion, as when a new stepmother is unsure of whether to be a disciplinarian or a buddy to her teenage stepdaughters.

Families also draw their character and identity from family *rules*. These may be reflections of broad social norms, or they may be specific to the family. All institutions have their rules, reflected in codes of conduct, ways of handling crises and conflicts, and means of daily operation. Families, like educational, medical, or business institutions, also have their rules. As with other institutions, these rules may be *explicit* or *implicit*. Explicit rules are the "rules of the house." These are the stated—and often repeated—codes of conduct: Don't use foul language, keep your room clean, show respect, ask before you borrow, and so forth.

Families also often operate on a variety of implicit rules that are unspoken but can be very powerful in controlling behavior: Don't show anger or weakness, stay away from Mother when she is in one of her moods, avoid Father when he has been drinking, appease Grandma at whatever cost, don't praise anyone directly, and so forth. Not all implicit rules are destructive, but an excess of implicit rules may point to a family under stress or with weak communication links.

Family values, traditions, stories, and scripts may also function as implicit rules. *Values* are those behaviors that are esteemed, rewarded, and emphasized: hard work, educational attainment, a sense of fairness, control of emotions, togetherness, honesty, etc. Despite diversity of forms, most families endorse similar values. They may place differing emphases on each, however. An emphasis on learning hard work and discipline through early work experience has been characteristic of many working-class families. Other families may emphasize higher education as a way to get ahead. For example, although they associate with a strong work ethic, many middle-class Asian American families discourage their children from holding jobs that might interfere with academic studies.

Family traditions are practices that are rooted in the family's history. They may be rooted in an ethnic or cultural history: special foods on particular holidays or music and customs that preserve a heritage. They may also be family-specific: The Christmas gathering is always at the old farmstead, and anyone who misses the event will need to make apologies for the rest of the year. Traditions can thus become a powerful form of family rule.

Family stories are those accounts that are often retold and perpetuated, giving the family a special identity. These stories may be "myths" whose moral is more important than the accuracy of the details: Grandfather immigrated to America with nothing but the shirt on his back; Father walked ten miles to school through the snow from the family farm and never complained. Such stories can maintain traditions, express values, and even convey implicit rules of behavior.

For Reflection

1. Think of your *family of origin*, the family in which you grew up. List its members and the roles they often played. Feel free to use your own labels to capture the image and expectations of these roles. Can you find examples of people who experienced role conflict, role strain, role transition, or role confusion?

2. What roles do you now play relative to your parents? Your siblings? Your partner, spouse, or children? How have these roles changed over time? Are there ongoing role transitions? New sources of role conflict or role strain?

3. Think again of your family of origin. What were the explicit and implicit rules? What were important family traditions? Can you remember important family stories?

4. Focus on your current family setting. Have the rules changed? In what ways? Are there new traditions and stories? Are there rules that you would like to change or eliminate? Are there new traditions that you would like to begin? If so, what would these be?

Family Relationships: Styles of Interaction

Family relationships are based on the family's rules and roles and also on their *interaction styles*. Miller, Nunnally, and Wackman (1991) have categorized the styles of talking most prevalent in families. These styles form the substance of parent-child, as well as couple, communication.

Style One, *Safe Talk*, is safe and routine. It includes *Small Talk*, the chatty discussion of happenings that keep families in touch; and *Shop Talk*, the organizing of tasks that can fill the family's days. You have heard plenty of examples of each in everyday conversation:
Small talk:

"I heard an interesting story at work today. . . ."

"Your mother said they had twelve inches of snow. . . ."
Shop talk:

"We need to get the car in for a tune-up. . . ."

"Adrienne's doctor's appointment is tomorrow. . . ."
Style One is both useful and necessary but limited. When families try to small-talk big issues, deep feelings will not be heard, and necessary understandings and agreements may never be reached.

The goal of Style Two is not to communicate but to control the situation. Light Style Two is *Control Talk* and includes efforts to per-

Table 6.2
Four Styles of Talking

Style I. Safe Talk
    A. Small Talk
    B. Shop Talk
Style II. Control Talk
    A. Light Style II: Light Control Talk
    B. Heavy Style II:
        1. Active: Fight Talk
        2. Passive: Spite Talk
Style III. Search Talk
Style IV. Straight Talk

Source: Miller, Nunnally, and Wackman, 1991.

suade, encourage, instruct, or direct. This is the taking-charge style, often used by supervisors and parents of young children. "Remember, homework before TV." "Let's finish this up so we won't be late." When the task at hand is straightforward, this is useful; otherwise, Control Talk may just breed resistance and resentment.

Heavy Style Two is the attempt to control the situation in spite of resistance and opposing points of view. It is almost always doomed to either fail in its attempt or to damage the relationship. Active Style Two is *Fight Talk*, often containing accusatory statements, broad generalizations, and emphasis on the shortcomings of the other. "That is the silliest excuse I've ever heard." "You never show any responsibility, do you?"

The closeness and intensity of family settings can easily provoke Style Two's struggle for control. A powerful way to improve family communication is to recognize when you are using Style Two and to decide if an alternative is called for. Fight Talk is often filled with accusatory "you" statements (Gordon, 1970) that put others quickly on the defensive. They are often conversation-stoppers and fight-starters.

Passive Style Two is *Spite Talk*. Whereas Fight Talk is a frontal assault, spite talk maneuvers behind the scenes to sabotage, undermine, and manipulate. It is often filled with "woe is me" statements, double meanings, and stony silences. "Well, if that's the way you want it. . . ." Spite Talk may also use rhetorical questions that do not seek information but press accusations or evade responsibility: "How should I know?"

Style Three is *Search Talk*. This is the style that researches the situation without premature commitments. Search Talk uses open-ended questions, wondering statements, and speculation to bypass quick blame and get to deeper issues. It is an excellent transition style to end the battles of Style Two or deepen the focus of Style One. Open questions, an element of Search Talk, probe for more information and invite a response: "I wonder why we always fight over this? Maybe we're both frustrated that things haven't turned out as we had hoped. What do you think?" Families can get stuck in Search Talk, however. At some point comes the need to self-disclose and work toward resolution.

Style Four, *Straight Talk*, involves this type of self-disclosure of sense, interpretation, feelings, intentions, and actions. Striving for resolution, Straight Talk is wasted on the small details of family life but is important when there are deep misunderstandings and conflicting intentions: "I saw you tense up as soon as the topic of moving came up, and it made me think how sensitive an issue this might be for you. But I want to try to make the best of it. I don't know what will come of it, but would you go with me to see the new house?"

For Reflection

1. Give an example you have heard of each of the following:

   a. Small Talk

   b. Shop Talk

   c. Control Talk

   d. Fight Talk

   e. Spite Talk

   f. Search Talk

   g. Straight Talk

2. Which styles predominated in your family of origin? Which styles predominate in your current family setting?

3. Moving from Style Two into the Search Talk of Style Three requires shifting from closed to open questions. Try to recast each of the following closed rhetorical questions into an open question:

    a. "Don't you ever listen?"

    b. "Why do you always try to annoy me?"

    c. "Why can't you understand?"

    d. "Aren't you ashamed of yourself?"

    e. "Why can't you discuss this like an adult?"

    Shifting from Style Two to the more self-revealing Straight Talk of Style Four requires letting go of the blaming and labeling of "you" statements that speak for the other in favor of "I" statements that speak for one's own impressions, interpretations, feelings, intentions, and actions. Sweeping generalizations need to shift to specifics that can be discussed. Try to recast each of the following "you" statements as an "I" statement that communicates rather than blames:

    a. "You make me mad!"

    b. "You never keep your promise!"

    c. "You are always making excuses!"

    d. "You were just trying to make me look bad!"

4. *Family Scripts* are patterns of family interaction that occur over and over again. It is as if each family member knows his or her part. Scripts are predictable, but negative scripts can mean that the same fight is re-enacted over and over. Can you think of scripts that reoccur in your family, or in families that you have observed? What causes these to be repeated? Scripts often draw their dialogue from Styles One and Two. How might the use of Styles Three and Four break these patterns?

5. *Sociograms* are ways of visually diagramming the relationships in a small group. Sociograms can be a useful

way to quickly see family patterns. To make a sociogram of your family of origin, select an age you remember very well. Decide who was the most central
person in your family at that time. Place a dot in the
center of the page for this person and label it with the
name. Now place yourself in relation to this person. If
you were close, place your dot nearby; if distant, place
yourself toward the outer edge. Now place each family
member in relation to the others. Those closely interacting should be placed close together, and distant relationships should be shown by physical distance.
Connect those who had a strong interpersonal bond
with a double line. Those frequently in conflict can be
connected by a jagged line. Broken relationships are
separated by double dash marks. Isolated individuals
will be distant from all family members with few connecting lines. Draw a dotted circle around any *family
coalitions*, groups of family members who stuck together as allies in times of conflict. Figure 6.3 is an example of a sociogram.

Figure 6.3
A Model; Sociogram

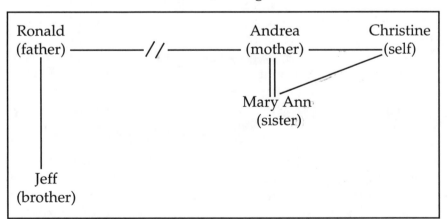

Note the broken relationship between the parents, the
isolated son who is only in contact with the father, and

the close cluster of ties between the mother and the two sisters.

What does the diagram you have drawn indicate about your family of origin and its relationships? Draw a sociogram for your current family setting. Is it similar or very different? Have patterns been repeated?

Siblings: The Ties That Bind (and Chafe and Blister)

Relationships with brothers and sisters are some of the most important in life. For one reason, they often last longer than other relationships—friends come and go, adult friends are rarely those from childhood, spouses and children may come later or not at all, and we will likely outlive our parents—but siblings may be there our entire lives. Literature, folklore, and personal stories are filled with important sibling relationships—some very good, others tragic. Yet for all this importance, until recently such relationships were studied and less frequently than other family relationships. (If you have an introductory sociology text, see if it contains a section on siblings; or if you have a marriage and family text, see if it has a chapter on siblings. Most of them do not.) Emerging research suggests that for many people, sibling relationships are indeed enduring and very important. However, even good sibling relationships often have difficulties that must be worked out over time.

The two aspects of sibling relationships that have received some attention, both scholarly and in popular media, are the numbers of children and birth order, or *ordinal position.* Studies of the effects of numbers have often sought to dispel the popular notion of "only children" as spoiled, lonely, or otherwise maladjusted. Rather, few clear personality characteristics have emerged, but "onlies" do tend to have higher educational and occupational attainment. Researchers have suggested a "dilution" model that argues that parents have limited resources—financial, emotional, and time—and these become more diluted in larger families. It may also be that onlies receive more parental attention and more parental pressure to succeed. Similar arguments are offered for the effect of birth order. The oldest children may be given more attention, as well as more responsibility (especially over their younger siblings), so they are more likely to be highly responsible achievers. Middle children may struggle for a unique identity in the family and continue that struggle into adulthood. Youngest children may find the parents more permissive (many parents relax their discipline over time or just get "worn out") and may have certain privileges as the "baby" of the family. Later in life, they may be more sociable and more permissive themselves. Note that in one important sense, siblings do not grow up in the "same" family. Eldest children spend some time as onlies before others come along; the youngest spend more time growing up in a bigger family. If the family changes dramatically over time, children may be affected in very different ways, depending on their ages at the time of the transition. Despite popular interest in birth order, ordinal position is in fact a fairly uncertain predictor of future characteristics. This is because factors, such as gender and temperament, may play an important role (for instance, older girls are often given more family responsibility than older boys), and because position or status is only important insofar as it is a predictor of likely roles. It is the actual role expectations and the interrelationships between those roles that can have powerful effects.

Parents of several children often struggle with stereotyped roles, as well as with problems of equity and consistency. Stereotyped roles can occur as parents overrespond to differences in age, gender, and temperament to create "the smart one," "the pretty one," the "good kid," the "problem child," and so forth. One young woman struggled with low self-esteem because of her belief that her parents always saw her as "the stupid one." In fact, they believed that she was much prettier than her sister, so they wanted to balance the scales by noting that her sister was "the smart one." Clearly, it is safer for parents to avoid such comparisons. Some problems, however, are difficult to avoid. Each child is different, yet siblings often demand strict equity: "If he can, why can't I?" or "She was always your favorite." Similarly, parents do tend to change their rules and standards over time, while siblings (especially older ones) often want to hold them to strict standards of consistency: "I never got to do that at his age."

Perceptions that they are being compared can lead siblings to rivalry and competition. Struggles for "rights" can lead to coalitions that exclude other siblings or to bullying. Although we tend to make little of sibling spats and bullying, evidence is mounting that physical and sexual abuse between siblings may be as common, severe, and lasting in its effects as abuse by parents.

Even when the childhood relationship was more positive than negative, siblings often have to work hard at re-establishing an adult relationship. Many have to deal with envy and bitterness coming from perceived inequities, with past conflicts and verbal or physical abuse, with stereotyped roles (e.g., a continued tendency to play the part of big sister or big brother), and with continuing rivalries. Most people report that their adult sibling relationships are strong and valuable, but many also find they are still carrying a great deal of baggage from a common childhood that they need to unload.

For Reflection

1. Examine your relationship with siblings, if you have any. What issues and patterns (problems of equal treatment, coalitions, conflict, etc.) do you see illustrated by your family?

2. How have your sibling relationships changed over time?

    If you have no siblings, have you experienced any negative assumptions about being spoiled or lonely? What are some of the ways that being an only child has affected you?

3. As a child, did you tend toward roles that were over-responsible (caretaking, substitute parenting, or being the super-achiever or family hero), under-responsible (the family clown, baby, rebel, scapegoat, outcast, or lost child), or reasonably balanced and self-responsible? How has this affected your aspirations, activities, and relations with others?

4. Many stressed or imbalanced families also have to deal with problems of guilt and blame. Sometimes, family members become "Charlie Browns," like the character in the *Peanuts* comic strip who internalizes blame: "Good grief, I blew it again." Others become "Lucys," externalizing blame and accusing, threatening, or psychoanalyzing others. Do you tend to fall into one cate-

gory or the other? Does this reflect your family of origin's rules and roles?

Parenting and Career: Maintaining Your Balance

Talk of family values must ultimately include both personal values and social values, personal responsibility and social responsibility. Nowhere is this more apparent than in the current strains of parenting and career. This has often been portrayed as primarily a woman's problem. Framing the problem this way reflects a continuing assumption that family problems are women's problems and the fact that working in professional careers is relatively new for women. Women, of course, have always worked, sometimes in paid labor, often in unpaid work. A few in the past have received higher education, but these most often were women from the upper classes who used their educations to become proper hostesses or to manage a household but never for paid labor. What is new is the large numbers of women who are combining education and work into a professional career. As a society, we are still sorting out the implications of this. Initially, the changes were seen as threatening. In *Esquire* magazine in 1954, Merle Miller argued in vain against "that increasing and strident minority of women who are doing their damnedest to wreck marriage and home life in America, those who insist on having both husband and career. They are a menace and they have to be stopped." Menace or not, two-career families have moved from a rarity to the norm.

Are career and family compatible? Arlie Hochschild, co-author of *The Second Shift* (1989), contends that the American career system was designed for a man with few family obligations. If he had a family, a man could still devote the vast majority of time and attention to work, since a full-time homemaker would handle home, children, and social obligations. This clearly does not work when there are two demanding careers in the same home. What are the effects of this relatively recent situation?

Much of the attention has focused on working mothers and the effect on children. Despite concerns, the overwhelming conclusion is that the important point is the quality of childcare. Researchers conclude that there is "near consensus among developmental psychologists and early childhood experts that child care per se does not constitute a risk factor in children's lives; rather, poor quality care and poor family environments can conspire to produce poor developmental outcomes" (Scarr, Phillips, and McCartney, 1989, p. 1406). Mary Jo Bane (1976) notes that mothers in the past had time-consuming chores and more children. Time spent actually interacting with children may be as great now as ever before.

Some still see a loss in two-career parenting. Ellen Galinsky of the Families and Work Institute notes the loss of "blue sky time"; that is, being there physically and psychologically to simply "hang out" with and enjoy the children's presence. She suggests that working and parenting may not be less effective but may be less satisfying. A recent survey conducted by the Institute asked children with two full-time working parents, "What do you want most; what do you wish was different?" Interestingly, the children did not frequently wish for more time with parents but for less stressed parents.

Two-career parents can face tremendous pressures on their limited time. "Cutting back" may not be easy, as the financial squeeze on families with children has increased. Some have even suggested that the new class distinction will be between parents and non-parents. Parents have greatly increased expenses and at the same time, they may have significantly reduced net income, whether they reduce work hours or pay for childcare. This was less of a problem in a time when it was assumed that women, with or without children, would be at home. Now, as James Coleman suggested (1987), many specialize either in making money or in having children. Such "specialization" clearly poses stresses for parents and risks for children.

Both the emotional and financial stresses result in part from the failure to provide institutionalized substitutes for extended kin. In simpler societies, grandparents, aunts, older siblings, or other members of family, kin, and community were more likely to be available. In most other industrial societies, there is much more government and industry support to replace lost kin and community support. For many parents in the United States, however, there is neither. Prominent pediatrician T. Berry Brazelton contends, "We're stuck with two biases: One is that we feel families ought to be entirely self-sufficient, and if they're not, they have to identify themselves as failures and get a handout from the government. The other is that we shouldn't encourage mothers to work by helping them" (quoted in Cadden and Kamerman, 1990).

The debate in Congress over the Family and Medical Leave Act did not even suppose more direct government support but mostly centered on what government could reasonably demand from industry. On their own, some companies have begun to provide more flexible work arrangements: job sharing, "flextime" with flexible hours and allowances for work at home, time off for family needs with the guaranteed right to return at the same level, and less demanding expectations for those with greater family needs. A proposal by Felice Schwartz in the *Harvard Business Review* (1989) for alternate expectations for women with children was given the unfortunate label "Mommy track" and touched off a furor. Some saw new flexibility, others saw gender discrimination and double standards returning in a new form. Rosabeth Moss Kanter has ques-

Table 6.3
Hours Spent in Household Tasks

Household Task	With Parents*	Living Alone*	Cohab- itating	Married	Divorced
	Living Situation				
Women					
Preparing Meals	3.64	6.74	7.99	10.14	8.15
Washing Dishes	3.92	4.38	5.51	6.11	5.14
Cleaning House	3.94	5.16	7.10	8.31	6.68
Yard Work	1.39	1.24	1.34	2.06	1.94
Car Maintenance	.48	.42	.28	.16	.40
Total Hours of Housework	19.26	25.04	31.12	36.67	31.37
Men					
Preparing Meals	2.23	5.06	3.71	2.69	5.50
Washing Dishes	1.92	2.77	2.63	2.15	3.24
Cleaning House	2.20	2.97	2.60	2.03	3.54
Yard Work	3.56	1.56	3.18	4.94	2.60
Car Maintenance	1.23	.92	1.51	1.37	.99
Total Hours of Housework	14.93	18.92	19.16	17.83	21.56

*never married
Source: South and Spitze, 1994.

tioned the focus on women: "Why not a family track open to fathers as well?"

The struggles are not limited to workplace but also often occur in the home. Studies have repeatedly borne out Hochschild's assertion that working women work a second shift, bearing a disproportionate burden of household responsibilities. Interestingly, this seems to be true almost everywhere in the world (Scarr, Phillips, and McCartney, 1989). It is also true regardless of the marital arrangement or stage in the life cycle (see Table 6.3). Women in every situation spend more time on household chores: They seem to be socialized to it in their family of origin, are more home-conscious as singles, and continue the pattern into relationships and marriage.

For Reflection

1. Agreement on the need for supporting families is common. There is less agreement on where the main need for change lies: with mothers, fathers, employers, government, or others. A particular problem is the issue of personal versus social responsibility. Should everyone pay for other people's children? Is childrearing a personal or a community concern, and how should these be balanced? Where does responsibility for change lie: with government, local communities, employers, families themselves, or in some combination thereof?

2. What can families do to make family and career more compatible? Is slowing down possible? Is hired domestic help an answer? Do you believe it is best for one partner to specialize in home and the other in work, or for both to strive for maximum role flexibility?

3. Why are unequal home and childcare arrangements so prevalent? Do the women need to insist on more equity? Women often complain that the man is sloppy or incompetent at home, and men often complain that the woman is watching over their shoulder in household tasks. What does this suggest about social rules, roles, and expectations?

4. How involved are you currently in domestic chores? How would you negotiate this in the future with other household members?

5. Do you plan to balance career and family responsibilities? What is the balance or compromise that you hope for? Will this affect your decisions in careers and relationships? How might you try to balance time for relationships, leisure, and work? What kinds of arrangements and agreements might this entail?

Living Well, Staying Well: What Will You Be When You Grow Old?

Our society is "graying" with a growing proportion of older adults. Yet Americans of all ages continue to view the later years of life with considerable uncertainty and ambivalence. On the one hand, publications for seniors show smiling retired people playing golf in some sunny location. On the other hand, we encounter images of the elderly slumped over in a wheelchair in an unsanitary nursing home, abandoned and forgotten.

Years ago, this was less of a problem: The main concern was whether one would live long enough to qualify as elderly. Now, we tend to assume that we will get there but wonder about what it will be like. The question often posed to children takes a new adult twist. It is no longer "What do you want to be when you grow up?" but rather "What do you want to be when you grow *old?*" Those nearing retirement wonder about maintaining independence, those in their middle years wonder about caring for aging parents, and those in their early earning years wonder if Social Security and Medicare will really be there for them when they retire.

In economic terms, the outlook is mixed. Senior citizens are no longer any more likely to be poor than the general population. A national commitment to Social Security has made major reductions in poverty among the elderly. Some groups, however, such as very elderly women who have outlived husbands and survivor benefits, are still at considerable risk of poverty. Can our society continue to support growing numbers of the elderly?

Demographically, this should not be as difficult as is sometimes suggested. Lower birth rates mean an older population with higher percentages of retired people to support, but they also mean lower percentages of the population in the pre-earning years of childhood and school. A convenient measure used internationally to assess how large the non-working population is relative to the working population is called *demographic dependency.* Combining estimates of the proportion of our population under age 18 and those over age 65 offers us a picture of quite stable demographic dependency (see Table 6.4).

Table 6.4
Demographic Dependency
Percentage of the Population in Non-Working Age Groups

Year	Under 18	Over 64	Total
1970	34	10	44
1980	28	11	39
1990	26	12	38
2000	26	13	39
2010	25	13	38
2020	24	16	40
2050	24	20	44

Source: Census Bureau. *Statistical Abstract of the United States: 1994.*

Socially, there is also not much reason for extreme pessimism. Those over age 65 are more likely to report that they are satisfied with their lives than any other group and most likely to select this period as their preferred time of life. They also seem to interact with friends and family members about as frequently as do others of any age. Part of this may be that increasingly, age 65 is not a very good measure of "elderly." Many people remain very active and involved through their sixties and even seventies. The problems and people's fears tend not to be of early retirement years but of late retirement, the final years. This is where we hear reports of "granny dumping" at emergency rooms and debates over the right to die with dignity.

It is still not easy to be truly elderly in American. But then, it never was. Laslett (1976) suggests that our perspectives are biased by what he terms "the myth of before and after." This myth contends that somewhere in the past, there was a golden age when elders were revered and respected and lived out their days in great dignity. Just as we found no golden age of family relationships, Laslett finds no golden age of aging. The multigenerational household with grandparents as an integral part of the family was rare for several reasons. First, Americans have always placed great emphasis on privacy. Second, they have always moved a great deal. These moves were not always from one coast to another, but before long-distance telephones and commercial aircraft, the parent's move could mean loss of almost all contact with grandparents.

Laslett also suggests that we have too readily accepted the "myth of abandonment" of today's elderly. Some of those lonely nursing home residents may be as much due to demographics as to ungrateful children. Of those born between 1901 and 1910, 27 percent never married or had children (they reached marriage and childrearing age at the peak of the Great Depression), so that half of those now living in nursing homes have no living children. Most of the rest were placed in a nursing home as a last resort. Many people are surprised to learn that less than two percent of the elderly population is in nursing homes or similar care facilities (see Table 6.5). Again, this is more of a problem for the very elderly, but even for those over age 85, only 20 percent are in institutional care facilities. As baby-boom parents reach later years, they will more likely have help and visits from their children, simply because they have more children. There is one new area for concern here, however: the rising numbers of divorced men. Older men often depend heavily on more able wives for support, as well as on their children. If the men are not remarried in later years, there is no spouse, and a substantial number of divorced men lose close contact with their children. This could be the new group that will seem "abandoned."

For many people, grandparents are more of a present part of their lives than ever before. In the past, fewer knew their grandparents well, because there were far fewer grandparents to know. The probability of a 15-year-old child having three or more living grandparents increased from 17 percent in 1900 to 55 percent in 1976. Cherlin and Furstenberg (1987) note that grandparents are more likely to be around to enjoy grandchildren; more likely to have the cars, telephones, and means to stay in touch; less likely to still be raising their own children (as was often common when a couple's children were spread over many years); and more likely to be financially independent.

Although many elderly are eager to stay in touch with family, many others are not as eager to move in. Many of them greatly value independence and are unwilling to undergo the role transition from provider to dependent. Rabushka and Jacobs (1980) note, "Most elderly people want love and attention from their children, but not necessarily help with money, housing, or other charitable gestures. Indeed, some prefer to do things for their children and grandchildren, rather than be on the receiving end of things." For answers to how to best meet the needs of the elderly, it is older adults themselves who are often the least likely to suggest living with children as a good solution (see Table 6.6)

Table 6.5
Living Arrangements of the Elderly, 1994
Percentage in Each Category

Living Arrangement	Men	Women
Living alone	16	40
Living with spouse	75	41
Living with other relatives	6	17
Living with nonrelatives	2	2
Living in nursing home	1	1

Source: U.S. Bureau of the Census, 1995. *Current Population Reports.*

Most older adults favor the maximum independence possible: living with spouse or alone. When this is not possible, many people, old and young alike, face a quandary about what to do. "Nursing home" remains an ugly word for many. Some try to help their aging parents live alone by "helping out" as much as they can. This can work if the needs are not too great and works best if there is maximum family involvement. This is a real strain, however, on only children. Even when there are several children, often the majority of the tasks will fall to one of them, usually a daughter.

New options are emerging in many communities: separate but close living arrangements; older adult communities that provide some services, while retaining maximum independence; so-called adult day care to provide activities while family caregivers are at work; and others. Their effectiveness often depends a great deal on the quality of prior family relationships, on widely distributing caregiving tasks among family members (both men and women), and being able to mix family support with social services that provide meals, transportation, counseling, and medical services.

Table 6.6
Preferred Living Arrangements:
Percentage of Those Agreeing That Elderly Parents Should Move
in With Their Children When They Can No Longer Take Good
Care of Themselves

Age of respondent	Agree	Disagree
Total	40	60
18-24	50	50
25-34	46	53
35-44	43	57
45-54	33	67
55-64	31	68
65 and over	26	74

Source: *Public Opinion,* December/January, 1986; 1,230 respondents

For Reflection

1. What are some of your images of older families and of being elderly? Do the prevalent living arrangements shown in Table 6.5 support or challenge your images?

2. Many researchers report the importance of staying active and involved for older adults, sometimes professionally—an emeritus professor continues to offer a favorite class, a retired lawyer continues to do pro bono work, a retired doctor in a rural area still assists with local patients. Others find new opportunities to volunteer: a grandparent becomes "grandma" or "grampa" to twenty children in a Head Start program. Others find new time for meaningful hobbies and family interaction. If you could write the script now, what would you want to be when you grow old?

3. Which of the ways of caring for the needs of elderly adults seems preferable? What are the advantages and

disadvantages of three-generation households? Are there ways to ease the stress on the "sandwich generation" that may be both raising or launching children and caring for parents?

4.   In your experience, has the greater possibility of knowing grandparents been realized in practice? How has your relationship with your grandparents compared with your parents' relationship with their grandparents?

Toward a New Intergenerational Contract

What are our "family values?" And whose family, as well as whose values, are included in this term? What responsibilities do we have to our children? What responsibilities do we have to our parents? Are we responsible for other people's children? Are we responsible for other people's parents? As a society, we are still deciding our response to these questions. Agrarian societies in both Europe and Asia operated on what has been termed the *intergenerational contract*. Parents cared for their children when the children were too young to work, with the knowledge that some of those children would care for the parents when they were too old to work. This practice has become more informal in industrial societies and in some cases has broken down altogether: Many are unable to provide completely for their children, are unable to provide completely for their aging parents, have no children, or have no parents.

Perhaps we need to broaden the intergenerational contract from a familial to a community, societal, and generational level. One generation will accept responsibility for the next—one's own children and "other people's children"—in the knowledge that the new generation will someday provide for them—one's own parents and "other people's parents." Such a commitment will require a willingness not only to address needs close to home but also needs that we might prefer not to face.

For Reflection

1.   Economist Sylvia Ann Hewlett (1991) asserts that the United States is one of the least child-friendly nations in the world. The United States spends less of its GNP on children's needs and has a greater percentage of its

children in poverty (about 20 percent) than any other industrialized nation. Most people will agree that children should be a priority, but the political debate often centers on where the changes should occur. One side tends to focus on societal change, as does Hewlett, and on community change, as in Hillary Clinton's *It Takes a Village* (1996). The other side often stresses personal and family changes, as in Bob Dole's rejoinder, "No, it takes a family." This is a debate about levels of analysis and to some extent, about changes in culture versus changes in social structure. How might meeting the needs of children be approached from multiple levels? How are personal, family, community, and societal responsibilities interconnected? What specific propositions or policies need to be part of a new intergenerational contract?

2. Some observers see the United States locked in a "culture war" (Hunter, 1991) battling to define our basic values. In this view, on one side are religious and political conservatives, typified by such groups as the Christian Coalition, stressing the values and cultural patterns of earlier times. On the other side are religious and political liberals, demanding a renewed commitment to progressive reforms. Other analysts, however, suggest that this is too simple a division, and that in fact there at least two dimensions to this variation. A social/moral dimension contains issues related to lifestyle, sexuality, sex roles, and free speech. An economic/social justice dimension covers regulation of social and economic behavior to promote equity. Consider Table 6.7 on the next page.

    The percentages in each category can vary considerably, depending on how the specific issues are framed, but note how equally divided the population tends to be among categories. The differences in the four perspectives became clear in the 1996 presidential primaries. Politicians are never eager to claim a label that contains only one-quarter of the population but are often eager to label one another. Pat Buchanan was labeled a populist, Steve Forbes a libertarian, Bob Dole a conservative, and Bill Clinton a liberal.

Table 6.7
American Political Orientations
(Percentage of the Population for Each Type)

		SOCIAL/MORAL ISSUES: Restrictions on Lifestyle, Sexuality, Sex Roles, and Free Speech	
		Oppose	Favor
ECONOMIC/ SOCIAL JUSTICE ISSUES:	Favor	Liberal 28%	Populist 23%
Regulation of social and economic behavior to promote equity	Oppose	Libertarian 25%	Conservative 24%

Source: Olson, forthcoming (revised from Maddox and Lilie, 1984).

Religious groups as a whole do not fall into a single category but tend to span the categories (Olson, forthcoming). White evangelicals tend to have conservative views, while black evangelicals are more likely to have populist perspectives. Liberal Protestant laypersons tend toward more libertarian views, while Jews are more likely to have liberal perspectives. Roman Catholics are equally likely to be found in any of the four cells.

What social influences and personal characteristics might affect someone's position on the two dimensions in Table 6.7? Do you see American public opinion moving toward a two-side culture war, a plurality of perspectives, or a moderate middle ground of consensus on key issues? How will this affect the way family needs are addressed in the next century?

3. In their widely read critique of American individualist culture, *Habits of the Heart* (1985), Robert Bellah and his co-authors suggest that Americans need a

new language of community and commitment in family life, as well as in other spheres. Francesca Cancian (1987) challenges this perspective, arguing that the growing focus on self-development has been positive and liberating for both men and women. In place of what she sees as the "Durkheimian" perspective of Bellah, stressing the need for social control, she posits a perspective that she sees in accord with the humanist ideals of Karl Marx, stressing the freedom to become unique apart from restrictive roles. Some of the key elements of each perspective are placed side by side below:

A. *"Durkheimian" Perspective:*	B. *"Marxist" Perspective:*
Robert Bellah et al.	Francesca Cancian
Habits of the Heart	*Love in America*
Key Elements:	*Key Elements:*
Stability and belonging	Self-development
Long-term commitment	Freedom to become unique self
Enriched by tradition	Freely express individuality
Secure: Roles are known	Free from role confinement
Commitment makes it work	Communication makes it work
Focus on community	Focus on choice

Which side do you find most in accord with your own perspective? Are family and community traditions enriching or confining? What is the more urgent need, for greater moral constraint or for greater personal freedom? Is there a way to have a third position, the best of both, or to begin with one side then add the other?

Reaching Out, Digging Deeper

Family Portraits

This chapter has focused on the family as a social institution and the way ideas of family have become a lightning rod, attracting emotionally charged critiques, warnings, and anxiety stemming from broad social changes. A better understanding of our past and the full range of diverse family experiences can help you to provide a truer picture of the challenges ahead and allow you to better critique the critics.

For a good account of family systems theory, illustrated by a fascinating account of a family going through turmoil and therapy, see Napier and Whitaker, *The Family Crucible* ([1978] 1988), as well as Napier's follow-up book on marriage patterns, *The Fragile Bond* (1988). On communication styles, see Miller, Nunnally, and Wackman's communication manual, *Talking and Listening Together* (1991), and their earlier book, *Straight Talk* (1981). A provocative look at the myths and realities of families of the past is provided by Stephanie Coontz's *The Way We Never Were* (1992) and Arlene Skolnick's *Embattled Paradise* (1991). For strong and well-documented critiques of public policy and the needs of children, see Sylvia Ann Hewlett's *When the Bough Breaks* (1991) and Ruth Sidel's *Keeping Women and Children Last* (1996). Glimpses of challenges in family and economic life are provided by Carol Stack's *All Our Kin* (1974) on low-income black family networks; David Harvey's *Potter Addition* (1993) on low-income, urban-fringe white families; Lillian Rubin's *Families on the Fault Line* (1994) on working-class families; and Arlie Hochschild's *Second Shift* (1989) on the challenges of double-income families.

To further explore family experiences, family needs, family diversity, and family change, consider the following project ideas:

In Your Family

1. Discuss the four styles of talking with other family members. How do they perceive your family communication? Brainstorm about ways to improve your family's communication. What ideas are generated? Examine communication styles in your own family of origin or in your current household. What styles predominate? What styles are the hardest? How has this changed, or has it?

2. Have other family members draw a sociogram of the family. Place the diagrams side by side and compare the results. How similar are the diagrams? Do people see things differently?

3. Family history is not necessarily remote. We are still learning about our recent domestic history, especially in regard to issues that were much less discussed in the past. Talk with a grandparent, older friend, or relative about their experiences and observations. What was their family life like? What were their expectations of marriage? What changes have they experienced personally? Ask about the families they can remember forty or fifty years ago. Did they know of friends or acquaintances who married quickly because "they had to?" Did they know of cases of desertion or chronically absent spouses and parents? What are their fondest memories of family life? Are there aspects of family life that they are glad have long vanished? Be gentle and sensitive in asking appropriate questions, but don't be surprised if you find a wealth of personal family history that you hadn't expected.

4. A *genogram* is also a way to document family relationships over time. Genograms are used by therapists to gain a brief overview of a personal family history. They can also be a fascinating way to look at your family, its changes, and patterns that continue over time.

To break a genogram into components, squares indicate males and circles indicate females. Ages are listed in the squares and circles, an "X" indicating death. Solid horizontal lines indicate marriage or intimate relationship; double slash marks on the line indicate divorce. Vertical lines indicate children, left to right from oldest to youngest; an "A" beside the line means adoption. Double lines indicate closeness, jagged lines indicate conflict, and dotted lines indicate emotional distance. Double slash marks on the vertical show a severed parent-child relationship. Identifying data next to the person includes their name and can also include age, occupation, education, and an important identifying adjective or event.

Genograms may also be used to trace recurring family problems. A box around the name (often in red) can be used to indicate alcoholism and chemical dependency. Physical or sexual abuse can be indicated by a wavy line (often in green) connecting those involved;

Figure 6.4
A Model Genogram

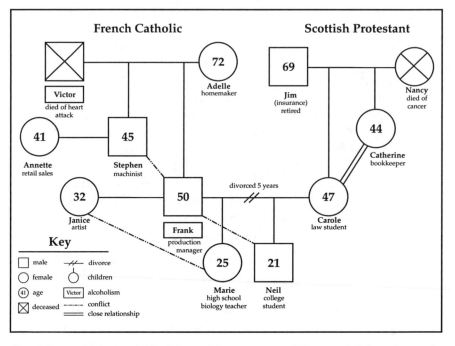

direction of abuse is indicated by arrows. Figure 6.4 is a sample
genogram for Neil, a college student:

Make a genogram for your family. Try to include at least three
generations. In completing a genogram, you may work from your
existing knowledge, but it is often interesting to have other (especially older) family members help you fill in information. New information and insights into your family history may emerge. Take
your rough-draft genogram to several family members and have
them fill in further information. If you choose to include information
about family conflict, trauma, and dysfunction, be sure to be sensitive in how you discuss this with family members.

In Your Community

5. New strains on family life have emerged, as many of
    the older "natural" support systems of kin and village
    have declined. To fill this gap, programs have been de-
    veloped privately and publicly at the national, state,

and local level. Many of these programs are eager to make the community more aware of their activities, and many welcome volunteers. Look in the Yellow Pages of your local phone directory under "Social Services" and "Human Services." What family-related agencies and programs are listed? You can find out more about local programs through the local United Way office. You can also find out more through your campus' counseling center or campus ministry office or through a volunteer or service-learning coordinator. Opportunities to consider include the following:

a. Head Start programs work with young children and their parents to encourage school readiness. This is a federally funded program that began during the War on Poverty in the 1960s and has continued to receive praise and support for its work in helping disadvantaged (mostly low-income, as well as some learning-disabled) children to be better prepared both socially and cognitively for school. Local centers must demonstrate local support in the form of donated space, materials, and volunteer time. Ideally, the teachers are assisted by both parent and community volunteers and are used to working with a changing stream of assistants and helpers. Contact the local Head Start office, ask for the volunteer coordinator, and ask to help in a location near your home, work, or school.

b. Area YWCA facilities often offer many programs beyond recreation. These may include programs for pregnant teens and victims of domestic violence and abuse, as well as many others. Similar programs may be offered by women's community centers, shelters, and other agencies. Visit one of these locations to find out about the range of programs offered. Some may welcome short-term volunteers to answer phones and help with activities.

c. Homeless shelters nationwide are finding that their populations have shifted to include more families. Find out if local shelters have family-oriented programs and activities. Often these programs depend heavily on community volunteer support.

d. Look for local church and community programs that are attempting innovative ways to meet family needs in areas of nutrition, health, education, housing, and self-sufficiency. Find out about the program and perhaps find ways to become involved.

e. Look into local programs to work with families and older adults in the areas of health, safety, and self-sufficiency. These might include meals-on-wheels, adult daycare, elderly support services, residential care facilities, transportation services, etc. If possible, volunteer to help with programs, meals, transportation, etc. Try to talk with program directors, as well as older adults and their families, about the needs, challenges, and opportunities they face.

To reflect on the experience, consider the following:

• What surprised, impressed, or interested you about this organization and the families it serves?

• What course-related issues and themes are addressed by the work of this organization? Are trends or patterns in family relations and family diversity apparent here?

• How effective is this project in meeting family needs? Did you observe any unmet needs or problems?

In the Media

6. Family interaction is a perennial staple of material for filmmakers. Some are unrealistic or sensationalized in their portrayal, but many include real insights into family problems and dynamics. Watch any of the following films then reflect on the social forces that forge and shape the family dynamics and experiences. Note especially the effects of historical events, gender expectations, social class, race and ethnicity, and social situation in these films:

Alice Doesn't Live Here Any More. Think about women's roles, abusive relationships, and self-esteem.

The Color Purple. Observe issues of family, race, gender, and class.

Driving Miss Daisy. Think about interaction styles, issues of race and class, and problems of aging.

My Family, Mi Familia. A depiction of a Mexican-American family in transition.

Fiddler on the Roof. A light but revealing look at Jewish family life in agrarian Russia. Reflect on the impact of changing family traditions.

The Grapes of Wrath. A classic on the Great Depression.

The Joy Luck Club (or read the novel). A forceful account of mother-daughter relationships in Chinese and Chinese American families.

Kramer vs. Kramer. What problems in the divorce and custody process are illustrated?

Mrs. Doubtfire. A light but revealing look at divorce and custody issues.

On Golden Pond. Look especially for communication styles and intergenerational dynamics.

Ordinary People. Note the power of family roles and interactions surrounding loss and grief.

Prince of Tides. Consider sibling relationships and lasting effects from abuse.

Return of Martin Guerre. Observe the dynamics of peasant family life.

Stella (or the novel, *Stella Dallas*). Note the consequences of class differences.

Roommates. A grandfather-grandson relationship, relating across generations.

Rudy. Note the values, struggles, and interaction styles
of this working-class family.

7. Literature can be a good source of family history. Many
elements of family life that were ignored by historians
have turned up in fictional accounts. Realize that some
novels and stories reflect biases and stereotypes held
by their authors, and some may only treat certain social
classes (often the upper classes, just as they do in night-
time soap operas). Others, especially those with a
strong autobiographical approach, truly reflect important elements of earlier home and family situations.
John Steinbeck's *The Grapes of Wrath* is a classic account
of the struggles of the Depression era in Oklahoma.
Pearl Buck's *The Good Earth* explores family life, kinship
structure, and gender roles in traditional China. Historical children's literature can be a good source, because it so often emphasizes the ordinary details of
home and family. Good examples include the *Little
Women* series (19th-century New England), the *Anne of
Green Gables* series (turn-of-the-century Eastern Canada), and Laura Ingalls Wilder's *Little House* series (the
frontier American plains; use the semi-autobiographi-
cal books, not the romanticized TV series). Skim these
for details of family life: experiences of childhood, expectations of children, gender roles and expectations,
discipline, communication, and the impact on the family of work, birth, and death. Are there common themes
and experiences? Are some elements surprising?

8. Look through old issues of magazines with a long history of covering family issues, such as *Life, Look,* and
The Ladies' Home Journal. Focus on views of domestic
life in the 1940s and 1950s, changes in gender roles or
views of the family between the 1950s and the 1970s, or
a related topic of interest. What values and lifestyles
are emphasized? What ideals or myths do the articles
and advertisements perpetuate? What changes in attitudes and expectations do you observe?

9. Contrast the views of parenting and family in a variety of popular magazines (e.g., *Parents, Mothering, Family Circle, Cosmopolitan, Esquire,* and *Working Mother*). What are the values, lifestyles, and subcultures emphasized? How do their views of family life differ? Which perspectives resonate with your own values?

10. Examine the coverage of family issues in a publication associated with conservative political opinion, such as *The National Review.* Compare this coverage with that in a publication associated with liberal political opinion, such as *The New Republic.* What types of issues are emphasized in each? How does the analysis of the problems differ? What evidence is presented? How do the proposals for change and reform differ? Are changes most often proposed at the individual, local, or national level?

7

The Home of Humanity

Thinking Globally, Acting Locally

A Beautiful Day 'n the 'Hood

From Mr. Rogers to the local street gang, neighborhoods are important to people. And neighborhoods often say a lot about the people who live there, whether by choice or because they have nowhere else to go.

Neighborhood types and characteristics give residents a sense of place and communicate something about them to outsiders. People sort themselves so thoroughly by social class, race, age, interests, and lifestyle that a whole field of *geodemographics* and targeted marketing has emerged, ready to pigeonhole you based on your zip code or your census tract. The market specialists can then sell your name and address to the appropriate catalog mailing list, so that you can receive customized, pre-selected junk mail. Though we usually assume that we are unique, we tend to gravitate toward people who are "unique" in many of the same ways. Hence, we are not really that difficult to target.

National Decision Systems catalogs residents into 48 groups, including Suburban Gentry, Young Urban Professionals, The Leave It to Beaver Cluster, Young Beginners, Young Hispanics, Golden Years, and Books and Beer Dorm-Escapees. The Claritas Corporation, originator of all this categorizing, suggests more than forty neighborhood types, ranging from Blue Blood Estates (e.g., "look for the Rolls") and Money and Brains (e.g., Princeton, New Jersey) down to Tobacco Roads (e.g., Southern black farm communities) and Hard Scrabble and Public Assistance (Weiss, 1988).

Neighborhoods have boundaries, some of which are geographical (e.g., railroad tracks, a freeway, or a river), while others are social (e.g., high-income versus low-income housing). Still others are social psychological in that they are largely places of the mind but are nonetheless identifiable places, because the boundaries are shared by many minds. Neighborhoods draw their characteristics from their placement within the larger community, as well as from their composition, including race, ethnicity and cultural heritage, social class, and lifestyle enclaves. Neighborhoods go through historical transition as the composition changes over time.

Cities are richer places for having what Mark Abrahamson (1996) calls "urban enclaves." Even small communities often have distinctly different types of neighborhoods. These places provide a meeting place and common ground for people with common characteristics to meet and feel at home. They also provide interest and "local color" for visitors. As the concern over Carter's comment about "neighborhood purity" reminds us, however, distinctiveness can result in isolation; identity preservation can lead to exclusion. At their best, distinctive neighborhoods practice "cultural hospitality," in which local pride fosters a commitment to the community and its heritage, and yet keeps a welcome mat out for those interested in visiting or joining.

For Reflection

1. Think about the neighborhood in which you grew up or spent a great deal of time. Give it a label. If you can, label neighboring areas. Why did you choose that particular label? What characteristics were predominant? What defines this neighborhood: architecture, geography, history, proximity, noise, conformity or non-conformity, or other distinctives? How is the identity maintained: zoning, social pressures, natural proximity, price, or other forces?

2. Consider the neighborhood in which you live now (at home or at school) and repeat the above. What label did you give it and why?

3. Try an exercise in *cognitive mapping*. Map the neighbor-
    hoods you described in 1 or 2 above. Are there distinct
    boundaries, such as rivers, major thoroughfares, or less
    well-defined transition zones around the edges? Are
    there distinct focal points (nodes), common paths
    (ways of traveling) for residents, or notable physical or
    architectural landmarks? How does this layout affect
    interaction?

Our Town: Metropolitan Sectors

Urban areas are organized not only into neighborhoods but into
larger sectors or districts of activity. The most important early attempt to systematically analyze the city was the Chicago school of
urban ecology, which focused on how these sectors and districts were
spatially organized. The approach was later criticized for focusing
too much on spatial dimensions and neglecting broader political
and economic forces. For a period of time in the 1960s and 1970s,
these elements were given primary attention under the umbrella of
political economy. Yet cities are spatial as well as political entities;
thus, the urban ecology and political economy perspectives are re-
emerging together under such rubrics as the "socio-spatial" approach of a new urban sociology (Gottdiener, 1994).

Urban theorists in the Chicago school tradition borrowed images from biology to try to analyze urban patterns and change. Unfortunately, the images they applied to sociology were often
oversimplified. This has evolved into a greater problem, as cities
continue to become more complex entities. The classic picture still
offered in many textbooks is one of concentric circles radiating out
from the city center, each ring holding a type of activity (residential,
commercial, or industrial) or a particular social class. This is elegant
in its simplicity, but it cannot accurately describe any urban environment today.

Further, it is more likely that any attempt to analyze a "city" as
an independent entity will be doomed to fail. When the word "suburb" was coined, suburbs were just that: sub-entities surrounding
a large city. American suburbs currently contain a higher proportion
of the national population than do cities themselves. Just as the
streetcar once redesigned urban life, the automobile has recreated
our cities and continues to do so as new highways allow more com-

muting options. Outward-bound urban dwellers have filled suburbs and absorbed outlying towns and countryside to create *exurbs,*
satellite communities and corridors of development that have
blurred the line between city and country. It is more realistic today
to think less in terms of city boundaries and more in terms of metropolitan regions. Although these regions may look more like mere
splatters of colored paint on a state map than clearly defined rings,
they do have a structure shaped by social, political, economic, and
geographic forces.

Despite regional variations, several common types of residential
sectors have emerged in this metropolitan pattern, as described below. They may encompass a variety of neighborhoods but share
some common defining characteristics, often dominated by a particular social class and sometimes by a specific racial or ethnic group.
Some are defined by recognizable landmarks, as well as by district
nodes (gathering points, such as a park or commercial district),
edges (the boundaries or undeveloped area that define them), and
paths (common ways of moving through the area).

Elite urban. Enclaves of the old rich have been so well-guarded
that they have remained elite addresses, although they are now often
shared with a few of the nouveau riche.

Depressed inner city. New downtown office towers quickly
give way to boarded up factories and warehouses and residential
streets with housing in serious disrepair, often owned by absentee
landlords. They are now often inhabited by a majority of African
American or mixed Latino and black residents.

Gentrified urban. Desirable urban "villages" have been re-
claimed by middle-class residents who have tired of commuting,
have become bored with the suburbs, or whose interests, color, or
sexual orientation were not welcomed in neighboring suburbs. Well-
kept townhouses, brownstones, and renovated historical houses
often predominate this sector.

Working-class urban. Small but tidy houses have been built on
small, often largely treeless lots, usually near places of former blue-
collar employment that no longer exist.

Middle-class suburban. This is the region of tract homes, cul-
de-sacs, and two-car garages. Ranch homes share the street with
two-story colonials and a few assorted "tri-levels."

Elite suburban. These suburbs are usually known locally by name as elite addresses (e.g., Something Heights, Something Hills, or Something Point) and are often distinguished by water or wooded hills. The subdivisions within them are typically marked off by gates that announce, for example, Something Estates. Large houses are frequently built here to evoke old traditional styles, though they are fully equipped with modern conveniences.

Exurban. This often exists where a highway or quick commuting route to the city has allowed developers to push beyond the ring of suburbs into the countryside, offering new homes to residents with the promise of "the best of both worlds."

Satellite town. At one time probably a completely independent town or village built around a rural hub, railway depot, mill site, or some other attraction, this sector now holds mostly urban commuters.

Small town rural. This is the traditional small town in the vein of Norman Rockwell-styled Americana. Many of them once served agricultural needs, and some continue to thrive on a mix of farming and small industry; others are graying, as their young people leave for jobs and education elsewhere.

Open country rural. Scattered farm houses, trailers, and sometimes a few out-of-place newer homes comprise this region. Some residents farm full- or part-time and some work out of their home; others work for rural employers (e.g., the county) or commute over long distances.

Rural pocket. Often not big enough to be incorporated, this area is occupied by a cluster of homes with an occasional business at the junction of secondary roads and highways, in a "hollow" or valley, or at some other congregating point.

Specialty community. Small and sleepy, such communities sometimes have a college, tourist attraction, artist's colony, a unique history or identity, or some other draw. Included here are newly built retirement communities and clusters of second homes owned by urban escapees.

For Reflection

1. Map your city and its outskirts, ideally where you live right now, although it can be some other place you know better. Note the major districts and communities.

You can use the labels above or modify them to fit your own situation. Note landmarks, district nodes, edges, and paths. Are some areas well-defined or others less clear in your mind? What does your map reveal about your interests and uses of your city?

2. How might this "cognitive map" look different if you were part of a different class or racial background? Consider some area that you would like to explore or learn more about. What activities might give you some familiarity with or increase your knowledge of this area? What are some ways to make a city or region "your own"?

3. Each of the areas above has its own promoters who are ready to explain why it is such a good place to live. Even low-income areas have been cited as having "people who are real folks" or being "where the action is." Each area also has its own detractors who claim they would never want to live there. Here are a few common responses:

Community:	Promoters:	Detractors:
large city	activity, excitement	noise, crime, crowding
small city	"best of both worlds"	"worst of both worlds"
suburban	quiet, family-oriented	dull, homogenous
exurban	convenient yet country	ugly sprawl
small town	quiet, friendly	dull, intrusive, closed
open rural	beauty, space, freedom	isolated, few options
specialty	shared interests	homogeneous, transient

Which of these community types do you find appealing or could tolerate? What factors would improve your perception of a particular community type?

Places Rated: The New Geography of Choice

The considerations above would have been inconsequential to many people from our agrarian and industrial past, many of whom lived wherever they could afford a plot of farmland or could find a job. Employment in those days was often in locations determined by one's access to shipping or rail transport or to a local power supply or a manufacturer of raw materials. Strong regional and family ties, in turn, reinforced a commitment to one's "hometown," unless economic necessity forced a move out of the location.

Increasingly today, this geography of necessity has given way to a geography of *choice.* Air conditioning and new light industry has opened up the sunbelt to newcomers, and portable social security checks have promoted gray flight to warmer climates. New job opportunities in the Western states, along with ever-expanding utilities and services, have opened new options near mountains and oceans, sunny dry deserts, and other attractive but previously less accessible locations. Many people still move on the basis of necessity or in the wake of family members, but many others make choices based on the need for a better physical, social, or business climate.

Freed from geographical constraints, many of those in transition select a place to live by focusing on common criteria: locations that are convenient to shopping and recreation yet away from traffic and crime, or those that offer both community and access to unspoiled beauty. On the other hand, it would pose a problem if everyone tried to relocate based on this criteria, because too many people in one area could spoil the very objective they are seeking. This becomes the classic dilemma of individual choices and collective consequences.

A similar process, for example, often occurs during school lectures, town meetings, or church gatherings in large auditoriums or congregation areas. Many people like to sit at the back of the crowd, where they can observe everyone and everything that happens with relative anonymity. The first arrivals, on the assumption that the room will be about half full, may sit in the middle. Later arrivals then end up sitting behind them, so that the place fills toward the back. Consequently, the front rows are all empty, and everyone is too far back to see, hear, and participate comfortably.

In metropolitan regions, this same process can be played out: New residents settle on the geographical edges where they can have ready access to the city in one direction and to open space and countryside in the other. This unravels when everyone tries to play the same game. The edges keep moving back as newer arrivals occupy one step beyond the previous residents, and the space closer to the city is left neglected and wasted, to everyone's detriment. This situation is further exacerbated by the fact that many residents and businesses prefer to build from scratch rather than repair, reuse, and reclaim existing structures. New houses go up in distant suburbs and exurbs with the latest styles, conveniences, and landscaping; more central properties deteriorate and are eventually abandoned. New mega-stores, mega-malls, and smaller strip malls provide convenient alternatives to the more central shopping districts, which in turn fall into a serious decline.

If these were the only forces at work, cities would continue to sprawl outward in all directions like a wildfire, leaving a charred, barren core in the middle. In some places, this has indeed occurred with ever-widening circles of suburbanites who can travel to work and shop in edge cities without ever approaching the core. Other forces, however, contain this process somewhat, especially as cities try to concentrate cultural and convention attractions near the inner core. More and more, interesting old city sectors have become prime areas for revitalization (e.g., San Antonio's Riverwalk, Baltimore's Inner Harbor, Cleveland's North Coast Harbor and Gateway Development, or Pittsburgh's new riverfront developments). These are usually reincarnated as select, upscale, and high-priced locales, though they offer little to nearby lower-income urban residents, who are merely shifted from one deteriorated neighborhood to another without the opportunity to partake in the much-publicized "urban renaissance."

This continual remaking of the metropolitan landscape has major environmental, as well as social, impacts. The abandonment of central city industry and its replacement with glittering, new commercial and entertainment ventures has often been accompanied by a cleaner environment. At the same time, however, new suburban and exurban housing developments served by endless "mall-sprawl" have consumed woodlands, filled wetlands, displaced wildlife, and paved over some of the nation's most productive agricultural land.

The "miracle growth" of California's Silicon Valley, for example, has eliminated huge areas of orchards, nut groves, and farms. The irony of this collective pursuit of the "best of both worlds" is echoed in the subdivision names themselves, which often evoke images of the very things they destroyed: Quail Ridge (the ridge was bulldozed and terraced, and the quail have fled), Clear Creek Farm (the creek is now a series of concrete culverts, and the original farm was razed), Forest Trail (the forest is limited to a few wooded lots, and the trail is now four lanes of rush-hour traffic), and so forth.

Another problem with geography of choice has arisen in interstate migrations. For the first time, the last census noted more people moving out of California than moving into it, though international immigration into California has maintained a growing state population. This new movement was based on economic forces (e.g., slow-downs in electronics production), political forces (e.g., military base closings and defense cutbacks), and social forces, as people sought less crowding, traffic, and pollution. Some of the very people who had first come to California seeking the good life have now moved on to such "less spoiled" places as Colorado and Arizona. Yet, as Denver and Phoenix and their respective regions have quickly expanded (along with traffic and smog), others have decided to look for new opportunities and space in Utah. Now, as the Salt Lake City to Provo metropolitan strip has grown at an explosive rate, still others are starting to move on to Nevada. When they arrive there, however, they are more likely to find the other half of the people leaving California.

For Reflection

1. Examine Figure 7.1 below. What patterns do you note? Where are the biggest population losers and gainers? How does international movement affect this? What regions are most affected by internal migration? What regions are most affected by movers from abroad? What social and economic forces might explain the patterns you noted?

2a. Examine Figure 7.2 below. How is the distribution of the American population changing? How would you interpret and describe the changes: Is this a picture of the urbanization of America or the suburbanization of America or something else? What is happening to the populations of major metropolitan areas? Is this a picture of urban decline or urban realignment? Think about the implications of population shifts? What might the effects be for the natural environment, for political power and decisionmaking, for city budgets

and services, for public schools, for the urban poor, and
for urban employers?

b. Table 7.1 below shows the patterns of migration that
are continuing to reshape city and countryside. What
happened to the "rural exodus" in 1994 (note the exchange of migrants between metropolitan and non-
metropolitan)? What about the migration within the
metropolis between central city and suburb? How

Figure 7.1
Immigration and Internal Migration, 1994

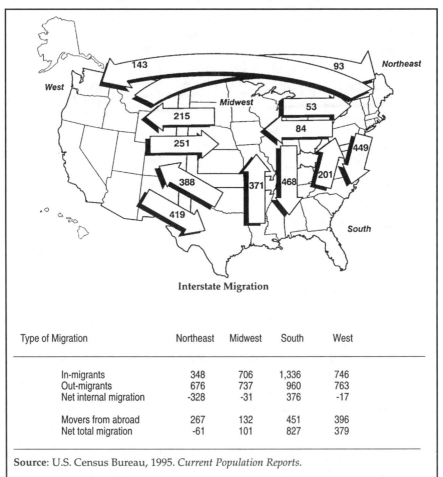

Type of Migration	Northeast	Midwest	South	West
In-migrants	348	706	1,336	746
Out-migrants	676	737	960	763
Net internal migration	-328	-31	376	-17
Movers from abroad	267	132	451	396
Net total migration	-61	101	827	379

Source: U.S. Census Bureau, 1995. *Current Population Reports.*

Figure 7.2
Changing Distribution of the American Population

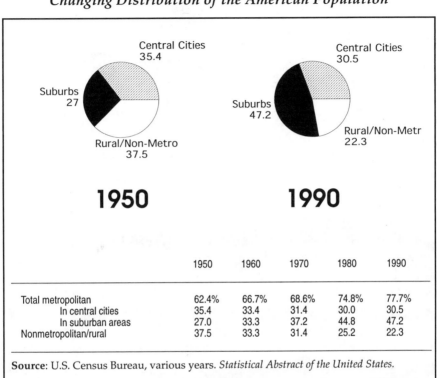

	1950	1960	1970	1980	1990
Total metropolitan	62.4%	66.7%	68.6%	74.8%	77.7%
In central cities	35.4	33.4	31.4	30.0	30.5
In suburban areas	27.0	33.3	37.2	44.8	47.2
Nonmetropolitan/rural	37.5	33.3	31.4	25.2	22.3

Source: U.S. Census Bureau, various years. *Statistical Abstract of the United States.*

does immigration and international movement affect this picture? Immigrants once concentrated in "urban villages" and ghettoes; where did the most movers from abroad settle in 1994?

Power Among: Power, Elites, and Community Mobilization

One answer to the endless search for a better place is that perhaps the quality of life which we seek cannot be found but must be built though concerted community efforts. But how much power do ordinary citizens have to reconstruct their neighborhoods and communities? Is the power to change held only by a few? Two differing answers to these questions have become known as the *elite perspective* and the *pluralist perspective*.

Table 7.1
Metropolitan Migration, 1994
(Numbers in thousands)

Type of Migration	Metropolitan Status			
	Total Metropolitan	Central Cities	Suburbs	Non-Metro
In-migrants	1,770	3,516	6,721	1,856
Out-migrants	1,856	6,452	3,871	1,770
Net internal migration	-86	-2,936	2,850	86
Movers from abroad	1,095	447	658	150
Net total migration	1,009	-2,489	3,498	236

Source: U.S. Census Bureau. 1995. *Current Population Reports.*

In a book by the same name, C.W. Mills (1956) contends that the United States as a whole is dominated by a *power elite,* consisting of corporate, political, and military leaders who dominate and control what he terms our "military-industrial complex." In *The Lonely Crowd* (1953), David Riesman proposed a different view: Certainly, elites may exist, but they do not always have a common agenda; they may even exist as "veto groups," checking one another's power. In *Who Rules America* (1967) and subsequent books, G. William Domhoff argues that the controlling elites do have a common agenda, even if it is only to preserve their hold on power and privilege. He maintains that they can coordinate their activities as they interact in elite clubs, select alumni associations, and other exclusive social gatherings, and as they work together through interconnected associations, foundations, and boards of directors. So common is the practice of "interlocking directorates," in which prominent executives and financiers sit on one another's boards, that Domhoff's charts of network affiliations resemble dense spider webs, interlinking together a powerful, wealthy elite.

The debate over the power elite has also extended to the local level. Examining the decisionmaking process in New Haven, Connecticut, Robert Dahl (1961) finds a wide range of differing positions and agendas in conflict with one other. Looking at the same city, Domhoff suggests that the real decisions have already been worked out in the back rooms, and that the agenda was set long before the complex and contentious process that Dahl noted ever began. John

Walton (1970) has examined elites and elite behavior in a wide variety of times and places, concluding that whether one finds support for the elite position or the pluralist position may depend largely on the measures used—reputations, affiliations, decision making, and so forth—and on the community involved. He suggests that different local communities have different patterns of power, based on differing economic and social histories.

In many places, groups of citizens have felt excluded from real power and are determined to challenge the existing order of institutionalized power through *collective action.* Collective action may consist of a single event, such as a protest march, riot, strike, or prayer vigil. When a series of such collective acts begin to build momentum, coherence, and a broad common agenda, they become *social movements.* A powerful example of this process in the United States was the Civil Rights movement. A series of bus boycotts, cafeteria sit-ins, voter registration drives, and related activities began in the 1950s. These actions drew strength from one other and from an inevitably more sympathetic national climate, thus developing the leadership and articulate agenda needed to become a concerted ongoing movement.

Early studies of social movements tended to stress such factors as *deprivation* (either absolute or relative), the failure to meet rising expectations, and the alienation of people in an impersonal *mass society.* In each case, an irrational, impulsive "mob mentality" was automatically assumed. When government spokespersons in Beijing commented on the student actions in Tiannemen Square, and when government spokespersons in Los Angeles commented on the 1992 riots, both used strikingly similar terms like "random acts of hooligans." Careful research into most social movements, however, rarely finds many "random acts" of mass hysteria nor a leadership made up largely of "hooligans." Often, an educated leadership carefully plans how to build support, use media coverage, and maneuver the political process to achieve its desired ends. People become involved through their social contacts with other activists, as they see attainable goals that are worth the risks involved. The dominant sociological views of collective action now focus on this as *resource mobilization* and *political process.*

Studies of social movements also suggest a common life cycle: The movement grows and flourishes at first then declines or stagnates. Revolutionary social movements that have changed whole societies have become fossilized and inflexible over time.

China and Cuba's struggles with the aging guardians of their revolutions and Mexico's "frozen revolution" are notable examples of this. In the United States, even as more African Americans rise to important positions of political leadership, the original fervor and vision of the Civil Rights movement seems lost and stagnant. It may be that revolutionary or reformist vision is hard to sustain, or that greater access to power eventually undermines movements as it corrupts the leadership. Since the last century, such sociologists as Gaetano Mosca and Robert Michels have suggested that this "iron law" is inevitable, with each successful movement creating only a new power elite that distances itself from its original constituencies. This is the pessimistic assessment of George Orwell's famous tale, *Animal Farm:* the new masters quickly come to look and act more like the old. Is there any escape from this iron law?

The term *empowerment* was first used to describe the agenda of the political left and has now been frequently adopted by the political right. But if the price of becoming empowered is alienation from one's community of origin, is this truly a goal to strive for? One answer is that we need to rethink our ideas of power. There is "power over," the position of being near the top of the chain of command, as discussed in Chapter Three. There is also "power among," the community-based power of being central to a web of interaction. "Power among" requires an understanding of local problems and the ability to communicate among diverse groups. In this case, to "lose touch" is also to lose power, for it means stepping out of this web of interaction. Strong network ties with people able to bridge the gap between various community circles of common interest is the process of *community building.* It also forms the basis for *community mobilization* in response to a particular crisis (Granovetter, 1973). Once the many positive and balanced ties between residents are in place, the start-up costs and the time needed to mobilize the community are less, and the benefits of being a cooperative participant are likely to increase. Over time, the power among of community building also creates greater community solidarity, "a sense of place" that allows more than just a short-term cry of protest. It also provides a long-term effort toward sustained change.

Although these efforts may be local and small-scale, they can have broad ramifications. The term *new social movements* has been coined to describe broad national and international movements that are loose affiliations of local efforts. These often focus on quality-of-life concerns that can be discussed in global forums but frequently need to be enacted locally. The environmental movement has become at once more local and more global. Likewise, the women's movement has broadened into a worldwide discussion of gender and family concerns. The peace movement, too, has begun to encompass racial and ethnic tensions, as well as the conditions of violence on all levels of human society. International conferences and internet communications are now balanced by new community centers and local action. This phenomena is too new for anyone to gauge its effectiveness. Although some doubt that new social movements can challenge the established seats of power, others see them as the only way to move the locus of power from elite control to broader, more informed community control.

For Reflection

1. As you look at national controversies and the political process, do you find greater evidence for control by a power elite or for the pluralist position? Does your answer depend on what the issue is, and why or why not?

2. When you look at your local community, do you find evidence of local elites? Is local power based on reputation and prestige, on the control of wealth, on the control of the political process, or on some other factors? Are these factors dispersed throughout the community or concentrated in a few hands?

3. Examine Figure 7.3 below. Apply its model of community mobilization to a recent local controversy, for example, in your hometown, your present neighborhood, or your campus community. What factors were important in people's ability or inability to organize and voice their concerns? What factors were key in affecting the eventual outcome?

Figure 7.3

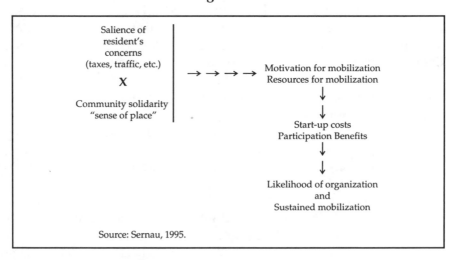

4. Find examples of people and groups whom you see as exercising "power among." Have they been able to remain true to their original vision and concerns? Have elites emerged, or has power remained dispersed? Have they been effective in fostering change?

Toward a Community of Communities: Change, Equity, and Sustainability

Social Change: Facing the New World Disorder

Rapid social change has led to a geography of choice and new opportunity for some but also to a geography of desperation for others. Around the globe, villagers and rural dwellers who are unable to support their families or have been forced off their land by bigger enterprises, flee to urban areas. In much of the world, this has created growing mega-cities with populations of more than 10 million people. In Table 7.2, the "Big Ten" of the year 2000 includes only one city in the United States and none in Europe.

Urbanization has dominated the advanced industrial countries as well, as people are drawn from rural areas by the attraction of higher-paying urban jobs. This draw continues in some places in the developing nations, such as in Shanghai, China, or Bangkok, Thailand. Many more, however, are forced by desperation and face few job prospects. In the past, Europe and the United States have experienced such major migrations as Britain's rural clearances, the mid-American Dust Bowl of the 1930s, and the flight of African Americans from Jim Crow oppression in the rural South. But the current international movement has been developing on a colossal scale.

Table 7.2
The New Mega-Cities
The World's Ten Largest Metropolitan Areas in the Year 2000

Metropolitan Area	Population (in millions)
Tokyo-Yokohama, Japan	30.0
Mexico City, Mexico	27.0
São Paulo, Brazil	25.4
Seoul, South Korea	22.0
Bombay, India	15.4
New York, United States	14.7
Osaka-Kobe-Kyoto, Japan	14.3
Tehran, Iran	14.3
Rio de Janeiro, Brazil	14.2
Calcutta, India	14.1

Source: Projections based on United Nations data 1993.

Because the burgeoning cities of the developing world can neither supply the constant stream of people with basic services—housing, water, electricity, sewage, etc.—nor with jobs, many end up in the sprawling peri-urban slums or shantytowns that ring the city.

Here, people often build homes from what they can scavenge, and they create their own jobs in the informal economy: buying and selling small articles and foodstuffs, scavenging and "recycling" garbage, making or fixing articles to sell, pawning or swapping, and so on. These urban newcomers are often determined and energetic; but incorporating them into the broader social fabric of the metropolis, so that they can provide for themselves and enjoy a decent standard of living, remains an enormous challenge for governments, international agencies, community organizations, and the organizations that these newcomers have themselves created to be their voice.

With the close of the Cold War, then-President Bush expressed optimism about a *new world order,* and many looked forward to the new "peace dividend." Instead, bloody conflicts erupted in the Persian Gulf, Liberia, Rwanda, Burundi, Somalia, and the former regions of Yugoslavia. Even where war has been avoided, tensions remain high: in Haiti and Cuba, in parts of South Asia, between North and South Korea, between mainland China and Taiwan, throughout the states of the former Soviet Union, and for that matter, on our own American borders and in such major "international cities" as Los Angeles and Miami.

The world has witnessed with considerable surprise the power of two seemingly opposite forces: national integration and national disintegration. After decades of relative stability on many borders, we now find that maps are obsolete by the time they are printed. Many national states have broken apart: the Soviet Union, Yugoslavia, Czechoslovakia, Ethiopia. Many others are currently struggling with movements for independence within their own borders. At the same time, countries are coming together. European nations continue to push toward greater unity in a growing common market, NAFTA is binding North American economies together, and similar accords are being negotiated around the world. In large measure, the two seemingly opposite forces of integration and disintegration may indeed be complementary. One reason that a small state like Slovenia can survive and hope to thrive is through its close economic ties to an integrated Europe. Economic integration and political disintegration may, in fact, work hand in hand.

We have come to accept the modern nation-state as the natural order of the world. Even larger organizations are based on this premise: The United Nations is just that, a union of nation-states. Historically, however, people were more likely to be organized into smaller ethnic regions or into larger empires. The rulers of Britain, France, Spain, and others had to work hard to forge the image of a common people with a common language and identity. But people do not always accept this process, so today there has been a flourishing of regionalism and a new interest in regional languages. The entity of the nation-state, therefore, may prove to be too big to address people's desire for local autonomy, regional distinctiveness, ethnic identity, and community-based solutions. At the same time, it may be too small to cope with global economic, social, and environmental problems.

What lies ahead is less clear. Barber (1996) observes two opposing and equally dangerous forces at work: "McWorld," the tendency to pull together into a uniform global marketplace; and "Jihad" (from the Muslim term for a holy war), the tendency to pull apart into hostile religious and ethnic factions. He suggests that neither is very promising for democracy—in one, matters are decided by dollars; in the other, by demagogues and bullets. The Gulf War could be viewed in these terms: on one side, a leader clearly evoking the language of Jihad; on the other, the combined forces of global economic interests. Even if international economic interests do prevail, as they did in the Gulf War, Barber's vision raises the specter of ever more Jihads from groups threatened or excluded by the global market.

A more appealing prospect is that these changes will lead to both a greater appreciation of global diversity and a greater commitment to building a community on all levels. In this case, national divisions are replaced by a global village of communities. This vision has been detailed by Amitai Etzioni in a series of recent books, as well as being his choice of theme at a recent American Sociological Association Annual Meeting. In place of a world of individual actors competing in a vast McWorld marketplace or a world of bitterly divided Jihad factions, Etzioni's view looks to local community commitments nestled within a broader commitment to a world community that mediates common interests.

This challenge is similar to the theme of the growing Green Party that has been adopted by environmental groups: "Think globally, act locally." If it is to be successful, however, such action will require renewed commitment to a global social system dedicated to both *equity* and *sustainability*.

Equity: Confronting Global Apartheid

If the world is becoming a single global village, it is also a segregated village. The enormous divisions between the haves and have-nots are so great and so entrenched that Gernot Kohler (1978; see also Richmond, 1994) has referred to the world system as *global apartheid*. In a system similar to that which used to prevail in South Africa, a small minority, divided but mostly white, controls the vast portion of the world's wealth and uses both institutional legitimation and military force to guard its horde. Excluded from this enclave of wealth and power is the majority of the world's people, living in nominally independent entities but nonetheless dependent on this minority, thus providing a vast reserve of cheap labor. Although formal apartheid in South Africa was condemned and dismantled, informal apartheid in the world system continues to thrive (see Table 7.3).

Some countries are not just being left behind—they are losing ground. Incomes in some African nations have declined nearly 20 percent since 1977 (Jones and Kiguel, 1993). The scattered success stories—Chile in Latin America, Ghana in Africa, Thailand in Asia, the Czech Republic in Eastern Europe—have seen rising incomes but also rising inequality. The result are economies of exclusion, whose formal labor markets have no place for a growing global underclass:

> We have glimpses of a new world economic order. I suspect the best glimpses will not be found primarily in the high rises of Tokyo and Manhattan, nor in the desolation of Mogadishu, Somalia and Kinshasa, Zaire. A more likely glimpse of the future can be seen in Bangkok, Thailand, where economic miracles and social nightmares coexist daily. We might include Juárez and Tijuana in Mexico, São Paulo and Rio de Janeiro in Brazil, Kuala Lumpur and Jakarta in Southeast Asia, perhaps Lagos and Nairobi in Africa, probably Los Angeles and Miami in the United States—all those hot, noisy, hazy mixtures of hope and despair. They provide the products and services for a growing global middle class, along with the prospect of a door into that class for the otherwise excluded. Without fundamental changes, however, for many it will be a rapidly revolving door, offering an invitation, a quick glimpse of air conditioned affluence, and a rapid return to the street. (Sernau, 1994, p. 137)

For several decades, the debate over the causes of prevailing world poverty has divided into two broad camps. From the 1940s through the 1960s, the dominant perspective in North America and Europe clustered around what has come to be known as *modernization theory*. The poor remained poor, this theory contended, because they lacked the following aspects:

1. *Modern personalities.* People still thought in "traditional" ways.

2. *Modern institutions.* They lacked efficient governments, businesses, and financial institutions.

3. *Modern technology.* Their means of production were "backward."

Once these things were acquired, largely through participation in world trade and public and private investment from wealthy nations, the situation would change. A process of *diffusion* was set in place by key actors, such as international business, that would eventually bring all three modern aspects to the poor. Urbanization would only facilitate this process. Progress might be slow but at least certain.

In direct and conscious opposition to this line of thinking, scholars and leaders in Latin America began to develop an alternate line of thought that has come to be known as *dependency theory.* This approach was the minority position from the 1940s through much of the 1960s. But by the 1970s, it had become the most common social science perspective on development, even though dependency thinkers had gotten used to thinking of themselves as the underdog and still often refer to modernization approaches as "the dominant paradigm."

Modernization theory was an evolutionary perspective that drew heavily on structural-functional thinking, while dependency theory grew out of a classic conflict approach response. Dependency theorists argued that the poor were not poor because they were traditional or *undeveloped,* but because a history of imperialism involving colonial domination (followed by the subtler but real practices of *neo-colonialism*) at the hands of wealthy nations had made them *underdeveloped.* Being *dependent* on the wealthy nations resulted in three things for the rest of the world:

1. *Exploitation.* Their labor and resources benefitted only local and foreign elites, not the people themselves.

2. ***Domination.*** The poor countries were not free to chart their own course but were controlled by big powers and international financial interests.

3. ***Distortion.*** The economies of poor countries were shaped around exports and foreign interests and could not serve local needs. Some developing economies did grow, but it was argued that this was "growth without development" and only benefitted national elites rather than the masses.

Early modernization thinking eventually retreated under attacks claiming that it was ethnocentric in its assumption that everyone should adopt Western values and practices, and that it was merely a system of justification for continued global inequity. In part, too, a decade-long recession and many failures in development policy simply left most observers far more pessimistic than before.

In the 1980s, however, a new conservative spirit and renewed growth in the West (coupled with the rapid growth of the Pacific Rim nations and the slow decline of socialist alternatives) revived the emphasis on free trade, open markets, and the role of an unfettered private sector to produce growth. *Neo-liberalism*, the free-market economics associated with Adam Smith in the utilitarian and rational choice tradition, became the favored policy. Neo-liberal approaches recommend less government spending, balanced budgets, and privatization of production. This policy still continues to dominate the national agenda of many countries, as well as international lending policies and trade agreements.

About the same time in the early 1980s, dependency thinking increasingly focused on a series of ideas known as *world systems theory*, mostly associated with Immanuel Wallerstein (1974, 1984). According to Wallerstein, the world system is dominated by a core of wealthy capitalist nations, a semi-periphery that acts as something of a buffer, and a periphery of the poorest nations. Economic success was less dependent on an individual nation's policies than on its position in this world system. The failure of poor countries to show much progress and the difficulty of individual socialist systems were to be expected, as long as the world was dominated by a single core-controlled capitalist system.

As we approach the end of the century, the evidence is still mixed, though both modernizing processes and dependency processes are very much in evidence. Compartmentalizing them into separate ideological camps probably did little to advance our understanding of social and economic development. Neo-liberal "reforms" deliver sporadic periods of growth but frequently at the price of growing inequality. Heavy state intervention can reduce inequality and provide basic needs, such as universal health and education, but often at considerable cost to the economy. Both the capitalism of the West and socialism of the old Soviet-bloc "East" seem to have proceeded with little regard to the social or physical environment. Consequently, neither seems to offer any acceptable models of lasting progress or *sustainable development*. Many scholars have now joined the search for workable alternatives.

Sustainable Worlds

Given the realization of the limits of both the public sector (government) and the private sector (business) to effect meaningful change, many have started to consider a third alternative, sometimes called the *social sector* or *civil society* (e.g., see Henderson, 1996 [1978]). This encompasses a wide range of social movements and nongovernmental organizations dedicated to interrelated causes: racial and gender equity, human rights, peaceful conflict resolution, and environmental protection. Often, their approach to progress involves a grass-roots development built on the strengths inherent in local communities. Interestingly, both those on the political right (traditionally suspicious of big government) and those on the political left (traditionally suspicious of big business) are looking increasingly toward community control and community-based solutions. In no way can the social sector replace the public and private sectors, but it can help to hold both government and industry accountable for responsible action. Solutions are often neither completely "top down" nor completely "bottom up" but involve an interaction between levels; for instance, government policy can facilitate community action which may, in turn, further shape national policy. At their best, the three sectors can work together in concert for a common cause.

A growing realization, such as that echoed by the world environmental conference in Rio de Janeiro, Brazil, and the women's conference in Beijing, China, is the interdependence of all people—

of both human and natural communities. Conservation and development have often been seen in the past to be at odds; yet we are beginning to realize that they are inseparable (Weaver, Rock, and Kusterer, 1997). Strong, healthy cultures and communities supply the resources to nurture the next generation, just as a healthy environment provides the resources to sustain and inspire future generations. Whether under the banner of "ecological economics" or "social ecology," it is becoming all too apparent how desperately we need to see the bigger picture.

Two-year-old children, for example, are known to be *egocentric*, seeing themselves in the center of everything. Cultures work diligently to socialize these youngsters, so they can see beyond themselves, but instead often create adults who can only relate to like-minded individuals who are *ethnocentric*. The urgent challenge for the social sciences, in concert with growing social movements, is to help us all to mature and become *geocentric*—caring for the earth as a whole.

For Reflection

1. Examine Table 7.3. The heading "Real Purchase Power" refers to the gross national product per capita, adjusted for differences in the cost of living. "Quality of Life Index" measures health, education, and well-being. Note that the income estimates in the table under "Real Purchase Power" have been adjusted to take into account differences in the cost of living. The spread of actual dollar incomes, based on official exchange rates, is much greater. Also, you should realize that life expectancy, often used as a measure of health and welfare, is more affected by child and infant mortality than by the numbers of extremely elderly. Find the wealthiest and healthiest nations and compare them with those with the poorest and least healthy economies. How closely correlated are the two? What might explain the differences in the two measures, particularly those countries that are doing much better or worse than one would expect from their wealth? How closely correlated is formal education? How might income, education, and health be interrelated?

Table 7.3
Income and Well-Being in 30 Nations

Country	Real Purchase Power	Life Expect. at Birth	Mean Years of Schooling	Quality of Life Index
Canada	$19,320	77.2	12.2	.932
Switzerland	21,780	77.8	11.6	.931
Japan	19,390	78.6	10.8	.929
Sweden	17,490	77.7	11.4	.928
Norway	17,170	76.9	12.1	.928
France	18,430	76.6	12.0	.927
Australia	16,680	76.7	12.0	.926
United States	22,130	75.6	12.4	.925
Netherlands	16,820	77.2	11.1	.923
United Kingdom	16,340	75.8	11.7	.919
Germany	19,770	75.6	11.6	.918
South Korea	8,320	70.4	9.3	.859
Russia	6,930	70.0	9.0	.858
Costa Rica	5,100	76.0	5.7	.848
Poland	4,500	71.5	8.2	.815
Mexico	7,170	69.9	.9	.804
Brazil	5,240	65.8	4.0	.756
Saudi Arabia	10,850	68.7	3.9	.742
Iran	4,670	66.6	3.9	.672
South Africa	3,885	62.2	3.9	.650
China	2,946	70.5	5.0	.644
El Salvador	2,110	65.2	4.2	.543
Kenya	1,350	58.6	2.3	.434
India	1,150	59.7	2.4	.382
Haiti	925	56.0	1.7	.354
Nigeria	1,360	51.9	1.2	.348
Cambodia	1,250	50.4	2.0	.307
Ethiopia	370	46.4	1.1	.249
Chad	447	46.9	.3	.212
Afghanistan	700	42.9	.9	.208

Source: *United Nations Human Development Report, 1994.*

2. Looking down the table's list of countries, notice that the United States is the world leader in years of formal education and in income relative to the cost of living (the Swiss have the world's highest absolute income); yet it ranks only eighth in the world in the overall Quality of Life Index, due to poorer performance in measures of health (in this case, overall longevity). Marion Wright Edelmann of the Children's Defense Fund often points out that infant mortality in the United States for

nonwhite infants is similar to that in Botswana and Albania. Thinking back to the issues that we have discussed in the last three chapters, why do you think the United States fares so poorly on this measure?

3.   Earlier, we considered the theoretical debate over "nature versus nurture." The present world situation suggests that we need activities that promote both nature *and* nurture, cultural preservation as well as natural preservation. The concern for nature may lead to an emphasis on waste reduction, less intense or wasteful consumption, and so forth. The concern for nurture, on the other hand, may lead to an emphasis on ways to strengthen family ties, protect cultural heritage, promote gender equity and so on. Filling in the two columns provided below, list what you see as the crucial needs in each category.

Nature   Nurture

4.   Take one example from each of the two columns. Who would be the key social actors in addressing this need: individuals, families, businesses, churches, civic organizations and voluntary associations, local communities, national or state government, or others? How would the actions of these various entities interrelate?

5.   How might the concerns you listed affect your involvement in the private sector (business ethics, consumer behavior, etc.), in the public sector (voting, lobbying, etc.), and in the social sector (joining and supporting groups and organizations)?

Reaching Out, Digging Deeper

The ability to assess demographic patterns and trends is a valuable tool for making a wide range of decisions: where to put a new store, business, or franchise; whether to build (or to close) an elementary school; what the market for a particular product or service will be; or what challenges a community is likely to face. Demographic data is readily available at most libraries and increasingly available electronically. The mother of all domestic sources is the U.S. Census Bureau, with its decennial (ten-year) census and periodic updates. In addition, the Labor Department, Commerce Department, Education Department, and many others release frequently updated data. We most often encounter these in the news media as brief clips of a new report or newly released index. The more complete original sources are readily available, however, and can serve to better ground general impressions. With a bit of practice, you will find that these sources can provide a wealth of information.

1. A good source with which to be acquainted is the *Statistical Abstract of the United States.* Almost any reference library will have a current copy, and much of this material is also now available on CD-ROM as a database entitled US CENSUS. Included are data on vital statistics (births, deaths, marriages, divorces, etc.), as well as educational and business trends and others. Locate a recent copy of the *Statistical Abstract* and look at the demographic data in the first part. For each of the following questions, photocopy the relevant tables (if you can) and circle your data source.

    a. What is the birth rate for the United States? How does it vary by age and race? What are the trends?

    b. What is the mortality rate for the United States? How does it vary by age and race? What are the trends?

    c. Consider the data on immigration and internal migration. What areas are receiving the most immigrants? Which countries are the major sources of migration? What areas are gaining and losing population most rapidly?

    d. Select an area of interest to you—marriage, divorce, abortion, educational attainment, etc.—and "unpack" this issue by noting dimensions, trends, and differences by region, race, age, and gender. How does

this compare with the initial impressions you had of
this topic?

2. Several publications offer a variety of local information.
    A good source commonly available is a supplement to
    the *Statistical Abstract,* called the *County and City Dat-
    abook.* Its data is organized by state then by county
    (much of this data is also now available on CD-ROM
    as a database entitled US COUNTIES). Select the county
    in which you now live, the county of your hometown,
    or another county with which you have some familiar-
    ity. Pay particular attention to trends and to compari-
    sons with neighboring areas.

    a. What is the age structure of this county? Where are
        the "bulges" in the age structure: a young population
        with a preponderance of children, a large number of
        young adults, a graying population with many retir-
        ees, or a more balanced pattern?

    b. What is the sex ratio (number of women per 100 men)?
        What might be the reason for unbalanced sex ratios?

    c. What is the racial and ethnic make-up? What are the
        trends in race and ethnicity?

    d. What are the trends in industry and commerce—
        growth, decline, or general stability?

    e. How does this county compare with neighboring
        counties?

3. A quantitative glimpse of the world situation can also
    be gleaned from a number of sources. United Nations
    publications often contain a wealth of measures of na-
    tional economic development and social well-being.
    Many countries publish a statistical abstract of their
    own with this data. Each year, the World Bank publishes
    its *World Development Report,* which contains a large
    number of tables of national indicators: income, educa-
    tion, natural resources, fertility and mortality, women's
    status, etc. These tables are organized by country, start-
    ing with the poorest nation in the world and proceeding

to the wealthiest. Find the *World Development Report* for a recent year (again available in almost any research collection).

a. Look at the maps that precede the country tables. What general impressions emerge?

b. Examine "Table 1. Basic Indicators." Which are the world's richest and poorest countries? Which are the middle-income countries? How do the United States and Canada rank in comparison? Do you notice any surprises in this ordering of countries? Look at life expectancy in the same table. How closely does it correlate with income? Also look at literacy (simple measures of education). Are there relatively poor countries doing surprisingly well in terms of life expectancy and literacy? Are there wealthier countries not doing as well? Why might this be? Note the level of rank on each measure of the United States, Canada, and Japan. How do they compare?

c. Look through the tables for another area of interest. Some tables are quite technical, while others can be easily interpreted. What international trends and patterns do you observe?

d. A similar source with a somewhat different emphasis is the United Nations *Human Development Report,* from which Table 7.2 is drawn. How does this report compare with that prepared by the World Bank? How do the emphases of these reports differ? How might this reflect two different perspectives on the important aspects of development?

4. Many people are unaware of the full range of activities and services offered in their community. Campus life offices, community resource centers, and local United Way offices often provide a wide range of referrals for specific needs and for volunteer and service opportunities. A simple way to get a quick glimpse of a community is through the telephone book.

a. Open the Yellow Pages to "Social Service Organizations." How many organizations are listed? What
   types of groups are most common?

b. What social needs and concerns seem to be well-ad-
   dressed locally? Do you notice any areas that seem to
   be lacking?

c. Are you familiar with most of the organizations, or
   do you find many unfamiliar groups or activities?

To further explore social change and social action in our communities, our society, and our world, consider the following project
ideas:

In Your Family

1. If you have children of your own—or have ready access
   to nieces and nephews, young siblings, grandchildren,
   friends with children, etc.—look through their collection of books. Alternatively, study the new children's
   books in a library or a bookstore. What social and environmental themes have become common? How have
   these themes changed over the last twenty-five years?
   Are the presentations realistic? What impressions do
   they convey? How much should children be exposed
   to societal and global problems and how much should
   they be sheltered from them? How would you do this
   in your own family? What themes and values would
   you prefer to stress?

2. Examine your family's lifestyle in the following areas:
   energy consumption (e.g., heating and cooling, electric
   appliances, and gasoline consumption), range and
   quantity of material recycled, types and cost of food
   eaten, types of materials discarded (e.g., using a quick
   "content analysis" of the trash can, what are the biggest
   contributors to bulk?), types of materials reused (including clothing), and areas of growing or declining
   consumption. Which aspects do you consider the
   strongest and which the weakest? Do your family mem-

bers agree on this? Are there aspects that you hope to change?

In the Community

3. Explore the sector of your community with which you are the least familiar (using reasonable caution in your choice of place and time of day, of course). What are its community resources, gathering places, distinctives, escapes, and landmarks? Did you feel at home or uncomfortable in this sector? What gave you this impression, and did it change? Why have your travels and errands never or rarely taken you to this part of town before?

4. Spend time in a neighborhood that is undergoing a major transition: abandonment, gentrification, revitalization, shifts from resident owners to absentee landlords, commercial encroachment, loss of local jobs, or some other major change. What are some of the causes of this change? What are some of the effects? How do residents and businesspeople feel about these changes? What forces do you consider the sources of change: global, national, regional, local, or some combination thereof? Is the transition the result of political pressures, economic forces, social action, or some combination thereof?

5. Spend time in a location that is on or near the boundary of two socially or physically distinct neighborhoods. The distinctions can be based on social class, predominant age, lifestyle, or other defining characteristics. How do the physical boundaries of the area reflect the social boundaries between groups? In what ways do members of the two neighborhoods interact? Are there ways in which they never interact? How do residents convey their own sense of identity and their feelings toward the other neighborhood?

6. Select a community near you with a distinct cultural heritage. This could be a small town with a strong ethnic identity or an "urban village" within a large city

that has a distinct cultural heritage and identity. Approach the setting as a respectful inquirer and focus on community structures and cultural themes. Spend enough time in local businesses, community agencies, and gathering places to get a feel of the area. What gives this place its special character?

7. Look up one or more environmental organizations with a local chapter in your community. Widely distributed groups include chapters of the Sierra Club, the Nature Conservancy, the Audobon Society, the Isaac Walton League, and the National Wildlife Federation. How large is the membership of this chapter? What local facilities and activities do they have? What local projects are they working on? Do they have ties to international activities or organizations, such as Greenpeace or the World Wildlife Fund?

8. Find out if there is a local chapter of Human Rights Watch, Amnesty International, America's Watch, Witness for Peace, Veterans for Peace, or other human rights groups. What is their membership? What are the current concerns that they are addressing and their current activities? Are they currently focusing on specific issues or in certain parts of the world?

9. Visit a neighborhood center, neighborhood association, or neighborhood revitalization organization. They are often associated with low-income neighborhoods but may also form around historic districts, anti-crime programs, or just neighborhood beautification and betterment. Who is active in this organization? Try to note prevailing factors, such as age, gender, and vocation. Who are its leaders? How did the group form? What are its goals and activities? Have they met with success? What community characteristics have fostered or hindered their activities?

10. To explore community mobilization, find a citizen's group that has come together around a local issue: opposing a new road or development; keeping a school

Florida, Richard, and Martin Kenney. 1991. Transplanted Organizations: The Transfer of Japanese Industrial Organization to the U.S. *American Sociological Review* 56:381-98.

Frey, William H. 1995. The New Geography of Population Shifts. In Reynolds Farley (ed.), *State of the Union: America in the 1990s*, Vol. 2. New York: Russell Sage.

Gans, Herbert. 1979. Symbolic Ethnicity. *Ethnic and Racial Studies* 2:1-20.

Gilbert, Dennis, and Joseph Kahl. 1993. *The American Class Structure: A New Synthesis*, 4th ed. Belmont, CA: Wadsworth.

Gilligan, Carol. 1982. *In a Different Voice: Psychological Theory and Women's Development*. Cambridge, MA: Harvard.

Glass, Lillian. 1992. *He Says, She Says: Closing the Communication Gap Between the Sexes*. New York: Putnam.

Goffman, Erving. 1959. *The Presentation of Self in Everyday Society*. New York: Doubleday.

——. 1979. *Gender Advertisements*. Cambridge, MA: Harvard.

Gordon, Thomas. 1970. *Parent Effectiveness Training*. New York: Wyden.

Gottdiener, Mark. 1994. *The New Urban Sociology*. New York: McGraw-Hill.

Granovetter, Mark. 1973. The Strength of Weak Ties. *American Journal of Sociology* 81:1360-80.

Hacker, Andrew. 1992. *Two Nations*. New York: Ballantine.

Hall, Edward T. 1966. *The Hidden Dimension*. New York: Doubleday.

——. 1976. *Beyond Culture*. New York: Doubleday.

Hancock, Emily. 1989. *The Girl Within*. New York: Dutton.

Hannan, Michael T., and John Freeman. 1989. *Organizational Ecology*. Cambridge, MA: Harvard.

Hareven, Tamara. 1982. American Families in Transition. In Froma Walsh (ed.), *Normal Family Processes*, pp. 446-466. New York: Guilford.

Harrington, Michael. 1962. *The Other America: Poverty in the United States*. New York: Macmillan.

Harrington, Michael, and Mark Levinson. 1985. The Perils of a Dual Economy. *Dissent* 32:417-26.

Harris, Marvin. 1974. *Cows, Pigs, Wars and Witches: The Riddles of Culture*. New York: Random House.

Harrison, Bennett, and Barry Bluestone. 1988. *The Great U-Turn: Corporate Restructuring and the Polarizing of America*. New York: Basic Books.

Harrison, Roderick J., and Claudette E. Bennett. 1995. Racial and Ethnic Diversity. In Reynolds Farley (ed.), *State of the Union: America in the 1990s*, Vol. 2. New York: Russell Sage.

Harvey, David L. 1993. *Potter Addition.* New York: de Gruyter.

Hawley, Amos. 1986. *Human Ecology.* Chicago: University of Chicago.

Henderson, Hazel. 1996 [1978]. *Creating Alternative Futures: The End of Economics.* West Hartford, CT: Kumarian Press.

Hennig, Margaret, and Anne Jardim. 1977. *The Managerial Woman.* New York: Doubleday.

Hewlett, Sylvia Ann. 1991. *When the Bough Breaks: The Cost of Neglecting Our Children.* New York: Basic Books.

Hochschild, Arlie. 1979. Emotion Work, Feeling Rules, and Social Structure. *American Journal of Sociology* 85:3, 555-575.

Hochschild, Arlie, with Anne Machung. 1989. *The Second Shift: Working Parents and the Revolution at Home.* New York: Penguin.

Hunter, James Davidson. 1991. *Culture Wars: The Struggle to Define America.* New York: Basic Books.

Janis, Irving. 1972. *Victims of Groupthink.* Boston: Houghton Mifflin.

Jencks, Christopher. 1972. *Inequality.* New York: Basic Books.

Jones, Christine W., and Miguel A. Kiguel. 1993. *Adjustment in Africa.* Washington, DC: World Bank.

Kanter, Rosabeth Moss. 1977. *Men and Women of the Corporation.* New York: Basic Books.

———. 1983. *The Change Masters.* New York: Simon and Schuster.

———. 1989. *When Giants Learn to Dance.* New York: Simon and Schuster.

Kohler, Gernot. 1978. Global Apartheid. *World Order Models Project, Paper 7.* New York: Institute for World Order.

Kohn, Melvin. 1969. *Class and Conformity: A Study in Values.* Homewood, IL: Dorsey.

Kotlowitz, Alex. 1991. *There Are No Children Here.* New York: Doubleday.

Kozol, Jonathan. 1991. *Savage Inequalities.* New York: Crown.

———. 1995. *Amazing Grace.* New York: Crown.

Laslett, Peter. 1976. Societal Development and Aging. In R.H. Binstock and E. Shanas (eds.), *Handbook of Aging and the Social Sciences,* pp. 87-116. New York: Van Nostrand.

Leavitt, H.J. 1951. Some Effects of Certain Communication Patterns on Group Performance. *Journal of Abnormal and Social Psychology* 46:38-50.

Lenski, Gerhard. 1966. *Power and Privilege: A Theory of Stratification.* New York: McGraw-Hill.

Lukas, J. Anthony. 1985. *Common Ground.* New York: Knopf.

MacLeod, Jay. 1995. *Ain't No Makin' It.* Boulder, CO: Westview.

Mangione, Jerre. 1978. *An Ethnic at Large.* New York: Putnam.

McCall, Nathan. 1994. *Makes Me Wanna Holler.* New York: Random House.

McCurdy, David. 1994. Using Anthropology. In James Spradley and David McCurdy (eds.), *Conformity and Conflict,* 8th ed. New York: HarperCollins.

McPherson, Miller, Pamela Popielarz, and Sonja Drobnic. 1992. Social Networks and Organizational Dynamics. *American Sociological Review* 57:153-70.

Miller, Sherod, Elam Nunnally, and Daniel Wackman. 1981. *Straight Talk.* New York: Rawson, Wade.

———. 1991. *Talking and Listening Together.* Littleton, CO: Interpersonal Communication Programs.

Mills, C. Wright. 1956. *The Power Elite.* New York: Oxford.

———. 1959. *The Sociological Imagination.* New York: Oxford.

Momaday, N. Scott. 1976. *The Names: A Memoir.* New York: Harper and Row.

Morris, Martina, Annette D. Bernhardt, and Mark S. Handcock. 1994. Economic Inequality: New Methods for New Trends. *American Sociological Review* 59:205-219.

Myrdal, Gunnar. 1944. *An American Dilemma.* New York: Harper.

Napier, Augustus. 1988. *The Fragile Bond.* New York: Harper and Row.

Napier, Augustus, with Carl Whitaker. 1988. *The Family Crucible.* New York: Harper and Row.

Nesbitt, John. 1982. *Megatrends.* New York: Warner.

Olsen, Daniel V.A. Forthcoming. Dimensions of Cultural Tension Among the American Public. In Rhys Williams (ed.) *Culture Wars in American Politics.* New York: Aldine de Gruyter.

Ouchi, William. 1981. *Theory Z: How American Business Can Meet the Japanese Challenge.* Reading, MA: Addison-Wesley.

———. 1984. *The M-Form Society: How American Teamwork Can Recapture the Competitive Edge.* Reading, MA: Addison-Wesley.

Parenti, Michael. 1995. *Democracy for the Few,* 6th Ed. New York: St Martin's.

Park, Robert. 1914. Racial Assimilation in Secondary Groups. *Publications of the American Sociological Society* 8:66-72.

Park, Robert, and Ernest Burgess. 1921. *Introduction to the Science of Sociology.* Chicago: University of Chicago.

Piore, Michael, and Charles Sabel. 1984. *The Second Industrial Divide.* New York: Basic Books.

Rabushka, Alvin, and Bruce Jacobs. 1980. *Old Folks at Home.* New York: Free Press.

Reiman, Jeffrey. 1990. *The Rich Get Richer and the Poor Get Prison*, 3rd Ed. New York: Macmillan.

Richmond, Anthony H. 1994. *Global Apartheid: Refugees, Racism and the New World Order*. New York: Oxford University Press.

Riesman, David. 1953. *The Lonely Crowd*. New Haven, CT: Yale Press.

Ritzer, George. 1996. *The McDonaldization of Society*, 2nd Ed. Thousand Oaks, CA: Pine Forge.

Rodriquez, Richard. 1981. *Hunger of Memory*. Boston: Godine.

Rose, Mike. 1989. *Lives on the Boundary*. New York: Free Press.

Rose, Peter. I. 1990. *They and We*. New York: McGraw-Hill.

Rubin, Lillian B. 1976. *Worlds of Pain*. New York: Basic Books.

———. 1994. *Families on the Fault Line*. New York: HarperCollins.

Scarr, Sandra, Deborah Phillips, and Kathleen McCartney. 1989. Working Mothers and Their Families. *American Psychologist* 44, 11:1402-1409.

Schlesinger, Arthur Jr. 1992. *The Disuniting of America*. New York: Norton.

Schwartz, Felice. 1989. Management Women and the New Facts of Life. *Harvard Business Review*, 65-76.

Schwartz, John, and Thomas Volgy. 1992. *The Forgotten Americans*. New York: Norton.

Sernau, Scott. 1994. *Economies of Exclusion: Underclass Poverty and Labor Market Change in Mexico*. Westport, CT: Praeger.

———. 1995. A Sense of Place: Community Characteristics Affecting Community Mobilization. In Robert P. Wolensky and Edward J. Miller (eds.), *The Small City and Regional Community, Vol. 11*.

———. 1996. Economies of Exclusion: Economic Change and the Global Underclass. *Journal of Developing Societies* Vol. XII, 1:38-51.

Shaw, M.E. 1954. Some Effects of Problem Complexity upon Problem Solution Efficiency in Various Comunication Nets. *Journal of Experimental Psychology* 48:211-17.

Sidel, Ruth. 1996. *Keeping Women and Children Last*. New York: Penguin.

Skeels, H.M., and H.A. Dye. 1939. A Study of the Effects of Differential Stimulation in Mentally Retarded Children. *Proceedings of the American Association for Mental Deficiency* 44:114-136.

Skolnick, Arlene. 1991. *Embattled Paradise*. New York: Basic Books.

Smith, Anthony. 1981. *The Ethnic Revival in the Modern World*. Cambridge, UK: Cambridge University Press.

South, Scott, and Glenna Spitze. 1994. Housework in Marital and Nonmarital Households. *American Sociological Review* 59:327-347.

Spradley, James. 1994. Ethnography and Culture. In James Spradley and David McCurdy, eds., *Conformity and Conflict*. New York: HarperCollins.

Stack, Carol. 1974. *All Our Kin*. New York: Harper and Row.

Sutherland, Edwin H. 1940. White Collar Criminality. *American Sociological Review* 5:1-12.

Takaki, Ronald. 1993. *A Different Mirror*. Boston: Little, Brown.

———. 1994. *From Different Shores*, 2nd Ed. New York: Oxford.

Tannen, Deborah. 1990. *You Just Don't Understand: Women and Men in Conversation*. New York: Ballantine.

Terkel, Studs. 1992. *Race*. New York: New Press.

Thomas, Piri. 1967. *Down These Mean Streets*. New York: Signet.

Thurow, Lester. 1980. *The Zero-Sum Society*. New York: Basic Books.

Toennies, Ferdinand. 1988 [1887]. *Community and Society (Gemeinschaft und Gesellschaft)*. New Brunswick, NJ: Transaction.

Toffler, Alex. 1980. *The Third Wave*. New York: Bantam.

Turnbull, Colin M. 1961. *The Forest People*. New York: Simon and Schuster.

Uhlenberg, Peter. 1980. Death and the Family. *Journal of Family History* (Fall).

Veblen, Thorstein. 1912. *The Theory of the Leisure Class*. New York: Macmillan.

Wallerstein, Immanuel. 1974. *The Modern World System*. New York: Academic Press.

———. 1984. The Present State of the Debate on World Inequality. In M. Seligson (ed.), *The Gap Between Rich and Poor*, pp. 119-132. Boulder, CO: Westview.

Walton, John. 1970. A Systematic Survey of Community Power Research. In Michael Aiken and Paul E. Mott (eds.), *The Structure of Community Power*. New York: Random House.

Waters, Mary. 1990. *Ethnic Options*. Berkeley: University of California.

Weatherford, Jack McIver. 1988. *Indian Givers*. New York: Fawcett Columbine.

———. 1994. *Savages and Civilization*. New York: Fawcett Columbine.

Weaver, James H., Michael T. Rock, and Kenneth Kusterer. 1997. *Achieving Broad-Based Sustainable Development: Governance, Environment, and Growth with Equity*. West Hartford, CT: Kumarian Press.

Weber, Max. 1996 [1930]. *The Protestant Ethic and the Spirit of Capitalism*. Los Angeles: Roxbury.

Weiss, Michael. 1988. *The Clustering of America*. New York: HarperCollins.

White, Ralph, and Ronald Lippitt. 1953. Leader Behavior and Member Reaction in Three 'Social Climates.' In Dorwin Cartwright and Alvin Zander, eds., *Group Dynamics*. Evanston, IL.: Row, Peterson.

Whyte, Jr., William H. 1956. *The Organization Man*. New York: Simon and Schuster.

Wilson, Kenneth, and Alejandro Portes. 1980. Immigrant Enclaves: An Analysis of the Labor Market Experiences of Cubans in Miami. *American Journal of Sociology* 86:295-319.

Wilson, William Julius. 1987. *The Truly Disadvantaged: The Inner City, the Underclass, and Public Policy*. Chicago: University of Chicago Press.

———. 1996. *When Work Disappears*. New York: Knopf.

Wong, Jade Snow. 1945. *Fifth Chinese Daughter*. New York: Harper.

Index